Life Sciences Research Report 18
Evolution of Social Behavior:
Hypotheses and Empirical Tests

The goal of this Dahlem Workshop is:
To assess the validity of evolutionary theories of social
behavior; to identify the most promising modes of
research in the domain for the near future.

verlag
chemie

Life Sciences Research Report
Editor: Silke Bernhard

Held and published on behalf of the
Stifterverband für die Deutsche Wissenschaft

Sponsored by:
Stifterverband für die Deutsche Wissenschaft and
Senat der Stadt Berlin

Hubert Markl
Editor

Evolution of Social Behavior: Hypotheses and Empirical Tests

Report of the Dahlem Workshop on Evolution of Social Behavior: Hypotheses and Empirical Tests, Berlin 1980, February 18–22

Rapporteurs:
Marc Feldman · Paul H. Harvey · John R. Krebs ·
George F. Oster

Program Advisory Committee:
Hubert Markl (Chairman) · Norbert Bishof · Irvin Devore ·
Bert Hölldobler · Dan E. Koshland, Jr. · Hans Kummer ·
John Maynard Smith · George F. Oster · Donald S. Sade ·
E. O. Wilson

Verlag Chemie
Weinheim · Deerfield Beach, Florida · Basel · 1980

Copy editor: M. Cervantes-Waldmann
Photographs: E. P. Thonke

CIP – Kurztitelaufnahme der Deutschen Bibliothek

Evolution of social behavior, hypotheses and empirical tests:
report of the Dahlem Workshop on Evolution of Social Behavior,
Hypotheses and Empir. Tests, Berlin 1980, February 18–22/Hubert
Markl. Rapporteurs: Marc Feldman... [Dahlem-Konferenzen]. –
Weinheim, Deerfield Beach (Florida), Basel: Verlag Chemie, 1980.
  (Life sciences research report; 18)
  ISBN 3-527-12020-3 (Weinheim, Basel)
  ISBN 0-89573-033-2 (Deerfield Beach)

NE: Markl, Hubert [Hrsg.]; Feldman, Marc [Mitverf.]; Workshop on
Evolution of Social Behavior, Hypotheses and Empirical Tests
<1980, Berlin, West>; Dahlem-Konferenzen

Verlag Chemie GmbH, D-6940 Weinheim

Table of Contents

Evolution of Social Behavior: Hypotheses and Empirical Tests, ed. H. Markl,
pp. 1-10. Dahlem Konferenzen 1980. Weinheim: Verlag Chemie GmbH.

Introduction

H. Markl
Fachbereich Biologie, Universität Konstanz
Postfach 5560, 7750 Konstanz, F. R. Germany

Considering the fact that some essential resources are ultimately
limiting the expansion of all animal populations, and that some
form of competition for these resources is therefore inevitable,
social cooperation is not exactly what the evolutionary biologist would expect to find frequently in the animal kingdom.
However, quite to the contrary, it is there, alive and thriving
in ecological success in numerous evolutionary lines. Mankind
itself derives its evolution from social animal ancestors.

Thus, in fitness, it evidently pays to live in social groups,
and students of animal behavior have assembled evidence of what
it is that makes social life superior to coping with life's
exigencies in splendid isolation. Given that social cooperation
entails moderation of competition for resources, which leads to
sharing of resources, and the tendency for any socially inclined
individual to lose out against more selfish competitors, one
question still remains: By which evolutionary mechanisms are
animals brought over the threshold of sociality?

Evolutionary biologists have lived with this problem since Darwin
and have tried to explain it away with foggy notions of behavior,
adaptive for the species if not for the individual performing

it. It was the inestimable merit of W.D. Hamilton's seminal
papers of 1964 (3) that destroyed the complacent illusion of
these traditional views by being able to explain the evolution
of social behavior and by showing how a rigorous population
genetical explanation of social evolution in animals could proceed. Termed "kin selection" by J. Maynard Smith (5), this did
not remain the only genetical model for social evolution. However, it did set the stage for an entirely new way of thinking
about animal behavior and its strategies of adaptation to the
environment. Game theory models supplemented the more classical genetical models and thus enriched the hypothetical reper-
toire tremendously. Insights from decades of productive work
by ethologists, population geneticists, ecologists, and evolutionary biologists merged rather suddenly into a unified approach to an understanding of the evolution of social behavior
in animals - labeled "Sociobiology" by E.O. Wilson (9). Within
a few years, this area of research proved its vigor as an in-
novative field, rich in new theoretical concepts, and thus stim-
ulated a wealth of empirical studies on many aspects of animal
social life never looked at before. Prone to premature simplifications as any exciting new field, its grasp ranged from molecular genetics to social sciences, and consequently it received
all the controversy expected for such daring generalizations.
Nevertheless, due to this development there has been a fresh
wave of enthusiastic interest in animal behavior and evolution,
both in the adherents of sociobiological theories and in their
opponents. This interest has lead to thorough theoretical and
empirical investigations of animal sociality.

Sir Karl Popper has remarked in his scientific autobiography (4)
that new scientific disciplines tend to have a typical ontogeny -
a phase of revolutionary innovation followed by a period of
dogmatism, whereby a set of promising theories is solidified
into paradigms that make bargaining with textbook publishers
profitable. This is eventually followed by a critical phase
of dismantling the scaffolding of premature assertions and convictions and replacing them by a solid base of carefully evaluated theoretical and empirical foundations. Although the close

observer of the sociobiological scene will have noticed ingredients of all these phases from the very beginning, it is certainly true as stated by G. Oster during the Workshop that
"the Romantic Age of sociobiology is over."   It was the aim
of this Dahlem Conference and the hope of its organizers
that this week's efforts serve not only for the stocktaking
of the sociobiological inventory at the end of this romantic
period, but also to contribute to the ushering in of Popper's
critical phase for this field.

In order to do this, the four working groups concentrated on:
a) clarifying and classifying what the alternative theoretical
core concepts are for the explanation of evolution of social
behavior; b) spelling out the undisputed and generally accepted
state of empirical knowledge about the social animal systems,
the controversies, and the need for further investigation; and
finally c) trying to define the most urgent questions and the
most promising methods for answering them by future research in
this field.

To achieve this, a well-balanced mixture of evolutionary theoreticians and mathematical model specialists on the one side and of
students of animal behavior in the field and laboratory on the
other was invited. Of course everyone realizes that most questions on evolutionary biology would be easier to answer if either
the theoreticians were left alone among themselves - ugly empirical facts being often only a pain in the neck to the makers of
beautiful models, or if the field-working ethologists were left
alone, because then the logical flaws in their plausible evolutionary speculations would not be discovered by cold-hearted
model makers. Though indispensable tools for clarifying hidden
assumptions and logical consequences of verbal arguments, mathematical models never explain anything in behavioral reality.
They select permissible explanations from flawed ones, thereby
also defining what kind of empirical evidence the ethologists
or population geneticists have to look for in order to select
among the admissible models. If that is so, then an interaction
between those who habitually skip formulas and proofs when leafing

through the Journal of theoretical Biology and those who like to
sprinkle bits of ant, bee, baboon, or Yanamamö behavior as an
embellishing frosting over a hard-core cake chock-full-of abstract
reasoning, assumed alleles, letters, numbers, and operators, was
certainly essential for the success of this Workshop. The goal
was to make theoreticians more intensely aware of what needs to
be realistically modeled in order to produce testable hypotheses
and empiricists aware of what really needs to be measured in order
to test the models.

Let me bring up just one point as an example of the difficulties
in trying to understand evolutionary models of social behavior.
These models generally seem to rely on social interactants performing specified pure or mixed strategies with defineable probabilities under specified conditions. However, there is one
element, most impressively characteristic of many social systems
for the behavioral biologist, which is not considered - adaptive
modification of behavior through feedback from social experience,
i.e., social learning. This complicates everything, clear theory
as well as neat experiments, but it is of major importance to
many social animals and of course even more so to man. To turn
to the ethologists - rarely do we really know what social modification and learning can do and what they do in social animal systems under evolutionarily relevant conditions. We all too often
like to regard our animals as exchangeable fixed entities with
static or well-defined probabilistic properties given by genotype,
sex, age, and present behavioral state. However, we tend to neglect
what an individual's history of social experience does to his behavior since it is so difficult to assess. Are we then not looking for the key where it is light and not where it has been lost?

This also seems to entail difficulties for the application of the
beautiful concept of Evolutionarily Stable Strategies to real
social behavior: how can a successful strategy be a stable one
in a learning, i.e., a continuously adapting, social system? Is
not "evolutionarily stable" a contradictio in adjecto; should we
not rather name it an Evolutionarily Superior Strategy (in order
to keep the acronym ESS); and is it not a changing, tracking

strategy rather than a stable one which is apt to be superior
in social animals able to learn?

Or, let me toss up two other problems which seem far from being
answered by the present state of our understanding of social
evolution. First, what is really meant by the adaptiveness of
a behavioral trait? Made simple, one can say that a trait is
adaptive if it confers superior fitness to its producer as compared to individuals who do not produce it under otherwise identical conditions. This could be open to experimental tests,
i.e., if we accept the short-term reproductive success of a
trait-bearer (what we usually at best can measure) as the estimate for long-term fitness (the evolutionary relevant quality).
W.D. Hamilton has, of course, taught us that what we really
ought to measure is the trait-bearers inclusive fitness, to be
exact, both present and future direct and indirect fitness effects (see J. Brown, this volume). Second, since, as a rule we
cannot measure the fitness effects of those genes that are actually involved in controlling the expression of a particular
behavioral trait under study, we have to be content with estimating genotype fitness. Considering the highly polygenic control of most behavioral traits, we may not even do so poorly
with that - although perhaps we ought to worry more about effects
of meiotic recombination and change of genetic environment on
gene fitness. Yet, if we obtain a convincing set of data for
assessing the adaptiveness of the trait for its producer, are
we then allowed to conclude that it therefore has been selected
for in evolution, which means selectively retained in competition with non-producers of this trait? This is a rather dangerous post hoc-propter hoc-type of correlation, a conclusion
from association to causality, and we have known about the reliability of inductive reasoning since David Hume. The trait
might as well have been co-selected as a neutral epiphenomenon
of a very different adaptive process and only become functional
under changed circumstances, maybe even only under our imposed
measuring conditions. Take, as an example, the alternative explanations (which, however, are not at all mutually exclusive)
of concealed ovulation and continuous sexual receptivity in the

human female by Alexander and Noonan (1), Spuhler (6), or
Burley (2). Evidently we have to be very careful about what
we mean when stating that a behavior is adaptive or, even more
so, that it has been selected for this function. There can
also be epistemological doubts as to whether the equation
"adaptive = selected for" can at all be applied to particular
behavioral traits, since it is always the whole phenotype that
is tested by the environment. Therefore, single trait analysis, as well as single gene analysis, may not correctly grasp
the essence of the selective interactions between the environment, the organism, and its genotype. There are, of course,
immunizing strategies around these problems, e.g., the postu-
lation of modifier genes, the course of selection at which one
looks. However, the nagging feeling remains that we may not be
studying behavioral evolution of the real world but only figments
in our imagination.

Most biologists will strongly agree that it is _fitness_ that
is selected for and optimized in social as in any natural evolution. Fair enough, but whose fitness are we talking about? It
ought to be most germane to the empirical biologist to quantify
fitness from the reproductive success of the individual, because he can quantify that in a limited-span field study. Of
course, we know now, that this will not do in social systems.
As already mentioned, we will want to quantify inclusive fitness in kin-lineages, which will consequently bring us to
look at gene fitness as the real thing. However, single genes
alone - even jumping transposons - can do little or nothing
for their fitness. They need an appropriate genetic environment. Thus we will tend to ascribe major evolutionary importance to complexes of genes that program fit phenotypes - taking
us back to the individuum again.

Furthermore, in social systems one can boost one's fitness not
only by maximizing inclusive fitness in one's kin-lineage, but
also by mutualistic and reciprocally altruistic interactions
with partners - who may or not be kin. (See reports by Oster
et al. (this volume) and Vehrencamp (8) for a discussion of

even more forms of fitness-affecting social interactions.) How
kin selection, mutualism, reciprocation, parental manipulation,
etc., together affect social evolution has hardly been scru-
tinized. But this has to be considered, because no component
can be neglected in long-lived, well-learning, cooperative
animals, and even less so in man. Thus, it would be a gross
oversimplification to regard, e.g., reciprocal altruism as
primarily a limited-term dyadic interaction. In a highly
evolved social community, an individual's fitness evidently
depends on a whole network of multilateral social interactions
and multitudinous, long-time behavioral contributions, especially when a system of division of labor exists. This gives the
social system emergent characteristics on which an individual's
fitness depends in the long run, probably much more so than on
its own behavioral endeavors. But, if any reductionist approach
is apt to destroy the very phenomenon to be analyzed, how are
we to model and measure these fitness-influencing factors?

I remain unconvinced that under the described conditions the
fitness that counts in evolution can be fully understood on
the individual level without considering group effects which
are consequently also subject to group selective pressures.

As discussed by Oster et al.(this volume) and in more detail
by Uyenoyama and Feldman (7), group selective effects can mean
many different things, from "hard" differential extinction to
"soft" transforming evolution. They, like the effects of all
other selective mechanisms, have to be considered separately
with respect to the incipient genesis of social systems and to
the continuing maintenance and differentiation of full-blown
social life. After all, the benefit/cost-term in Hamilton's
rule for alternative behavioral strategies may change tremendously along the path of the social evolution of a species.

These are only a few of the many fascinating aspects of evolutionary biology of social behavior. This Workshop will have
achieved much, if though solving none of these problems, it leads
to a better awareness of what it is exactly that we do not

understand about the social evolution of animals. There is, for
instance, the sociobiologists' peculiar obsession with directed
altruism in social systems, while non-random, kinship-related
aggression, and competition within and between social groups
may be as or even more important for social fitness.

This was not planned to be a conference on human sociobiology.
Social animals give us enough to chew on. Moreover, if we
do a good job in clarifying concepts, state of knowledge, and
ways for further research in the sociobiology of animals, including the primates, we may best do service to a sensible
and fruitful application of these insights to man - just as
the physiologist experimenting on the dog's heart lays the
foundations for an understanding of the human circulatory system. After all, if we cannot come to grips with how to understand social biology and social evolution of animals, how can
we expect to fathom successfully the biological basis of social
behavior in man? I feel that it will not suffice to state em-
phatically that anything in human behavior is subject to sociobiological explanation if it can be demonstrated to affect reproductive success and may therefore be postulated to be selected for this function. After all, even a love poem can have a
fitness-enhancing effect and can have been written in carefully
selected stanzas by virtue of the genetic endowment of a particular poet for inventing titillating verse - but still, I
would be reluctant to advertize this as the ultimate argumenta-
tion about it. I remain unconvinced that cultural evolution is
merely a continuation of natural evolution with other means,
and that cultures evolve primarily as mechanisms for maximizing
Darwinian fitness of their members, or even of their genes.
There are more "optimization criteria" (see J. Maynard Smith,
this volume) for cultural evolution than reproductive success,
which may not, of course, make biological reproduction entirely impossible for all members of a culture, but which are
also far from being just equivalent manifestations of Darwinian
fitness. This report testifies as to how far away biologists
are from really understanding what went on and goes on in the
evolution of animal sociality. It should make sober reading

for those who hope to find the masterkey to an understanding
of human social behavior in Sociobiology.

To those who participated in this Dahlem Workshop, this volume
represents more than a summary of scientific theories and arguments. It represents a permanent recollection of a week of
highly stimulating social interactions - altruistic and competitive in balance, which any really functional social system should
have. However, it could never have been the human and scientific experience that it was, without the unique blend of organiza-
tional efficiency and TLC of the Dahlem crew, which is the
trademark of the Dahlem Workshops.

The participants and above all the Chairman and Editor of this
Report acknowledge this indispensable support with sincerest
appreciation.

REFERENCES

(1) Alexander, R.D., and Noonan, K.M. 1979. Concealment of
     ovulation, parental care and human social evolution. In
     Evolutionary Biology and Human Social Behavior, eds. N.A.
     Chagnon and W. Irons, pp. 436-453. North Scituate:
     Duxbury Press.

(2) Burley, N. 1979. The evolution of concealed ovulation.
     Am. Natur. 114: 835-858.

(3) Hamilton, W.D. 1964. The genetical evolution of social
     behavior. I. and II. J. theoret. Biol. 7: 1-16; 17-32.

(4) Popper, K. 1974. Unended Quest. An intellectual Auto-
     biography. London: Fontana/Collins.

(5) Maynard, Smith, J. 1964. Group selection and kin selec-
     tion. Nature 201: 1145-1147.

(6) Spuhler, J.N. 1979. Continuities and discontinuities in
     anthropoid-hominid behavioral evolution. In Evolutionary
     Biology and Human Social Behavior, eds. N.A. Chagnon and
     W. Irons, pp. 454-467. North Scituate: Duxbury Press.

(7)   Uyenoyama, M., and Feldman, M.W. 1980. Theories of kin
      and group selection: a population genetics perspective.
      Theoret. Pop. Biol., in press.

(8)   Vehrencamp, S.L. 1980. The roles of individual, kin, and
      group selection in the evolution of sociality. In Handbook
      of Behavioral Neurobiology. Social Behavior and Communica-
      tion, eds. P. Marler and J.G. Vandenbergh, vol. 1, pp. 351-
      394. New York: Plenum Press.

(9)   Wilson, E.O. 1975. Sociobiology. The New Synthesis.
      Cambridge: Belknap Press.

Evolution of Social Behavior: Hypotheses and Empirical Tests, ed. H. Markl,
pp. 11-26. Dahlem Konferenzen 1980. Weinheim: Verlag Chemie GmbH.

Models of Kin Selection

B. Charlesworth
School of Biological Sciences, University of Sussex
Falmer, Brighton BN1 9QG, England

Abstract. Measures of genetic relationship are discussed, and
a population genetic model is presented that justifies the use
of inclusive fitness arguments in cases with weak behavioral
interactions among relatives. Some exact models of selection
on interactions between sibs are described, and it is shown
that inclusive fitness predictions may be inexact with strong
interactions. It seems that inclusive fitness arguments are
invaluable in providing insights about the likely outcome of
selection, but should be checked wherever possible by gene
frequency calculations.

INTRODUCTION

It is impossible in a brief report to give a comprehensive review

of the many significant contributions to kin selection theory.

Instead, I will present a short historical survey and then de-

scribe in some detail certain approaches to modeling kin selection

that I find especially illuminating. I shall concentrate on

problems associated with the construction and analysis of models

rather than on the predictions of the theory, which have been

repeatedly discussed elsewhere (14-17,30,36,38).

HISTORICAL SURVEY

In the Origin of Species, Darwin proposed that the anatomical

and behavioral specializations of the sterile castes of social

insects evolved because of the resulting benefits to the
reproductive members of the colony, whom he recognized as being
close relatives of the workers. This interpretation fits
Maynard Smith's definition of kin selection as "the evolution
of characteristics which favour the survival of close relatives
of the affected individual, by processes which do not require
any discontinuities in population structure" (24). In the 1930s,
Fisher (10) and Haldane (11) both discussed kin selection in
relation to the evolution of altruistic behavior. Haldane later
gave a brief but clear formulation of the role of the degree of
relationship between the donor and recipient of an altruistic
act in determining the strength of selection for altruism (12).
These ideas seem, however, to have had little influence on the
thinking of students of animal behavior, until the appearance
of Hamilton's papers (13-17), which provided a synthesis of
genetical ideas and behavioral data.

RELATIONSHIPS BETWEEN RELATIVES

The basic idea of kin selection is that behavioral interactions
between relatives influence the spread of genes controlling the
behavior patterns concerned, by virtue of the fact that relatives
have greater genetic similarity than unrelated individuals. The
measurement of genetic relationship is accordingly one of the
cornerstones of kin selection theory. The key concept is that
of identity by descent; two genes at a locus are said to be
identical by descent if they are both descended from a single
gene in some ancestral individual (23). It is difficult to give
a completely general description of genetic similarity, in the
sense of being able to state the probability that an individual
X has a particular genotype, knowing the genotype of a relative
Y (9,20). For example, if X and Y are inbred, the values of
nine identity coefficients must be determined from the pedigree,
even for the simple case of an autosomal locus. Fortunately,
certain simplifications are possible if we can assume that X
and Y are not inbred, so that the two genes at a locus within
each individual are not identical by descent. If we are interested in modeling random-mating populations, this is a reasonable
assumption, and one which I shall make from now on.

A single measure of relationship is adequate to describe the
dynamics of selection with both autosomal and sex-linked (haplodiploid) inheritance, at least to a first approximation. This
is what Hamilton (16) called the <u>coefficient of relatedness</u> when
correcting some errors in his original formulation, pointed out
by Crozier (8). In order to avoid some of the ambiguities concerning the definition of this quantity, which have appeared in
the literature, I define the relatedness r_{XY} between two individuals X and Y as the probability that X contains a gene identical by descent with a random gene at the same locus, sampled
from Y. r_{XY} is calculated from the pedigree on the assumption
that the locus concerned is neutral with respect to fitness, and
that the population is random-mating and infinitely large, so
that the coefficients are zero for unrelated individuals. With
diploid autosomal inheritance $r_{XY} = r_{YX}$ and is 1/2 for full-sibs,
1/4 for half-sibs, etc. With haplodiploidy, it is not necessarily
the case that $r_{XY} = r_{YX}$. If X and Y are full-sibs, for example,
$r_{XY} = 1/4$ if X is male and Y is female, but $r_{YX} = 1/2$. Tables
of values of r are given in the standard works (e.g., (34)).

The reason that r rather than any other measure of relationship
is relevant to kin selection may be seen by the following example.
Suppose we are interested in determining the fate of a rare gene
inducing altruistic behavior towards full sibs, which is introduced into a previously non-altruistic population. Since the
population is random-mating, we can neglect the possibility that
diploid individuals are homozygous for the gene. Suppose the
species is haplodiploid and that the gene causes heterozygous
females to behave altruistically towards their brothers, with
the effect of reducing their own fitness to 1 - c and raising
that of their brothers to 1 + b, relative to a value of 1 for
the initial, non-altruistic population. Ignoring gene frequency
differences between the sexes, an altruistic gene in a given
female Y therefore has a probability $r_{XY} = 1/4$ of being present
in a brother X. The effect of her altruistic behavior is thus
to decrease the number of copies of the gene by c and to increase
it by b/4. Assuming a 1:1 sex ratio, the net change in the

number of copies of the altruism gene transmitted to the next
generation is therefore b/4-c.   The gene will therefore only
increase in frequency if the benefit/cost ratio k = b/c exceeds
4.   Similar calculations can be done for other degrees of
relationship and display the fact that $1/r_{XY}$ (with the first
subscript referring to the recipient and the second to the donor)
determines the critical value of k that permits a rare gene for
altruism to invade a non-altruistic population (13-15).

This analysis makes a number of unrealistic assumptions.   In
particular, if selection is operating in the population, the
genotype frequencies in the population will be changed over the
course of a generation by an amount of order s, where s is a
measure of the strength of selection in terms of the difference
in fitness between the best and the worst genotypes.   The transmission probabilities given by the r_{XY} must therefore in general
be modified by the addition of terms of order s.   Similarly,
when there are sex differences in behavior, gene frequency
differences between the sexes cannot legitimately be ignored.
For these reasons, properly constructed models of kin selection
are necessary to supplement the insights gained by calculations
based purely on r values for the transmission of neutral genes
through pedigrees.   I next consider a model that is valid for
low intensities of behavioral interactions, based on Hamilton's
original approach (14), and then go on to discuss some recent
results on exact models of kin selection with interactions of
arbitrary strength.

INCLUSIVE FITNESS
A key concept in kin selection theory has been _inclusive fitness_,
first defined by Hamilton (14).   Hamilton himself stated clearly
that his well-known result that natural selection maximizes
inclusive fitness was derived from an approximate model, valid
only under certain conditions.   There has been a regrettable
tendency in the literature on behavioral evolution to apply this
idea indiscriminately, without examining its validity in circumstances where the original assumptions do not hold.   I give
below an outline of a model in which inclusive fitnesses provide

a reasonably accurate prediction of the course of selection,
in the sense of appearing in gene frequency equations which
have the same form as the equations in conventional selection
models. The model involves the assumption that behavioral
interactions of a selfish or altruistic nature are weak, by which
is meant that they are either rather infrequent or involve only
small changes to the fitnesses of the individuals concerned.

An Autosomal Locus

In the case of an autosomal locus, inclusive fitness can be
defined in the context of the following model. Consider a
discrete-generation, random-mating population segregating at a
locus with alleles A_1, A_2,...A_m, with frequencies p_1, p_2...p_m.
At the start of a generation, the frequency of the genotype
A_iA_j is p_ip_j (the first and second alleles in the genotype are
of maternal and paternal origin respectively). During the
course of a generation, individuals engage in pairwise interactions in which donors and recipients can be distinguished.
An individual of genotype A_iA_j has an expectation of $a_{ij}(r)$
interactions as donor towards individuals of relatedness r. Each
such interaction changes the fitness of the recipient by $b_{ij}(r)$
and the fitness of the donor by $-c_{ij}(r)$, the fitness of each
genotype in the absence of interactions being 1. The b's and
c's are positive if the interactions are altruistic, and negative
if they are selfish. Reciprocal effects are assumed to be
absent so that $a_{ij} = a_{ji}$, $b_{ij} = b_{ji}$, etc.

If the interactions are weak, so that $\sum_r a_{ij}(r)b_{ij}(r)$ and
$\sum_r a_{ij}(r)c_{ij}(r)$ for each genotype are small, the strength of
selection s (defined above) must also be small, so that terms
in s^2, $s \sum_r a_{ij}(r)b_{ij}(r)$, etc., can be neglected. Furthermore,
the genotypic frequencies among the donors and recipients will
be equal to the Hardy-Weinberg frequencies p_ip_j, plus terms
of order s. Utilizing these assumptions, the analysis presented
in the Appendix shows that we can usefully define the inclusive
fitness $\tilde{w}_{ij}$ of a genotype A_iA_j by the expression:

$$\tilde{w}_{ij} = 1 + \sum_r a_{ij}(r) \left[rb_{ij}(r) - c_{ij}(r) \right] \tag{1}$$

Equation (A.4) of the Appendix shows that, provided s is sufficiently small, the inclusive fitnesses play the same role in the equation for gene frequency change as genotypic fitnesses in the standard equation for weak individual selection at an autosomal locus. A similar equation was derived by Hamilton (14), who used its resemblance to the standard selection equation to deduce many of the well-known consequences of kin selection, e.g., the maximization of inclusive fitness, selection for an increased intensity of altruistic behavior if individuals have sufficiently close relatedness, and selection for concentrating altruistic behavior towards close relatives (14,15).

A Sex-Linked (Haplodiploid) Locus

A considerable amount of attention has been paid to the conse-quences of sex-linkage (haplodiploidy), both because of its intrinsic interest and because of its being the mode of inher-itance for all loci in Hymenoptera (15,16,30,34). It appears, however, that no general treatment yielding a gene frequency equation comparable to equation A.4 has been published. It is tedious but straightforward to extend the model that I have just described to the case of sex-linkage. The details are given in the Appendix. Equation A.6 is similar in form to the standard equation for weak individual selection at a sex-linked locus (19,27), justifying the definition of inclusive fitness by equations A.5 a and b. It is interesting to note that equation A.6 gives twice as much weight to selection on females as males, in accordance with the fact that twice as many genes are present in females as males. Equations A.5 a and b also demonstrate that the rarer sex gains a disproportionate advantage from altruistic acts by the opposite sex.

EXACT MODELS OF KIN SELECTION

The models described above suffer from the fact that weak behavioral interactions must be assumed for the approximations involved to be valid. There has recently been considerable interest in developing exact models that do not involve inclusive fitness directly (2,3,6,7,21,28). This type of approach goes back to the work of Maynard Smith (25) and Williams and Williams (37), although they used the approximation of assuming Hardy-Weinberg frequencies among the adults after selection, as did Scudo and Ghiselin (32) and Wade (35). In general this assumption cannot be made and the equations describing the dynamics of selection become correspondingly complex. Analytical results are therefore largely restricted to studies of the conditions for the spread of rare genes, where the system can usually be reduced to a set of linear equations. Computer studies are necessary for the full dynamics. I shall discuss here two classes of models of altruism between full sibs which bring out some interesting complexities. In particular, it appears that the inclusive fitness approach yields a quantitatively accurate prediction of the outcome of selection only under certain conditions, and there is often a kind of frequency-dependent selection for altruism, such that an intermediate level of altruistic behavior is evolutionarily stable.

The first class of model that I will discuss was developed by me (3) and is intended to provide a rough description of the early stages of the evolution of sociality in insects. Individuals of a given genotype are assumed to have a characteristic probability, π say, of sacrificing a fraction c of their fitness to aid members of the same brood of full sibs. The fitness benefit to a recipient, b, is assumed to be proportional to the product of c with the ratio of the numbers of donors to recipients within the brood. The constant of proportionality is k, corresponding to Hamilton's benefit/cost ratio (13,14). Altruists either exclusively aid sibs who are non-altruistic in phenotype (Model 1), or benefits are conferred at random on both altruists and non-altruists (Model 2). The net fitness of a recipient who is also an altruist is assumed to be $(1 + b)(1 - c)$. It was found that the critical values of k permitting the invasion of a non-altruistic population by a gene for altruism mostly exceed those derived from the inclusive fitness model (e.g., 4/3 for sister-sister interactions with haplodiploidy). The inclusive fitness values are, however, approached as $\pi \to 0$, i.e., as the

penetrance of the gene for altruism becomes low. This is because
with high penetrance, altruists have a strong chance of aiding
sibs who either do not carry the altruism gene (Model 1), or
themselves have sacrificed fitness (Model 2). I also examined
the evolutionary stability of the population mean values of π
and c to the introduction of modifiers with small effects. The
population value of π is generally adjusted to intermediate values
substantially less than 1, provided k exceeds the inclusive fitness critical value for selection of altruism, whereas c is
increased towards 1 with Model 1 but may attain an intermediate
level with Model 2.

In the second class of model, studied by Orlove (28), Charnov
(6), and Craig (7), the population at the start of a generation
is divided into potential donors and potential recipients by
some criterion wholly independent of genotype. The genotype
frequencies among the recipients are therefore unperturbed by
selection within the given generation and are identical with
those among the donors. The inclusive fitness approach is
therefore more likely to work than in the first sort of model,
particularly when the interactions involve relatives, such as
sibs, which are connected to a common ancestor by only one generation. In Orlove's model, intended to represent the evolution
of multiple foundresses of Polistes wasp colonies, a pair of
fertilized sisters come together and engage in a contest, which
each has a probability of one-half of winning. The loser is the
potential altruist; if she has a genotype conferring altruism,
she has a certain probability of remaining and sacrificing all
her own reproduction to aid her sister. Otherwise she founds
an independent nest. It can be shown that the condition for
an altruism gene to spread into a population in which all nests
have just one foundress is that $b > 4/3$, where b is the increment
in the number of offspring to a nest with two foundresses,
relative to the number raised by a nest with one foundress. This
agrees with the inclusive fitness criterion and with Orlove's
conclusions derived from a computer study.

Charnov and Craig both considered a model in which the distinction between donor and recipient is due to time. They imagined
a species of Hymenopteran in which the original population has
two generations a year. A female who produces a brood in the
first season may also produce a brood of the same size in the
second season. Her first-season offspring found their own,
independent nests. A mutation occurs such that a female who
emerges in the first season has a non-zero probability of staying
on and helping to rear the second-season offspring of her mother.
If she does so, she sacrifices her own reproduction but increases
the relative size of her mother's brood by b. If the sex-ratio
is 1:1, it is easily shown that the condition for the gene to
increase in frequency is $b > 1$. This agrees with the inclusive
fitness criterion, since the offspring which are reared by
the altruistic female have the same relatedness to her as her
own offspring ($r = 1/2$ in both cases), and both sets of offspring
reproduce in the same generation (6). A gene acting in the
mother, which enables her to compel some of her first season
offspring to act as altruists, has a selective advantage if
$b > 1/2$, and there is no counter-selection on the offspring to
resist this parental manipulation unless $b < 1$ (6). Thus, the
overlap of generations in this case has important consequences
for the conditions for the establishment of social behavior.

These results at first sight indicate that the inclusive fitness formulation provides a precise description of some classes
of kin selection models with arbitrarily strong interactions.
But both Craig and Orlove found that the direction and rate of
gene frequency change in their models do not fit the inclusive
fitness predictions when the gene for altruism is common. More
importantly, a gene for altruism can sometimes invade a non-
altruistic population but not spread to fixation. This conclusion can be confirmed by analytic methods. As in the first
class of model, an intermediate value of the probability of
behaving altruistically may be evolutionarily stable.

DISCUSSION
The models described above show that Hamilton's inclusive fitness

theory seems to provide an excellent approximation when the
frequency of behavioral interactions is low or their effects
on fitness are small. It also accurately predicts the spread
of rare genes affecting the intensity of such interactions
between sibs under wider conditions. Nevertheless, quantitative
disagreement with the inclusive fitness predictions can occur
with strong interactions (2,3,6,7,28). An important extension
of inclusive fitness theory has been to problems in sex-ratio
evolution (29,30,34). Gene frequency analysis in this case
seems to show that it provides a good guide, apart from some
minor discrepancies (4,29). Similarly, gene frequency models
of parent-offspring conflict and parental manipulation (3,6,7,
18,22,31) have confirmed many of the insights provided by the
inclusive fitness approach (33) and refuted the suggestion that
parents will always win a conflict of interest with their offspring (1), as well as exploring fresh possibilities.

Many important factors have, of course, been left out of these
models. As stressed by West Eberhard (36), if there are genetic
or environmental fitness differences between individuals, inten-
sification of altruism by the less fit towards the more fit will
be favored. In particular, it has been suggested that altruism
of individuals of low reproductive value towards related individuals of high reproductive value is likely to be selected for
in an age-structured population (36). I have been able to confirm this suggestion by means of a gene frequency analysis for
the case of interactions affecting age-specific survival rates,
but not for interactions affecting fecundity. Further work on
the validity of inclusive fitness arguments in the context of
behavioral interactions between individuals of different age
groups seems desirable. Another topic that has been little
studied is kin selection in inbreeding populations. A recent
paper (26) seems to show that Hamilton's (16) heuristic approach
is valid only for semidominant genes, but is itself based on an
approximate analysis. Finally, it is important to note that
behavioral traits will usually have a polygenic basis. The
single locus models discussed here are relevant to polygenic

inheritance if the loci concerned are loosely linked and have approximately additive effects on the behavioral trait in question. It is then possible to consider the net change in the character as arising from the sum of the effects of the changes in gene frequencies at the individual loci. A direct attempt to model altruistic behavior as a polygenic character has recently been made (39) and gives results similar to those of the single locus models.

APPENDIX
Inclusive Fitness with Autosomal Inheritance

Justifications of equation 1 have been provided by several authors (4,14,18). Modifying their approaches slightly, we can proceed as follows. Let there be n individuals at the start of a given generation. Suppose we are interested in a particular allele A_i; there are $n_i = 2n\, p_i$ copies of A_i In the absence of selection (i.e., $\tilde{w}_{ij} = 1$ for all ij), assume the n initial individuals would contribute 2ne genes to the next generation, where e is the net expectation of offspring without selection. As a result of the behavioral interactions, however, the total number of genes transmitted is modified to

$$2n' = 2n\ e\bar{w} \tag{A.1}$$

where $\bar{w} = 1 + \sum_{jk} p_j p_k \sum_r a_{jk}(r)[b_{jk}(r) - c_{jk}(r)] + O(s^2)$.

$\bar{w}$ is the mean population fitness. The $O(s^2)$ term arises from the fact that the main term in $\bar{w}$ is the sole one only if the categories of donor and recipient are mutually exclusive, so that individuals who act as donors never behave as recipients, and vice versa. If the same individual can act as both donor and recipient during its lifetime, additional terms of the form abc (of order s^2) must be added.

A similar expression can be derived for the number of copies of A_i transmitted to the next generation, n'_i. To do this, we note that, in the absence of selection, the frequency of A_i in the gametes produced by an individual X who is related to another individual Y, of known genotype, is given by

$$p_X = r_{XY} p_Y + (1-r_{XY}) p_i \tag{A.2}$$

where p_X and p_Y are the frequencies of A_i among the gametes of X and Y respectively, and p_i is the population frequency of A_i (14,20). With selection, a term of order s must be added to the right-hand side of this equation. This result may be exploited as follows. Consider a heterozygote A_iA_j, for example. It behaves as a donor an average of $a_{ij}(r)$ times towards individuals of relatedness r; each interaction involves a change of $-e\ c_{ij}(r)$ in the number of copies of A_i which itself transmits to the next generation, and a gain of $e\ b_{ij}(r)\ [r + 2(1-r)p_i + O(s)]$ due to its effect on the recipient. Summing up over all genotypes and degrees of relationship, we obtain the expression

$$n_i' = 2ne\ \{p_i + p_i\ \textstyle\sum_{jr}\ p_j\ a_{ij}(r)\ [rb_{ij}(r)-c_{ij}(r)] +$$

$$p_i\ \textstyle\sum_{jkr}\ p_jp_k(1-r)a_{jk}(r)b_{jk}(r) + O(s^2)\}$$

(A.3)

The change in frequency between generations, Δp_i, is given by $(n_i'/2n') - (n_i/2n)$. Substituting from equations 1 and A.1-A.3, we obtain the final expression

$$\Delta p_i = p_i(\tilde{w}_i - \tilde{w}) + O(s^2)$$

(A.4)

where $\tilde{w}_i = \textstyle\sum_j p_j\tilde{w}_{ij}$ is the marginal inclusive fitness of A_i, and $\tilde{w} = \textstyle\sum_j p_j\tilde{w}_j$ is the mean inclusive fitness of the population.

Inclusive Fitness with Sex-Linked Inheritance

It is essential to distinguish behavioral interactions according to the sexes of the participants. Assuming male haploidy, we can write $a_i^m(r)$ and $a_i^f(r)$ for the expectations of the number of interactions as donor of an A_i male towards males and females of relatedness r. (Note that the numerical value of the relatedness coefficient may be different for males and females with the same relationship to the donor.) The costs and benefits associated with these interactions are $c_i^m(r)$, $c_i^f(r)$, $b_i^m(r)$, and $b_i^f(r)$. Similar terms characterize the interactions of an A_iA_j female as donor, except that double subscripts are used (e.g., $a_{ij}^m(r)$ for the expected number of interactions with males). Let α be the ratio of the number of males to the number of females at the period of the life-cycle at which interactions first occur. Inclusive fitnesses for males and females can be defined as follows

A_i male: $\tilde{w}_i^m = 1 + \sum\limits_r a_i^m(r) [rb_i^m(r) - c_i^m(r)] +$

$$\sum\limits_r a_i^f(r) [\alpha rb_i^f(r) - c_i^f(r)]. \tag{A.5a}$$

$A_i A_j$ female: $\tilde{w}_{ij}^f = 1 + \sum\limits_r a_{ij}^m(r) [\frac{1}{\alpha}rb_{ij}^m(r) - c_{ij}^m(r)] +$

$$\sum\limits_r a_{ij}^f(r) [rb_{ij}^f(r) - c_{ij}^f(r)] \tag{A.5b}$$

With sex differences in behavior, the frequencies of a given allele A_i in eggs and sperm, p_i^f and p_i^m, will generally differ. With selection of strength s, however, an expression of the following form can be obtained for the change in overall gene frequency $p_i = 1/3\ p_i^m + 2/3\ p_i^f$:

$$\Delta p_i = p_i(\tilde{w}_i - \tilde{w}) + O(s^2) \tag{A.6}$$

where $w_i = 1/3\ w_i^m + 2/3 \sum\limits_j p_j w_{ij}^f$ is the marginal inclusive fitness of A_i, and $\tilde{w} = \sum\limits_j p_j \tilde{w}_j$ is the mean inclusive fitness of the population.

REFERENCES

(1)   Alexander, R.D. 1974. The evolution of social behavior.
      Ann. Rev. Syst. Ecol. 5: 325-383.

(2)   Cavalli-Sforza, L.L., and Feldman, M.W. 1978. Darwinian
      selection and "altruism." Theor. Pop. Biol. 14: 268-280.

(3)   Charlesworth, B. 1978. Some models of the evolution of
      altruistic behavior between siblings. J. Theor. Biol.
      72: 297-319.

(4)   Charnov, E.L. 1977. An elementary treatment of the
      genetical theory of kin-selection. J. Theor. Biol. 66:
      541-550.

(5)   Charnov, E.L. 1978. Sex ratio selection in eusocial
      Hymenoptera. Amer. Nat. 112: 317-326.

(6)   Charnov, E.L. 1978. Evolution of eusocial behaviour:
      offspring choice or parental parasitism? J. Theor. Biol.
      75: 451-465.

(7)   Craig, R. 1979. Parental manipulation, kin selection, and
      the evolution of altruism. Evolution 33: 319-334.

(8)   Crozier, R.H. 1970. Coefficients of relationship and the
      identity of genes by descent in the Hymenoptera. Amer.
      Nat. 104: 216-217.

(9)   Elston, R.C., and Lange, K. 1976. The genotypic distribu-
      tion of relatives of homozygotes when consanguinity is
      present. Ann. Hum. Genet. 39: 493-496.

(10) Fisher, R.A. 1930. The Genetical Theory of Natural Selec-
      tion. Oxford: Clarendon Press.

(11) Haldane, J.B.S. 1932. The Causes of Evolution. London:
      Longmans, Green.

(12) Haldane, J.B.S. 1955. Population genetics. Penguin New
      Biology 18: 34-51.

(13) Hamilton, W.D. 1963. The evolution of altruistic behavior.
      Amer. Nat. 97: 354-356.

(14) Hamilton, W.D. 1964a. The genetical evolution of social
      behavior. I. J. Theor. Biol. 7: 1-16.

(15) Hamilton, W.D. 1964b. The genetical evolution of social
      behavior. II. J. Theor. Biol. 7: 17-52.

(16) Hamilton, W.D. 1972. Altruism and related phenomena, mainly
      in social insects. Ann. Rev. Ecol. Syst. 3: 193-232.

(17) Hamilton, W.D. 1975. Innate social aptitudes of Man: an
      approach from an evolutionary point of view. In Biosocial
      Anthropology, ed. R. Fox. London: Malaby Press.

(18) Harpending, H.C. 1979. The population genetics of inter-
      action. Amer. Nat. 113: 622-630.

(19) Hartl, D.L. 1971. Some aspects of selection in arrheno-
      tokous populations. Amer. Zool. 11: 309-325.

(20) Jacquard, A. 1974. The Genetic Structure of Populations.
      Berlin: Spinger-Verlag.

(21) Levitt, P.R. 1975. General kin selection models for
      genetic evolution of sib altruism in diploid and haplo-
      diploid species. Proc. Nat. Acad. Sci. 72: 4531-4535.

(22) MacNair, M.R., and Parker, G.A. 1978. Models of parent-
      offspring conflict. II. Promiscuity. Anim. Behav. 26:
      111-122.

(23) Malécot, G. 1948. Les Mathématiques de L'Heredité.
      Paris: Masson.

(24) Maynard Smith, J. 1964. Group selection and kin selection:
      a rejoinder. Nature 201: 1145-1147.

(25) Maynard Smith, J. 1965. The evolution of alarm calls.
      Amer. Nat. 59: 60-63.

(26) Michod, R.E. 1979. Genetical aspects of kin selection:
      effects of inbreeding. J. Theor. Biol. 81: 223-233.

(27) Nagylaki, T. 1979. Selection in dioecious populations.
      Ann. Hum. Genet. 43: 141-148.

(28) Orlove, M.J. 1975. A model of kin selection not invoking
      coefficients of relationship. J. Theor. Biol. 49: 289-310.

(29) Oster, G.F.; Eshel, I.; and Cohen, D. 1977. Worker-
      queen conflict and the evolution of social castes. Theor.
      Pop. Biol. 12: 49-85.

(30) Oster, G.F., and Wilson, E.O. 1978. Caste and Ecology in
      the Social Insects. Princeton: Princeton University Press.

(31) Parker, G.A., and MacNair, M.R. 1978. Models of parent-
      offspring conflict. I. Monogamy. Anim. Behav. 26: 97-110.

(32) Scudo, F.M., and Ghiselin, M.T. 1975. Familial selection
      and the evolution of social behavior. J. Genet. 62:
      1-31.

(33) Trivers, R.L. 1974. Parent-offspring conflict. Amer.
      Zool. 14: 249-264.

(34) Trivers, R.L., and Hare, H.   1976.   Haplodiploidy and the
      evolution of social insects.   Science 191: 249-263.

(35) Wade, M.   1979.   The evolution of social interactions by
      family selection.   Amer. Nat. 113: 399-417.

(36) West Eberhard, M.J.   1975.   The evolution of social behav-
      ior by kin selection.   Quart. Rev. Biol. 50: 1-33.

(37) Williams, G.C., and Williams, D.C.   1957.   Natural selec-
      tion of individually harmful social adaptations among sibs
      with special reference to the social insects.   Evolution
      11: 32-39.

(38) Wilson, E.O.   1975.   Sociobiology.   Cambridge, Massachusetts:
      Harvard University Press.

(39) Yokayama, S., and Felsenstein, J.   1978.   A model of kin
      selection for an altruistic trait considered as a quanti-
      tative character.   Proc. Nat. Acad. Sci. 75: 420-422.

Evolution of Social Behavior: Hypotheses and Empirical Tests, ed. H. Markl,
pp. 27-34. Dahlem Konferenzen 1980. Weinheim: Verlag Chemie GmbH.

Power and Limits of Optimization

J. Maynard Smith
School of Biological Sciences, University of Sussex
Falmer, Brighton BN1 9QG, England

Abstract. Optimization is an appropriate method for the study
of phenotypic evolution when the fitnesses of phenotypes are
not frequency-dependent. The structure of optimization methods
is briefly described. If, as is generally the case in social
interactions, fitnesses are frequency-dependent, the appropriate method is the theory of games. The concept of an
"evolutionarily stable strategy" or ESS is described. Some
problems concerning stability are discussed. Symmetric and
asymmetric games are defined. The problem of analyzing games
between relatives is mentioned. Genetic constraints which can
prevent a population reaching an ESS are indicated.

INTRODUCTION

The aim of most of the people at this meeting is to find

"functional" explanations for social behavior; that is, to

identify the selective forces responsible for the evolution of

such behavior. The role of optimization theory in this enter-

prise is to help us decide, in particular cases, which types

of behavior will be favored by selection. Two somewhat dif-

ferent methods are available. Optimization theory is appro-

priate when the results of particular acts by an individual

do not depend on what others are doing. If this is not so (i.e.,

if fitnesses are frequency-dependent), the appropriate method

is game theory.

Optimization theory is a branch of control theory, developed
for application to engineering and economic problems. Suppose,
for example, we wish to control a fishery. There is a set of
possible control actions available (e.g., the imposition of
quotas for particular species). We must also specify our aim
or "optimization criterion" (e.g., to maximize the sustained
yield). There is in addition a set of equations, not under
our control, which govern how the fishery behaves and how it
responds to our controls. The mathematical problem is then
to select those control actions which maximize our criterion.

In biological applications, the set of control actions is
replaced by the "phenotype set" - i.e., the set of phenotypes
assumed to be possible. The optimization criterion is ideally
the maximization of Darwinian fitness, but is often replaced
by optimization of some particular performance; for example,
in foraging theory it may be to minimize the time taken to
acquire a given quantity of food. Finally, there must be some
method whereby the fitnesses of different phenotypes can be
determined.

An example will make the basic method clearer. Mirmirani and
Oster (6) sought the optimal growth patterns for an annual
plant. They assumed that the rate at which a plant can accu-
mulate resources is a fixed function of its size. The control
variable, or phenotype set, is the proportion of the resource
accumulated which is allocated to further growth, as opposed
to seed production. The optimization criteria is to maximize
total seed production. For a given starting size and length
of season, they show that the optimal strategy is to allocate
everything to growth up to a threshold time T, and subsequently
to allocate everything to seeds, and they show how T could be
calculated.

As for all scientific theories, optimization models can be
tested by comparison with data, in this case, by a comparison
of actual and predicted phenotypes. It is important, however,

to be clear about what is being tested. Thus we are not testing the general proposition that all organisms optimize; still less are we testing the proposition that organisms have characteristics optimal for the survival of the species. What we are testing is the specific functional explanation of the behavior or structure under study. If predicted and observed phenotypes are different, it may be because we have wrongly described the range of phenotypes available or the ways in which phenotypic change alters fitness. A more serious methodological difficulty is that environmental conditions may have changed too rapidly for the species to adapt, so that a discrepancy between observed and predicted phenotypes may reflect evolutionary lag rather than a wrong identification of selective forces or possible phenotypes.

The concept of a phenotype set (a modified version of Levins' (5) "fitness set") raises problems. The essential feature is that some characteristics can change, whereas others are fixed. For example, in foraging theory it is assumed that behavior (e.g., length of time spent in a patch, or prey items taken) can change, but "skills" (e.g., ability to detect, catch, or digest prey) cannot. One can get some idea of what characteristics can change by looking at related species, or at intraspecific variation. One can sometimes get an idea as to how two characteristics may be jointly constrained from physical considerations. This is often true in functional anatomy (e.g., a given increase in speed of movement must be paid for by a corresponding decrease in strength), but rarely in behavior. The important point, however, is to remember that all optimization models contain assumptions, tacit or otherwise, about the phenotype set, and these assumptions may be wrong. For example, since Fisher (1), theories of the evolution of the sex ratio have been based on the assumption that the "costs" of male and female offspring are fixed, but the sex ratio is an evolutionary variable. A model in which these assumptions are reversed might be more realistic.

For all behaviors relevant in a social context, the payoff to
any strategy will depend on what others are doing. This is
true for many aspects of the phenotype classically dealt with
by optimization methods. Since the growth of a plant is influenced by its neighbors, Mirmirani and Oster (6) adopted a game
theory approach to find the optimal growth strategy for a plant
competing with others. If foraging occurs in flocks, Rohwer
(7) and others have shown that individuals adopt different
strategies whose payoffs are almost certainly frequency-dependent. It follows that evolutionary game theory, rather than
classical optimization, is the appropriate method of analysis.

The basic approach is as follows. We suppose that individuals
can follow any one of a set of strategies A,B,C.... These may
be "pure" (i.e., in situation x, always do X, and so on) or
"mixed" (i.e., with a stochastic element - in situation x, do
X with probability P and Y with probability 1-P). For any
strategy A, there is an expected "payoff" E(A,B) against any
strategy B. The payoff measures the change in fitness of an
individual adopting A if his opponent adopts B. Thus the set
of strategies is the phenotype set, and the payoffs determine
their fitnesses.

We assume that a population of individuals, each with an initial fitness of K, pairs with a series of randomly chosen opponents, acquiring in the process a changed fitness. A new generation is then produced by each individual reproducing its
own kind, in numbers proportional to its fitness. Thus the
model is one in which inheritance is parthenogenetic.

We seek an "Evolutionarily Stable Strategy" (or ESS), I, which
has the property that a population of individuals adopting I
cannot be invaded by a mutant adopting a different strategy.
Thus we consider a population consisting primarily of I individuals, with a small frequency p of mutant J individuals. Then,
if each individual engages in r contests, the expected fitnesses of I and J are

W(I) = K + r [(1-p)E(I,I) + pE(I,J)],
W(J) = K + r [(1-p)E(J,I) + pE(J,J)].
If I is an ESS, W(I) > W(J) for all J ≠ I. Since p is small,
this requires

either   E (I,I) > E(J,I)

or   E (I,I) = E(J,I) and E(I,J) > E(J,J).   (1)

These are the conditions for I to be an ESS, provided that the
contest is "symmetric"; that is, if there is no role differentiation between the contestants which would enable an individual to adopt the strategy "play A if in role 1; play B in
role 2." Examples of asymmetric contests are those between a
male and a female, or between the owner of a resource and an
interloper, or between a larger and smaller contestant (provided
that the size difference is known to the contestants and hence
capable of influencing their choice of strategy).

Most (but not all) pairwise contests are asymmetric. The
main application of the theory of symmetric games in biology
is to cases in which an individual plays, not against one or
more randomly-chosen opponents, but against the whole population. For example, Fisher's (1) theory of the sex ratio
in effect describes a game in which each individual plays
against all others. It is easy to see that the same mathematical model applies to cases of "playing the field" as to a
series of pairwise contests.

In discussing the stability of the equilibria given by Eq. 1,
it is convenient to consider the "Hawk-Dove" game, defined by
the payoff matrix:

		player 2	
		H	D
	H	-1	2
Player 1	D	0	1

The only strategy satisfying Eq. 1 is "Play H with probability
0.5 and D with probability 0.5." However, a genetically polymorphic population with equal numbers of Hawks and Doves would

also be evolutionarily stable. Is it always true that if there
is a mixed ESS satisfying Eg. 1, then the corresponding genetically polymorphic population is also stable?   Unfortunately
not.   If there are only two pure strategies, then the polymorphic population is necessarily stable, but with more than
two pure strategies it may or may not be. However, this does
not alter the fact that a mixed strategy satisfying Eq. 1 is
stable. Some authors familiar with classical developments in game
theory have stated that an ESS is equivalent to a Nash Equilibrium. This is not so, as is obvious from the Hawk-Dove game.
Thus the Nash equilibria for this game are "Player 1 plays H,
player 2 plays D," and "Player 1 plays D, player 2 plays H."
For either of these strategy pairs, it would not pay either
unilaterally to alter his strategy, and it is this which characterizes a Nash equilibrium.   However, these are logically
impossible as evolutionary strategies in a symmetric game.
This confusion led Mirmirani and Oster (6) to give the wrong
stability criterion for their problem of competing plants.

Most pairwise contests are likely to be asymmetric. Provided
that the asymmetry can be unambiguously perceived by both contestants, the analysis of such contests is relatively simple,
since Selten (8) has shown that an ESS of an asymmetric contest must be a pure strategy; that is, it must have the form
"In role 1, always do I; in role 2, always do J." Hammerstein
(3) has used these results to analyze contests with multiple
asymmetries (e.g., of size and of ownership). Difficulties arise,
however, when contestants have only partial information about
an asymmetry.

A further difficulty arises because many real contests occur
between relatives. A natural way of tackling this problem (6)
is to replace the payoff matrix by a derived "inclusive fitness
matrix." Thus if the coefficient of relatedness between
opponents is r, we replace matrix a by matrix b :

	a				b	
	H	D			H	D
H	a	b	⟶	H	a(1+r)	b + cr
D	c	d		D	c + br	d(1+r)

Grafen (2) has shown that this method does not always lead
to a correct solution. However, it turns out (4) that a true
ESS (by Grafen's method) is necessarily an ESS of the derived
inclusive fitness matrix, although this is not sufficient to
guarantee stability. If the ESS is a mixed one, it is necessary
that mixed strategists should exist and reproduce; the corresponding genetically polymorphic population will in general
not be stable.

An obvious weakness of this game theory approach is that it is
based on a model with parthenogenetic inheritance. Do the
conclusions hold for sexual diploids? Clearly they do if the
ESS, pure and mixed, can exist as a genetic homozygote. I have
analyzed the case of the two-pure-strategy game, when strategies are determined by two alleles at a locus, the three genotypes having different probabilities of adopting particular
strategies. It can be shown that (with trivial exceptions) the
population will either evolve to the ESS frequency or, if
this lies outside the range of genetic possibilities, it will
evolve as close to the ESS as possible. There will be cases
in which genetic constraints will prevent a population evolving to an ESS, but this does not seem likely to be a serious
limitation in applying the method.

REFERENCES

(1)   Fisher, R.A.   1930.   The Genetic Theory of Natural
      Selection.   Oxford University Press.

(2)   Grafen, A.   1979.   The problem of games between relatives.
      Anim. Behav. 27: 905.

(3)   Hammerstein, P.   1980.   The role of asymmetries in animal
      contests.   Anim. Behav., in press.

(4)   Hines, G., and Maynard Smith, J.   1979.   Games between
      relatives.   J. Theor. Biol. 79: 19.

(5)   Levins, R.   1962.   Theory of fitness in a heterogeneous en-
      vironment.   Am. Nat. 96: 361.

(6)   Mirmirani, M., and Oster, G.   1978.   Competition, kin
      selection and evolutionarily stable strategies.   Theor.
      Pop. Biol. 13: 304.

(7)   Rohwer, S.   1977.   Status signalling in Harris sparrows:
      some experiments in deception.   Behaviour 61: 107.

(8)   Selten, R.   1978.   A note on evolutionarily stable strate-
      gies in asymmetric animal conflicts.   Working paper,
      Institute of Mathematical Economics.   University of Bielefeld.

Evolution of Social Behavior: Hypotheses and Empirical Tests, ed. H. Markl,
pp. 35-58. Dahlem Konferenzen 1980. Weinheim: Verlag Chemie GmbH.

Mechanisms of Identification and Discrimination in Social Hymenoptera

B. Hölldobler* and C. D. Michener**
*MCZ-Laboratories, Department of Biology, Harvard University
  Cambridge, MA 02138
**Department of Entomology, University of Kansas
  Lawrence, KS 66045, USA

INTRODUCTION

Modern theories of the evolution by natural selection of insect societies, in particular the kinship selection theory (14,
15, 35) postulate social discrimination on the basis of differential degree of genetical relatedness. These theoretical concepts have raised again one of the central questions in experimental insect sociobiology: which behavioral mechanisms reg-
ulate colony cohesiveness, group recognition and antagonistic
behavior in social insects? What are the cues for identification of kin versus members of alien conspecific societies?

In part, these questions have been asked before by several investigators and some fragmentary answers have been given (see
reviews in (25,39). It was found that individually distinctive
or colony odors occur throughout the eusocial insects and that in
highly eusocial species they constitute the central mechanism of
colony integration and organization. Furthermore, the early evidence seemed to suggest that species-specific odors have an innate
basis, whereas colony-specific odors are acquired at least in part
from the environment.

ENVIRONMENTAL FACTORS

In some species of the social wasp genus Polistes West-Eberhard's considerations (38) suggest that environmental cues
which define the home range of a group might be responsible
for kin identification. Foundress groups, usually sisters, of some
Polistes species often aggregate at the parental nest. Individuals encountering one another within the group's home range
should behave as if they were sisters or close relatives, but
individuals that meet outside the home range should "assume"
that they are less related and therefore behave more antagonis-
tically. As West (37) pointed out, group founding in some Polistes
leads to less dispersal and consequently makes populations more
viscous, whereas solitary nest founding in other Polistes increases dispersion and lowers population viscosity. Starr (32)
recently summarized these considerations by stating: "It is al-
together reasonable, given the basic statement of kin selection
theory, that, in the absence of direct ability to assess the
relatedness of individuals, selection should favor a lower level
of intolerance or selfishness toward the population as a whole
in more viscous populations."

Michener (25) reviews similar observations in the primitively
eusocial bee Lasioglossum imitatum and other species. Adult
bees can be transferred into foreign nests without releasing
antagonistic behavior. However, if the bees had already begun
to forage and had become familiar with the environment of their
own nest, the transferred bees did not stay in the foreign nest
but returned to their own. Under natural conditions this home
range fidelity may very well suffice in maintaining colony cohesiveness.

It is reasonable to speculate that there is a focus for kin
selection favoring the evolution of colony-specific orientation cues that induce individuals to bring the resources they
have foraged to their own nests and relatives. Indeed, home
range fidelity and territorial exclusiveness are often enforced
by colony-specific chemical markers.

In the harvesting ant Pogonomyomex the foraging grounds are partitioned in irregular patterns among the colonies. The trunk
trails from the nests to the food sites are not only marked
by species-specific mixtures of compounds (hydrocarbons of
the Dufour's glands), but also by colony-specific components.
In addition Hangartner et al. (16) have shown that P. badius
workers are able to distinguish the odor of their own nest material from that of other nests. In a very recent study Trani-
ello demonstrated that colonies of the ant Lasius neoniger occur at high densities in which entrances of neighboring nests
may be as close as 5 cm. Foragers depart from the nest along
previously established trunk trails that partition foraging
territories by directing workers from nearby colonies away
from each other. These trunk trails are chemically marked with
colony-specific components, which originate from the hindgut.
In the African weaver ant (Oecophylla longinoda) Hölldobler and
Wilson discovered that workers mark their entire territory with
persistent pheromones that are distinguishable to the ants at
the colony level (21).   Workers detecting the deposits of an
alien colony respond with increased amounts of aversive and aggressive behavior. Since these colony-specific pheromones are
at least in part contained in the rectal fluid, it is possible
that their colony specificity is due to a different dietary
mix of neighboring colonies.

The evolution of the use of colony-specific chemicals into
group membership cues accompanied the development of long-
lived nests in which brood and food resources are stored. In
such insects the nest entrance is typically guarded by some
colony members which check each entering individual and behave
aggressively toward nonmembers. In the Meliponini (stingless
bees), colony members must guard food and nest construction
material against the intrusion of robbers belonging to the
same species. Honeybees (Apis mellifera), too, must guard
against hive-robbing by alien conspecifics when food is scarce,
and the frequency of nest entrance-guarding varies in relation

to food abundance (review in (25)). In the honey ant Myrmecocystus mimicus, raids on conspecific neighbor nests can lead to intraspecific enslavement of the worker castes of the raided colony (19).

What is the source of the colony odor? No particular pheromone has been isolated to account for individual colony odor in any social insect species.   The hypotheses that in bees the Nasanov gland and in ants the metapleural gland are responsible for a colony odor pheromone have been disproved. But it has been demonstrated that olfactory conditioning to local odors, particularly those associated with food and nest material, can profoundly influence colony odor discrimination. In a classic experiment with the honeybee, Kalmus and Ribbands (23) manipulated a decline in aggressive behavior between bees of different colonies by taking them all to an isolated moor where only a single flowering species was available. The reverse effect, different diets disrupting colony unity, was also demonstrated when colony subunits were separated and maintained on different diets.   In bumblebees, colony odor could be changed by simply confining bees near alien nests.   This demonstrated that the odors to which nestmates responded did not have to come from ingested food but instead originated at least in part as odors absorbed directly into the cuticle.

There exists a wealth of experimental evidence indicating that in most advanced eusocial insect species, newly emerged adults learn the colony-specific odor. Young callow ant workers accept nestmates with any colony odor. After a certain degree of aging, however, they clearly discriminate between the odor of their own colony and that of other colonies. Jaisson (22) suggested that this form of learning may be imprinting, because in Formica polyctena he found that there is a critical period of the first 10-15 days of adult life during which odor recognition is established.   Indeed it is possible to condition individuals olfactorily by transferring them among nests as larvae or pupae, so that they treat members of alien colonies

or even of different species as nestmates. If, as is often
assumed, the colony odor is caused by the absorption of a specific mixture of environmental odorants into the cuticle, it
is not clear why larvae, pupae, and callow workers should not
carry the odor of the colony in which they are raised and
therefore be just as subject to aggression from members of a
foreign colony as their older nestmates.   To explain these
contradictions we can hypothesize that in the brood stages the
colony odor is masked by the brood-tending pheromones, which
are not colony-specific. It is also conceivable that these
pheromones have a high position in a hierarchical order of a
pheromone system and "dominate" any other colony-specific
odorous cues.

The absence of brood discrimination has actually been exploited
by many socially parasitic ants that conduct so-called slave
raids, during which they rob brood of closely related neighboring species. When these kidnapped pupae eclose in the slave
raiders' nest, the young workers are "imprinted" with the odor
of their captors' colony and in the future behave in a hostile
manner toward their real sisters, who remained behind in their
mutual mother's nest. The assumption of a high position of the
brood pheromone in a pheromone hierarchy system would also imply that
the Q/K ratio, i.e., the ratio of pheromone molecules released
to the response-threshold concentration (40), should be very
low. A high Q/K would saturate the nest with the dominant signal, and colony odors and other chemical signals would become
almost ineffective. Indeed, recent findings by Walsh and
Tschinkel (36) confirmed that the brood pheromones are nonvol-
atile and are effective only at very close range. In addition,
Hölldobler has experimental evidence that these pupal pheromones
are at least in part contained in the exuvial liquid. During
eclosion from the pupa, callow workers are still contaminated
by these pheromones, which might be the reason that callow workers can also be transferred to alien colonies. The processes
of losing the pupal pheromone signal and adopting and learning
the colony odor after eclosion seem to be well coordinated.

In light of these findings it is quite clear why Ribbands (29)
concluded that colony odor in ants is primarily genetically determined, while being acquired from the environment in honeybees. This is not to say that there is no indication of a genetical basis of colony odor determination in social Hymenoptera.
There has been a tendency for investigators to take an either/or
approach to disentangling the contributions of genetic and environmental factors to the nestmate recognition cues, and too
frequently the conclusion has been drawn that because of the
demonstrable influence of environmental factors, genetic influences do not exist.

INTRINSIC FACTORS
Genetically specified strain (or in out-breeding populations,
individual) differences in odors occur not only in at least
certain social Hymenoptera, but also in Drosophila (2,12) and
probably in various nonsocial Hymenoptera. Before we discuss details of these findings, we define two terms as follows: Odor signals that differ among individuals of a population, when not of extrinsic origin, can be called discriminators or recognition pheromones (12). In known cases, discriminators must first be learned, after which recognition
or discrimination may occur. There is probably no such thing
as innate knowledge of degree of relationship, of colony membership, etc. Response to a given individual's odor will depend
entirely on whether that individual or one like it has or has
not been smelled before. Discriminators may have feed-back in
addition to pheromonal functions; thus an individual may respond to its own odor as distinguished from odors of other conspecific individuals. So far the chemical basis of discrimination
is not known for any insect species. The nest entrance marking
substances discussed below are probably discriminators as are
the substance responsible for recognition of individual females
by males of the bee Lasioglossum zephyrum (3,4) and the rare
male phenomenon in Drosophila (2,12). The expression discriminating substances is used when it is not clear whether identification of an individual is based on secreted odor substances

which are genetically controlled (discriminators) or on environmental materials that differ among individuals or colonies.

Different groups of authors (5,12) have independently pointed out the probability that discriminators consist of multiple active components (as do various chemically known insect pheromones). Such a system allows differences to exist and be recognized with relatively few compounds and receptors. Suppose a discriminator consists of 10 compounds, each of which can be recognized at four different concentrations relative to the others, then 4^{10} different mixtures will be distinguishable on the basis of only 10 compounds. The alternative of as many compounds as there are olfactorily distinguishable individuals or strains, etc., is unthinkable both from the standpoint of synthesis and perception.

In nonsocial Hymenoptera (as well as in social ones), discriminators may help individuals find their own nests. Many observers have marveled at the ability of nonsocial wasps and bees to return, each to its own burrow, even when there are many similar burrows nearby, and especially when the burrow entrances have been obscured and minor landmarks destroyed by trampling or other disturbances. Return to the correct vicinity is surely primarily by visual cues but olfactory cues are likely aids to a returning individual in selecting the right spot in an area of disturbed sand at which to dig down to its own nest.

Shinn (31) remarked that nests of a solitary, ground-nesting andrenid bee, Calliopsis andreniformis, may have different odors. Working with pairs of nests only a few centimeters apart, he exchanged the tumuli of loose soil at the burrow entrances while both bees were away foraging. On returning, over half of the bees went first to their own tumuli at artificial locations. Presumably such bees recognized their own or their nests' odors in contrast to their neighbors' odors. The lemon-like odor of this bee can be perceived by man in the tumuli, showing that

the bees do leave secretions there. Unfortunately, Shinn's numbers were small (14 bees) and his controls were not explicitly
described; the studies are suggestive but should be repeated.
Although differences in Calliopsis nest odors could be due to
different soils or foods, the nests were close together, about
the same depth, in apparently homogeneous soil, and all the
foraging appeared to be on nearby flowers of Trifolium. It
therefore seems probable that nest recognition was based on
secreted, individually different odors, each bee having learned
her own.

A study of short-range orientation to nest entrances by solitary
bees and wasps, in this case Megachilidae and Sphecidae, nesting
in numerous adjacent hollow bamboo stems, was made by Steinmann
(33,34). He sawed off 4 cm long nest entrance sections and replaced them (as controls), exchanged them with adjacent nests,
or extracted them in alcohol and ether before replacing them,
and observed the behavior of bees returning to their nests.
The bees and wasps successfully entered their own nests in the
controls, but the great majority (70 to 97%) did not do so if
the nests had the wrong entrances or if the entrances had been
extracted. He therefore postulated individually different
marking substances on the entrances of the nests. He believed
these substances to be of glandular origin - what we have called
discriminators - but did not experimentally exclude the possibility
that they might be of environmental origin.

Among highly social insects, inherited colony odors probably
exist in some cases, and discriminators for recognition for individuals may also play a role. In the primitive ant genus
Myrmecia, pupae can be transferred from one colony to another
conspecific colony, but when the adult workers eclose they are
attacked by the conspecific aliens (17). Although there is some
reason for caution in interpreting these results as proof of the
existence of genetically determined colony-specific recognition
cues, the experiment nevertheless demonstrates a greater degree

of identification signal integrity than found in most other ant species (11). Workers of honeybees frequently kill one after another of the queens produced in a colony, before finally accepting one. M.D. Breed, S.K. Smith, and C.D. Rasmussen (personal communicaton) have shown that queens probably produce discriminators. Workers might preferentially accept queens with discriminators like their own, i.e., closely related to themselves, so that the inclusive fitness of the workers would be maximized.

The most convincing evidence for a genetic component in kin recognition was recently found in the primitively eusocial bee Lasioglossum zephyrum. This is the first experimental evidence that individual social hymenopterans not only can distinguish between nestmates and nonnestmates but are also able to respond differentially to degree of relatedness of individuals within a group of nestmates.

The following concerns only females of Lasioglossum zephyrum. In this species, caste determination occurs in the adult stage and there is a continuum in ovarian sizes from largest (queen) to smallest (principal forager) (28). The bees in a rather small colony of say six females are usually distinguishable behaviorally as a queen, a principal guard, a principal forager, and "other workers," more or less intermediate between the principal guard and principal forager (10,27).

There is evidence that a female is able to recognize the caste (or position in a social hierarchy) of another female regardless of colony of origin. This recognition is likely to be by odor although behavior has not been excluded. For example, a guard's response to a forager from another colony is different from that to another guard (9). Since caste recognition apparently occurs regardless of familial relationship and regardless of the nest from which bees are selected, it must be mediated in a different way than by the discriminators.

"Colony odor" may well be in part or wholly different from a
combination of individual odors. It has been little studied
in L. zephyrum but discriminators or other compounds do influence attraction of a bee to its own vs. foreign nests. This
response varies, depending on whether the bees in the nest are
sisters or a mixture of unrelated bees. Therefore, it is likely
that there is a genetic component in nest or colony odor (24).

As to the odors of individuals, discriminating substances have
been studied at nest entrances by introducing foreign bees (or
nestmates, as controls) into the nest entrance tubes. Such a
bee is either accepted or rejected by the guard (7,8). Rejection responses often begin when the introduced bee is still
several millimeters from the guard, showing that volatile substances are involved. Results are essentially the same whether
the introduced bee is dead or alive. Visual signals and vibra-
tions are thus eliminated as possible cues, and odor is left as
the only likely explanation for the observed behavior.

Several experiments involving transferring bees between nests,
blowing air continuously from one nest to another, transferring
soil from one nest to another, and adding foreign odors (pepper-
mint, molasses) failed to show that guards respond to distinctive odors of environmental origin on bodies of introduced bees.
Hence it was decided several years ago that discriminators were
probably involved (6). However, since it was wished to study
discriminators, all experiments except as specifically indicated
were conducted so as to minimize environmental factors: in each
series of trials the only foods ever provided were mixed Typha
pollen from a single jar and honey from another jar; nests were
in soil from a single batch, sifted and mixed before use.

Artificially assembled groups of unrelated females form functional "mixed colonies" with a queen, principal forager, and
principal guard (5,10,28). Bees at nest entrances usually
accept nestmates and reject foreign bees (6-8). In different
series of experiments 7 to 14% of the foreign bees were accepted,

however, suggesting that there may be odor mimics, i.e., individuals with similar or identical odors.

One concludes that bees learn the odors of their nestmates
either as individuals, or as a group (i.e., a mixture) of
familiar odors, and then accept nestmates or bees that smell
like nestmates, and reject other bees. Young females (up to
about two days old) are regularly accepted, as is necessary to
permit colony growth; presumably as such individuals develop
their odors, these are learned by the nestmates. Isolation
experiments on bees from mixed colonies suggest that guards
progressively forget nestmate odors, so that after 12 days of
isolation only 10% of the nestmates are accepted (24).

Greenberg (13) verified that guards are reacting to discriminators
by proving the existence of a major genetic component of kin recognition in L. zephyrum. At nest entrances he introduced bees to
guards having known relationships to them. All colonies consisted
of sisters. He bred bees in the laboratory to produce colonies
having 12 different levels of geneological relationship to one another, from "unrelated" to colonies whose members, even though living
in two separate nests, were sisters in inbred (brother-sister
mated) lines. Eleven of the levels of relationship (unrelated
plus various aunts, nieces, and cousins) involved bees reared
in different nests, while three involved sisters produced in
cells of the same nest, but the bees were removed and established in separate nests before they emerged from their cells.
(As noted by Michener (26), isolation and defecation make it
unlikely that such a bee would carry much environmental odor
from its parental nest. It might, however, have learned odors
as a larva that could influence its behavior as an adult.) In
all cases, bees tested (introduced bee and guard) had never
seen or smelled one another. Thus odors of environmental origin could not influence the results for non-sisters and probably
did not for sisters. The results showed a striking positive
relationship between the coefficients of relatedness of the bees
tested (introduced bee and guard to which it is presented) and
the frequency with which guards permitted introduced bees to

pass. This relationship was significant even when the sister data were excluded.

Greenberg's results were based on 1586 introductions, for which only data on acceptance or rejection were analyzed. However, in fact, there are various degrees of response by guards, from immediate acceptance to permanent rejection, and these appear to be correlated with relatedness (L. Greenberg, personal communication).

Greenberg's illustration showed a linear regression line having an origin at about zero for acceptance or unrelated bees. Actually a power function fits the data better, but not significantly so (L. Greenberg, personal communication). We believe the curvilinear relationship better represents biological facts, however, because it would have an origin above that of the straight regression line at 8 to 10% acceptance of unrelated bees, a level that has been approximated not only by Greenberg but also in other studies. Moreover, at the opposite extreme, the points are above the straight regression line for foreign bees that are sisters (in inbred lines) of guards; such bees are nearly all accepted.

Continuing to use the differences between closely related bees (presumably smelling alike) and distantly related bees as a tool, Buckle and Greenberg (in preparation) shed further light on discriminators by making special types of artificial mixed colonies. One type (3 + 3 colony) consisted of six females comprising two groups of three sisters from unrelated inbred lines. A guard in such a colony normally accepts not only its five nestmates but their other sisters kept in different nests, and never previously presented to the guard. This result was expected since, as noted earlier, mixed colonies can be formed, and since Greenberg (13) has already shown that guards confuse nestmates with nestmates' sisters (especially in inbred lines).

An important point is that the guard accepts at virtually equal rates its own non-resident sisters and the non-resident sisters

of its unrelated nestmates. Thus there is no evidence that the
guard draws any distinction among nestmates based on similarity
to itself.

Buckle and Greenberg made similar artificial colonies consisting
of five sisters from an inbred line and one unrelated bee (the
odd bee). When one of the five sisters was a guard, it normally
accepted its own sisters kept in different nests and also the
sisters of the odd bee. This is basically not a different result from that described for 3 + 3 colonies (therefore the test
was only repeated a few times).

Most unexpectedly, however, the odd bee seemingly learns the
discriminators of its nestmates but does not learn or know its
own odor. Several experiments indicate this. For example, the
odd bee accepts its own sisters much less frequently than do its
nestmates.

Some interpretations of the behavioral findings described above
are: Guards are able to recognize degrees of similarity of arriving bees to nestmates; they are more likely to accept a close
relative of a nestmate than a distant one. This does not mean
that they have any innate ability to assess kinship. The odors
are genetically controlled but the responses to them are learned,
as shown in the mixed colonies. A bee acting as a guard has
learned to accept its nestmates; the more similar in odor a foreign
bee is to a guard's nestmate, the more likely it is to be accepted
by the guard; and the more closely related the foreign bee is to
the guard's nestmate, the more likely it is to be similar in odor
to the nestmate.

The question arises as to whether the discriminators used by
guards to admit or reject females arriving at nest entrances are
the same substances as those used by males in distinguishing among
females. Kukuk et al. (24) postulate that they are different substances, because a young female attracts males but elicits no
agonism from guards until she is two or three days old. However,
the same results might come from guard and male responses to the

same mixture of compounds but at different concentrations or in
different contexts. An argument suggesting possible identity
of discriminators for the two functions is that female bees of
all ages including workers that do not ordinarily mate, stimulate
male pouncing and mating attempts. Why should these non-receptive
females secrete a mating pheromone through their lives unless
it also has another function, e.g., nest or individual discrimination?

This brings us to the consideration of two genetic models for
the innate components of colony odor in social Hymenoptera recently suggested by Crozier and Dix (11):
1. The "individualistic model" proposes "that innate colony-
odor differences between the colonies of social Hymenoptera
are determined by allelic variation at a number of colony-odor
loci. Workers recognize each other as nestmates if they share
at least one allele for each odor locus."
2. The "Gestalt model" proposes that colony-odor components
are transferred between all individuals of the colony. The
blend of the many individual odors represents the specific
"colony odor Gestalt." Only those colonies with the same genetic
mix of workers will have the same "colony odor Gestalt" and
therefore will not discriminate against each other.

The Lasioglossum data do not support the "individualistic,"
model which proposes that the colony constitutes a homogeneous
group in the terminology of Barrows, Bell, and Michener (5), i.e.,
a group whose members are recognized by one or more common features resulting from the common alleles which they possess. For
discriminators this is not valid in L. zephyrum. The ability of
unrelated bees in mixed colonies to accept nestmates and reject
other bees (unless closely related) is contrary to this model.

The alternative, the "Gestalt model," proposes that colony odor
is a blend of the individual odors, transferred among colony
members, and that it is this "colony odor Gestalt" that is used
to accept nestmates. Although the colony might be heterogeneous
in compounds that the various individuals produce, it is homogeneous in the odor mixture absorbed on them. This model also

is not supported by the data on L. zephyrum. If it were correct,
the associates of the odd bee should have acquired enough odor
from the odd bee that even if it could not smell itself, it should
have detected its own odor on its nestmates and admitted its
sisters. Perhaps more telling, differences between the "odor
Gestalt" of a mixed colony such as a 3 + 3 colony and odors of
unmixed groups of sisters of members of that colony should prevent acceptance of such sisters. But such sisters (especially
if in inbred lines) are readily accepted in the mixed colony.
Moreover, when bees from a 3 + 3 colony are introduced to guards
of colonies consisting of unmixed sisters of bees in the 3 + 3
colony, there is again no support to the contention that bees acquire the odors of their nestmates; acceptance depends on familial
relationship, not on colony make-up.

A problem with both of the Crozier and Dix models is that they
do not involve learning; for that reason, neither is appropriate
for L. zephyrum. Generally Crozier and Dix favor the "Gestalt
model," because, besides other reasons, "many species have
multi-queened colonies or multiple insemination, or both; such
a colony make-up would very often lead to severe internecine
strife under the "individualistic model," but not under the
"Gestalt model," unless inbreeding or other factors maintained
very high levels of relationship."

For insects living in large colonies it is likely that a homogeneous group (whether homogeneous because of shared alleles,
exchanged secreted odors, or environmental odors) provides the
simple and probably the usual mechanism for recognition of colony
members. For the reasons indicated above, however, we believe
that for insects in small colonies, differences among heterogeneous individuals are perceived, as is also probable in the nonsocial ancestors. Such individual differences might be memorized by
colony members and could result in individual recognition. On
the other hand, the differing familiar individuals could constitute, for the guard, a heterogeneous group of "individuals
smelled before" (no memory of individually distinguishing features), contrasted to unfamiliar individuals. Nothing in the

data on L. zephyrum so far collected, either on mating behavior
or on guard behavior, indicates which of these alternatives is
most likely. As Barrows, Bell, and Michener (5) say, however, the
simple mechanism may be one which, in spite of the input of individual differences, perceives the familiar individuals as a group.

Another important point rarely mentioned in discussions about
colony odor is that this odor seems usually less distinct in
truly polygynous ant species than in monogynous species*. Queens
of truly polygynous species such as Formica polyctena, F. exec-
toides, or Monomorium pharaonis are usually not aggressive toward
one another. In fact, they are often found clustered together
in large numbers, and so far as known all lay eggs and are not
organized into dominance orders. Queens of monogynous colonies,
in contrast, do not tolerate other queens in their vicinity. The
difference is maintained among mature colonies: workers of polygynous colonies display little or no aggression toward conspecific neighboring colonies. Sometimes the whole population of
nests can be considered as one large polydomous colony, because
workers, brood, and even queens are frequently exchanged between different nests. In contrast, workers of most monogynous species discriminate aggressively against members of
conspecific neighbor colonies, and they are often highly territorial.

By comparing the mating and colony founding strategies we can
further conclude that within-nest matings occur quite frequently in polygynous species. This in turn leads to a relatively
high degree of inbreeding, with new colonies being mostly
founded by budding. In monogynous species, within-nest matings
are extremely rare. Usually all alate sexuals leave the nest
during the nuptial flight period, and individuals from many
different nests mix in massive mating aggregations. This procedure assures a high degree of outbreeding. After mating, the
young females of most monogynous species found their colonies

---

*The special cases of oligogyny and functional monogyny are not
considered here.

independently, usually far away from their mother colony. Consequently, neighboring colonies of many polygynous species can be expected to be genetically much more closely related than neighboring colonies of monogynous species.

If genetic differences play a role in the determination of colony odors in ants, the simplest mechanism would appear to be for the queen to provide the essential ingredients. In the simplest conceivable case, where two alleles influenced odor at each locus, only ten such loci would generate $3^{10} = 59,049$ diploid combinations; three alleles at ten loci could yield 9^{10} such combinations (20). Monogyny would make such a system easily operable; polygyny would tend to break it down.

This mechanism of colony odor determination by queens is also functionally simple given the central importance of the queen to colony social organization and control of worker reproductivity. An ant queen is highly attractive to workers in her colony. She is continuously licked and groomed, thus facilitating the chemical communication of her presence. With the aid of radioactive tracers it has been demonstrated that queen-derived substances are distributed from worker to worker through the whole colony. Experimentally presented queen pheromones have been found to attract the workers of a variety of ant species.

Control of workers by queens seems to us a major principle in the organization of monogynous ant colonies, and consequently the queen appears to be a logical source for the colony odor. It is entirely conceivable that genes responsible for colony odor determination are only switched on in the reproductive queen caste, and that workers are imprinted on the queen odor shortly after eclosion.

Recent observations suggest that in monogynous outbred colonies multiple inseminations of the queen are much more common

than previously assumed (18). This means that the average relatedness between individual sisters can be lower than the 1/2
relatedness between a queen and her offspring, and that the
worker groups are relatively heterogeneous genetically. It is
reasonable to speculate that only by the unifying power of the
queen odor can the social integrity of the worker groups be
maintained.   These considerations support the parental manipulation theory (1,27), according to which selection acts on
queens to produce manipulated worker castes whose major tasks
are to secure nest sites and other essential ecological resources and to assist the queen in raising her reproductively
fully competent offspring. In our view, many of the physiological mechanisms of social control in monogynous colonies of ants
and also bees are better explained by the parental manipulation
theory than by the kin selection theory.

On the other hand, in truly polygynous ant colonies the life
span of individual queens seems to be considerably shorter
than that of queens of most monogynous species. A large percentage of multiple queens are not the mothers of the workers
but their sisters, because after mating, many of the young
queens are readopted into their mother-colony. In addition,
it is not unusual for mating to occur within the nest. It
is difficult to imagine how the parental manipulation theor-
ry can explain the social organization of these polygynous
colonies. Hamilton (14) postulated that inbreeding should fa-
cilitate the evolution of altruism and might account for the
existence of polygyny in some wasp species. Later Hamilton (14)
and also Trivers and Hare (35) argued that although inbreeding
should favor selection against "selfishness," it should not
necessarily favor the development of sterile castes. Several
characteristics of most polygynous ant species seem to support these assumptions:

1. The morphological difference between workers and queens is
considerably less distinct in polygynous species than in most
monogynous species.

2. In polygynous species worker fertility does not seem to be suppressed by queen pheromones but rather by other nutritional-
physiological factors, and it is even possible that at least
in some polygynous species workers regularly contribute to the
male production by laying unfertilized eggs (see reviews in (30)).

3. Finally, the very fact that in truly polygynous colonies
thousands of queens frequently coexist, behaving towards each
other passively, seemingly nonselfishly, and that frequently
whole local populations of polygynous colonies can be considered as one enormously enlarged family unit, supports
Hamilton's theoretical considerations.

No colony or individual discriminating mechanisms other than
chemical signals are known in social insects. In summarizing,
we list four different conceivable modes of colony or individual recognition:
1. Individuals produce discriminators which serve for individual or group recognition.
2. Individuals produce substances which are distributed among
all colony members to produce a collective discriminating substance characteristic of the colony.
3. The queen produces her discriminators which are distributed
to the workers to produce the colony odor.
4. Environmental odors (for example, from food and/or nest
material) can be the source of colony specific discriminating
substances.

All of the above involve learning. Other possibilities, we
believe unlikely ones, involve non-learned (innate) recognition of discriminators. Moreover, any combination of the modes
listed above is possible.

It is interesting to consider the evolution of discriminator
function in nonsocial and social forms. In Drosophila it seems
that unfamiliar discriminators secreted by males elicit increased acceptance by females. In Lasioglossum it seems that

unfamiliar discriminators secreted by females elicit increased
copulatory attempts by males. A familiar discriminator at the
nest entrance of a bee or wasp may elicit return to its own nest,
or an unfamiliar one may cause departure from a foreign nest.
Discrimination among conspecifics at the nest entrance of L.
zephyrum, however, may be different in that a familiar discriminator may inhibit the defensive action usual to a bee facing an
intruder. It seems probable that a solitary bee or wasp will
ordinarily attack any other insect, including a conspecific, that
enters its nest. A major early step in becoming eusocial must
have been acquisition of the ability to tolerate conspecifics.
Yet as shown by L. zephyrum, at a very early stage if not at
the inception of eusocial evolution, the ability arose to discriminate between nestmates and foreign conspecifics. Familiar
discriminators appear to elicit admittance, while unfamiliar
discriminators permit the probably ancestral defense reaction
to take place. Even in highly social Hymenoptera, such as honeybees, discriminators may have similar functions, inhibiting attack on individuals with familiar odors, although odors of environmental origins are sometimes more important as colony odors.

Acknowledgements. The following persons read and commented on
portions of our manuscript: L. Greenberg, G. Buckle, P. Kukuk,
and E.O. Wilson.

We appreciate the support for the work leading to this review
from the National Science Foundation Grants.

REFERENCES

(1) Alexander, R.D. 1974. The evolution of social behavior.
     Ann. Rev. Sys. Ecol. 5: 325-383.

(2) Averhoff, W.W., and Richardson, R.H. 1976. Multiple
     pheromone system controlling mating in D. melanogaster.
     Proc. Nat. Acad. Sci. USA 73: 591-593.

(3) Barrows, E.M. 1975a. Individually distinctive odors in
     an invertebrate. Behav. Biol. 15: 57-64.

(4) Barrows, E.M. 1975b. Mating behavior in halictine bees.
     III. Copulatory behavior and olfactory communication.
     Insectes Sociaux 22: 307-332.

(5) Barrows, E.M.; Bell, W.J.; and Michener, C.D. 1975. Indi-
     vidual odor differences and their social functions in
     insects. Proc. Nat. Acad. Sci. USA 72: 2824-2828.

(6) Bell, W.J. 1974. Recognition of resident and non-resident
     individuals in intraspecific nest defense of a primitively
     eusocial halictine bee. J. Comp. Physiol. 93: 195-202.

(7) Bell, W.J.; Breed, M.D.; Richards, K.W.; and Michener, C.D.
     1974. Social, stimulatory and motivational factors in-
     volved in intraspecific nest defense in a primitively
     social halictine bee. J. Comp. Physiol. 93: 173-181.

(8) Bell, W.J., and Hawkins, W.A. 1974. Patterns of intra-
     specific agonistic interactions involved in nest defense
     of a primitively eusocial halictine bee. J. Comp. Physiol.
     93: 183-193.

(9) Breed, M.D.; Silverman, J.M.; and Bell, W.J. 1978. Agonis-
     tic behavior, social interactions, and behavioral specializa-
     tion of a primitively eusocial bee. Insectes Sociaux 25:
     351-364.

(10) Brothers, D.J., and Michener, C.D. 1974. Interactions in
     colonies of primitively social bees. III. Ethometry of
     division of labor in Lasioglossum zephyrum. J. Comp.
     Physiol. 90: 129-168.

(11) Crozier, R.H., and Dix, M.W. 1979. Analysis of two gene-
     tic models for the innate components of colony odor in
     social Hymenoptera. Behav. Ecol. Sociobiol. 4: 217-224.

(12) Ehrman, L., and Probber, J. 1978. Rare Drosophila males:
     the mysterious matter of choice. Am. Sci. 66: 216-222.

(13) Greenberg, L. 1979. Genetic component of bee odor in kin
     recognition. Science 206: 1095-1097.

(14)   Hamilton, W.D.   1964.   The genetical evolution of social
        behavior, I and II.   J. Theor. Biol. 7: 1-52.

(15)   Hamilton, W.D.   1972.   Altruism and related phenomena,
        mainly in social insects.   Ann. Rev. Ecol. Syst. 3: 193-
        232.

(16)   Hangartner, W.; Reichson, J.W.; and Wilson, E.O.   1970.
        Orientation to nest material by the ant Pogonomyrmex ba-
        dius (Latreille).   Anim. Behav. 18: 331-334.

(17)   Haskins, C.P., and Haskins, E.F.   1950.   Notes on the
        biology and social behavior of the archaic ponerine ants
        of the genera Myrmecia and Promyrmecia.   Ann. Entomol.
        Soc. Am. 43: 461-491.

(18)   Hölldobler, B.   1976.   The behavioral ecology of mating
        in harvester ants (Hymenoptera: Formicidae: Pogonomyrmex).
        Behav. Ecol. Sociobiol. 1: 405-423.

(19)   Hölldobler, B.   1976.   Tournaments and slavery in a de-
        sert ant.   Science 192: 912-914.

(20)   Hölldobler, B., and Wilson, E.O.   1977.   The number of
        queens: An important trait in ant evolution.   Naturwis-
        senschaften 64: 8-15.

(21)   Hölldobler, B., and Wilson, E.O.   1978.   The multiple
        recruitment systems of the African weaver ant Oecophylla
        longinoda.   Behav. Ecol. Sociobiol. 3: 19-60.

(22)   Jaisson, P.   1975.   L'imprégnation dans l'ontogenèse des
        comportements de soins aux cocons chez la jeune fourmi
        rousse (Formica polyctena Foerst).   Behaviour 52: 1-37.

(23)   Kalmus, H., and Ribbands, C.R.   1952.   The origin of the
        odours by which honeybees distinguish their companions.
        Proc. Royal Society (B) 140: 50-59.

(24)   Kukuk, P.F.; Breed, M.D.; Sobti, A.; and Bell, W.J.
        1977.   The contributions of kinship and conditioning to
        nest recognition and colony member recognition in a prim-
        itively eusocial bee, Lasioglossum zephyrum (Hymenoptera:
        Halictidae).   Behav. Ecol. Sociobiol. 2: 319-327.

(25)   Michener, C.D.   1974.   The Social Behavior of the Bees.
        Cambridge, MA: The Belknap Press of Harvard University
        Press.

(26)   Michener, C.D.   1977.   Aspects of the evolution of castes
        in primitively social insects.   Proc. 8th International
        Congress, Internat. Union. Stud. Soc. Insects, Wageningen,
        Netherlands, pp. 2-6.

(27)   Michener, C.D., and Brothers, D.J.   1974.   Were workers
        of eusocial Hymenoptera initially altruistic or oppressed?
        Proc. Nat. Acad. Sci. USA 71: 671-674.

(28) Michener, C.D.; Brothers, D.J.; and Kamm, D.R. 1971. Inter-
      actions in colonies of primitively social bees: artificial
      colonies of Lasioglossum zephyrum. Proc. Nat. Acad. Sci.
      USA 68: 1241-1245.

(29) Ribbands, C.R. 1965. The role recognition of comrades
      in the defence of social insect communities. Symp. Zool.
      Soc. London 14: 159-168.

(30) Schmidt, G.H., ed. 1974. Sozialpolymorphismus bei In-
      sekten. Stuttgart: Wissenschaftliche Verlagsgesellschaft
      MBH.

(31) Shinn, A.F. 1967. A revision of the bee genus Calliopsis
      and the biology and ecology of C. adreniformis (Hymenop-
      tera, Adrenidae). Univ. Kansas Sci. Bull. 46: 753-936.

(32) Starr, C.K. 1979. Origin and evolution of insect sociality:
      A review of modern theory. In Social Insects, ed. H.R.
      Hermann. New York: Academic Press.

(33) Steinmann, E. 1973. Über die Nahorienterung der Einsied-
      lerbienen Osmia bicornis L. and Osmia cornuta Latr. Mitt.
      Schweizer. Ent. Gesellsch. 46: 119-122.

(34) Steinmann, E. 1976. Über die Nahorientierung solitärer
      Hymenopteren: Individuelle Markierung der Nesteingänge.
      Mitt. Schweizer. Ent. Gesellsch. 49: 253-258.

(35) Trivers, R.L., and Hare, H. 1976. Haplo-diploidy and the
      evolution of the social insects. Science 191: 249-263.

(36) Walsh, J.P., and Tschinkel, W.R. 1974. Brood recognition
      by contact pheromone in the red imported fire ant, Solenop-
      sis invicta. Anim. Behav. 22: 695-704.

(37) West, M.J. 1968. Range extension and solitary nest found-
      ing in Polistes exclamans (Hymenoptera: Vespidae). Psyche
      75: 118-123.

(38) West-Eberhard, M.J. 1969. The social biology of polistine
      wasps. Misc. Publ., Mus. Zool. Univ. Michigan 140: 1-101.

(39) Wilson, E.O. 1971. The Insect Societies. Cambridge, MA:
      Belknap Press of Harvard University Press.

(40) Wilson, E.O., and Bossert, W.H. 1963. Chemical communica-
      tion among animals. Rec. Prog. Horm. Res. 19: 673-716.

Evolution of Social Behavior: Hypotheses and Empirical Tests, ed. H. Markl,
pp. 59-80. Dahlem Konferenzen 1980. Weinheim: Verlag Chemie GmbH.

Behavioral Adaptations That Constrain the Gene Pool in Vertebrates

M. C. Baker* and P. Marler**
  *Department of Zoology and Entomology, Colorado State University
   Fort Collins, CO 80523
**The Rockefeller University, New York, NY 10021, USA

Abstract. For adequate description of vertebrate social systems, and in particular to assess the genetic consequences and
correlates of kin-related behavior we need to know how kin are
distributed in nature. The potential for kin-correlated behavior is rooted in the basic processes that determine genetic
population structure. The relative levels of cooperative and
competitive behavior may indeed be adjusted by the degree of
inbreeding, as suggested by kin selection theory. The prospect cannot be assessed, however, without a full understanding
of dispersal (gene flow) size and spacing of groups (population subdivision), and mating systems (gametic combination).
Indications are that in general, adult terrestrial vertebrates
tend to be faithful to a breeding site. Young are constrained
by a variety of social and other mechanisms, including philopatry, imprinting and xenophobia, to stay close or return to
their birth place for breeding. The degree to which this is
achieved varies in relation to a variety of factors, including
species and sex. There are strong forces favoring some degree
of homozygosis, especially if groups are small and relatively
closed. We suggest that these conditions may be satisfied
more often than is supposed, with populations composed of relatively close kin being maintained by a variety of communicative and other behavioral mechanisms. If correct, this will
have important consequences for the interpretation of matings
that may be extra-familial, yet involving neighboring members
of the same population.

INTRODUCTION

It is self evident that at some level spatial and temporal

patterns of the environment cause genetic structuring of ani-

mal populations. We propose here that this influence is felt

not only at the species level but also in local populations,

and that a considerable proportion of an organism's behavior,

social and otherwise, represents adaptations to maintain its
genome in concordance with the environmental pattern. We will
first elaborate and clarify this assertion and then review
some behavioral adaptations that appear to conform to our
model.

Diverse patterns of vertebrate social organization have been
attributed to variations in structure of the biotic environment, particularly the food supply, for about 15 years. The
work of J. Crook (24) and S. Gartlan (25) was seminal in
early efforts to find broad correlations between the spatio-
temporal arrangements of food or vegetation and the social
systems of birds and primates. This general theme was pursued
by others over the subsequent decade or more (20, 30, 74, 80,
98, 102).

Most often, mating system variations have been the focus of
attention, and current models are more refined then the earlier attempts. For example, the well-known polygyny threshold
model of Verner and Orians (74) has been extended to suggest
that the driving independent variable of habitat quality is
probably best represented by variations in vegetational structure for colonial birds but by variations in food availability
for non-colonial birds (109). As a further distinction it has
been suggested that polygyny may result from spatial variations in food abundance whereas polyandry may proceed from
temporal variations in food abundance (40).

In our view, however, the most profound advances in recent
years are the models of Bradbury and Vehrencamp (12, 13) which
explain group size and mating systems in tropical bats, and
the ecological model of Emlen and Oring (32), dealing with
mating systems of a broad array of vertebrates. The Bradbury/
Vehrencamp model seeks to map social dispersion onto resource
dispersion. Dispersion patterns are characterized by graini-
ness and degrees of packing. The model indicates that group
size is determined by the richness of the food patches and

that "territory" size is determined by the distance between
successively available patches and their rates of renewal.
Moreover, the defensibility of resources, or of mates whose
clustering may be determined by resources, appears to be the
main factor determining mating systems, in the views of both
the Bradbury/Vehrencamp and Emlen/Oring ecological models (see
also (107)).

It is of major theoretical significance that the variables
necessary to describe the social systems in vertebrate animals, namely, zygote-to-zygote dispersal patterns, size and
spacing of groups, and patterns of gametic combination or
mating systems, are precisely those necessary to describe
genetic population structure. Taken together, ecological
modeling of social dispersion and mating and the numerous
population genetics models (39, 45, 57, 62, 63, 83) suggest
that patterns of environmental heterogeneity may underlie both
social and genetic organization. Thus the role of environmental grain, or patchiness, in causing genetic variation among
populations, although complex, is becoming increasingly clear
(66, 82). On the basis of such explanatory theory, one can
ask what should be the predicted patterns of gene flow and
population structure, given a certain degree of environmental
patchiness. The problem is that, faced with widespread spatial
genetic variation, it is unreasonable to expect that throughout
the range of any genetically variable population there will be
uniformity of breeding or panmixia. How can a landscape of multiple adaptive optima be maintained under such conditions?

These problems can be addressed by advancing three types of
questions. First, we need to know about gene flow (migration).
What is the genetic neighborhood size expected from the dispersal function? Second, we must assess the spatial structure
of a population. What is the hierarchical pattern of subdivisions and what is the degree of isolation among sibling clusters, family or kin groups, local populations, area effect
trait groups, and geographic races or subspecies? Third, we

must describe and evaluate the rules of gamete combination
within such hierarchical subdivisions. For evolutionary biologists, these topics are grist for the mill because they represent the processes that determine the spread, the fixation, or
the loss of new mutations; in short, they are the fundamental
determinants of the rate and direction of evolutionary change.

DISPERSAL

For most vertebrates, dispersal is a behavioral process and
may be influenced by a variety of factors. By dispersal, we
mean to focus on the distance from birthplace to breeding
site. What may be called the zygote-to-zygote dispersal can
be used as a measure of gene flow in a population when an entire frequency distribution is accumulated for analysis.
Adult dispersal, from one site of breeding to another, may also
be important for some species but for many vertebrates this
component of gene flow is comparatively minor. In species
with long lives, most adults remain to breed or return to
breed year after year in the same place (4, 17, 42, 51).

Evidence from the shapes of the few vertebrate dispersal
curves available indicates that most young organisms return to
or stay close to their sites of origin. The predominant shape
is that of a strongly right-skewed distribution approximating
a gamma or negative exponential probability law (4, 10, 16,
26, 50, 73). One behavioral mechanism involved here is a form
of habitat "imprinting." Löhrl (59) identified such a process
by transplant experiments with young birds, and it may be a
widespread phenomenon (17, 47, 85, 104). There are parallels
with the host "imprinting" that may be responsible for the
occurrence of low migration rates and small effective population sizes in African indigobirds parasitic on the nests of
other bird species (77).

An interesting situation arises in White-crowned Sparrows
(Zonotrichia leucophrys) in which individuals from early
broods of the season are found a year later as breeders very

near the site of fledging, whereas later broods are located
considerably farther away from where they were fledged (5).
This pattern may be caused by some type of seasonally varying
"imprinting" process or may reflect competitive exclusion of
birds from late broods by birds from early broods who have
occupied habitat nearby their fledging sites. Our point,
then, is that young stay near their birthsite either passively
through learned attachment or actively by direct competition
for available sites. Retention of young in some group-living
birds may even be a more active process than is generally
realized (15, 60). We need to know more about the relevance
to the dynamics of active competition of such factors as different degrees of familiarity with the interaction site or
personal familiarity between potential competitors, whether by
vision, audition, or olfaction. Strangers are often the most
potent stimuli for attacking others and driving them away (61).

Although kin associations resulting from limited dispersal may
have obvious benefits from the perspective of inclusive fitness theorizing, we need to consider potential costs as well.
As a simple example of a cost accruing to the spatial clustering of close kin, we can consider the results on Darwin's
finches showing that more similar diets are correlated with
more similar bill dimensions in comparisons among pairs of
species (1). Furthermore the bill dimensions have large her-
etability values (11). If such results can be generalized to
within-population comparisons, there is an implied competitive
cost to spatial clusters of kin.

What are the consequences, for genetic neighborhood size, of
philopatric dispersal patterns? Analysis of the dispersal
functions available from the literature indicates that even in
species generally considered to be highly vagile such as birds,
the neighborhood population may frequently be on the order
of 100 (data in (16, 68) and (77)).   This is a first level
analysis and assumes that within the neighborhood population, mating is at random, progeny number is Poisson

distributed, population size is constant, and generations are
discrete. All of these assumptions are approximations at
best, but for most of them the probable departures cause further reductions in genetically effective size. Cases of even
smaller panmictic units have been reported in lizards (100)
and in deermice (86).

Dispersal is often sex biased. Male birds disperse shorter
distances on average (4, 16, 101, 111). The rusty lizard follows this pattern also (52). Important avian exceptions are
the snow goose, in which most of the exchanges between colonies are attributed to males (22), and several species of mi-
gratory ducks (96). Evidence is accumulating that various
species of primates have sex-biased dispersal with either females or more commonly males emigrating from their natal
group (19). Immigrant male primates are favored as mates over
home-born males in some primates (75).

The effects of these sex-biased migrations on genetic structure are to slow down the process of attaining homozygosis in
a local group; it is not stopped, however. The inbreeding coefficient can still build up to substantial levels if one sex
is fixed and the other emigrates randomly, the rates depending
on effective size, geographic dimensionality of the population, and the mating pattern within the population (88).

A further impact on the genetic consequences of dispersal
comes from the occurrence of sibships or kin groups migrating
together (37, 46). When this occurs, prediction of genetic
divergence among subpopulations becomes more complicated (see
also (87)).

POPULATION STRUCTURE
Wright (113) pointed out that natural populations are spatially structured and that this fact has important consequences
for evolutionary processes. The theoretical work of Slatkin
(91) and Nagylaki (69) indicates that if there exist even

imperfect barriers to dispersal then isolated populations result and gene migration will fail to swamp out local differences in gene frequencies. There is much active research on
population structure by analysis of allozymes or phenetic features sampled through various statistical procedures (94, 89,
67). The theoretical study of population structure has also
developed rapidly in recent years (18, 70, 92), and we foresee
that students of social behavior will find familiarity with
these developments increasingly profitable. Two readable general accounts of models and data related to gene flow, sub-
population differentiation, and genomic coadaptation are by
Endler (34) and White (106). Here we mention only some potential or realized behavioral mechanisms that are responsible
for population subdivision.

Perhaps the most versatile mechanism involved in maintaining
structured populations is communication. Several studies demonstrate the critical parameters of male bird song for repel-
ling others with varying degrees of intensity (31, 36, 78).
Geographic variations in vocal signals are also well documented but their significance for population structure is
obscure. Vocal dialects in numerous bird species have been
described. We now know that for one case study (3, 4) the
song dialect difference is characterized by correlated gene
frequency differences between contiguous dialect populations
and by reduced gene migration between them. Recent bird song
research also suggests that it is possible to describe a mo-
saic of song clusters within dialects. Work is in progress to
determine if they correspond to kin groups, as might be predicted from the dispersal distribution and from timing of the
song learning process.

Similar patterns exist in mammalian species as well. Colony
specific vocal patterns have been described in elephant seals,
pikas, and primates (41, 56, 95). The context and frequency
of vocal behavior of certain social ground squirrels has been
interpreted as evidence of kin selection (28, 90), though the

physical structure of the sounds themselves has yet to be examined for kin specific or spatial patterns. On the whole,
however, it seems likely that the most prevalent recognition
mechanism among small mammals, and perhaps large ones as well,
is based upon odor (6, 29, 38, 72, 81). Effects of olfactory
preferences on mating probabilities with respect to a restricted breeding pool deserve increased attention in the future.
There is a need for careful experimental studies on the perception of kin.

We emphasize the importance of communicative interactions because they are the essence of animal sociality and as such are
intimately involved in the social rituals that modulate peace-
ful proximity and aggressive dispersal (61). It is far from
clear at this time to what extent communication signals mirror
genetic population structure. For some purposes, however,
this is not especially critical. If a group of individuals is
reasonably small and partly isolated from free gene exchange
with other groups, then the genetic relatedness of individuals
will build up even under maximum avoidance of close inbreeding
(112). The modifying role played by explicit avoidance of
parent-offspring or sib matings is to slow down the process of
genetic homozygosis. The phenomenon of imprinting has the
appearance of a mechanism that results in inbreeding. Even if
an individual exhibits a preference for a slightly different
type than that on which it is imprinted (8), the end result
may not be very different as far as the gene pool of the local
population is concerned if it is small and relatively isolated. This holds true even in the isolation-by-distance model
of population structure if the neighborhood size is small. It
is interesting to note that the most dramatic effects on gene
pools occur with effective sizes on the order of 25 or less,
just the right magnitude for kin groupings. Several different
models (53, 65, 71) show that fixation of a new mutant allele
proceeds in relatively few generations when effective population size is in the vicinity of 50 or less.

GAMETIC COMBINATION

Patterns of within-group mating have a potential impact on genetic structure. From this viewpoint typological classifications of mating systems such as monogamy, polygyny, polyandry, lekking, etc., are of limited utility. These categories describe an approximation of modal behavior that allows us to converse conveniently about mating systems, but for evolutionary genetics we need a statistical description of how gametes combine in a population.

When studied intensively, bird species considered as classical examples of monogamy are often found to have some degree of bigamous matings in the population (73, 79, 93, 105). Furthermore, it is often, but not necessarily the case, that a male and a female remain paired for more than one reproductive episode (103). As far as the population genetic consequences are concerned these are important factors that are not revealed by the descriptive term monogamy. Within so-called polygynous mating systems, highly assortative mating occurs, with a tiny fraction of adult males, successful in some form of ritualized intrasexual competition, doing most of the matings (e.g., grouse (108, 110); manakins (58); seals (7, 23); baboons (44, 76)). However the precise genetic consequences are difficult to assess. Even with the best-studied, polygynous Red-winged Blackbird, one needs much more detailed description for effective comparison with other species. The genetically effective size of the population may differ by as much as 20-50 percent from one colony to another or up to 350 percent in comparisons among harems with a colony (calculated from data in Holm (48)). Not only is the number of females in each male's harem an important factor, but the degree of paternity certainty adds another dimension to analysis of genetic consequences.

Two experimental studies of paternity certainty in harem males (14, 99) demonstrated substantial gene leakage by virtue of mates of some vasectomized males becoming fertilized. In the

Red-winged Blackbird study of Bray et al., nearly 50 percent
of such clutches were fertilized! The crucial uncontrolled
variable in vasectomy studies, however, is that the influence
of recency and frequency of copulation is unknown. Thus paternity certainty may be much higher than the vasectomy studies imply if the resident male gains an extra advantage
through sperm displacement or stratification. Labeled sperm
could solve this issue in studies of natural populations but
this work remains to be done. Studies of domestic fowl (21)
indicate that the most recent insemination fertilizes most of
the eggs and the effect lasts up to a week or more. Nevertheless paternity uncertainty bedevils the genetic inferences
that can be drawn from most behavioral analyses of natural
vertebrate mating systems.

There is considerable interest in behavioral processes presumably leading to avoidance of close inbreeding as in parent-
offspring and sibling matings (8, 9, 64). The influence of
incest taboos on the genetic heterogeneity of a population,
however, cannot be assessed apart from the other two sources
of influence, population structure and dispersal. As Wright
and others have shown, even under maximum avoidance of close
consanguinity, the loss of heterozygosity proceeds inexorably,
albeit more slowly. In an isolated population, to take the
extreme case, the inbreeding coefficient builds up over time
irrespective of the mating pattern.

Moreover, the demographic profile of a population places constraints on the kinds of consanguinity possible. For example,
the expected number of reproducing siblings in a population is
given by:

$$E(S) = P + \frac{V}{P} - 1$$

in which V = variance in family size, and P = mean progeny reproducing (approximately 2 X R_o, the rate of population increase). For a simplified example, assume a Poisson distribution of family size so that V = P, and R_o = 1, i.e., a non-
growing population. This reduces the formulation to E(S) = 2.

For a passerine bird population in which the mean longevity is
roughly one year, there is little potential for sib matings.
With adults sedentary from one reproductive episode to the
next and a mean difference in male and female offspring dispersal, the probability of incest (parent-offspring, sib-sib)
is diminishingly small, in this example. With longer lived
animals, and/or $V > P$ (usually the case), $E(S)$ can be substantially larger, however.

The likelihood of close inbreeding, as predicted from theoretical expectations derived from demographic considerations and
sex-biased dispersal, is only part of the picture. Inbreeding
of any kind will have the same ultimate consequence, namely,
homozygosis. The closer the inbreeding the greater the loss
of heterozygotes and the fewer the generations to homozygosis.
But even with maximum avoidance of inbreeding within the population the end result is the same; the inbreeding coefficient, F, becomes unity.

As an example of the process by which heterozygotes are lost
from and homozygotes increased in a population, it is convenient to consider the formula:
$$P = \frac{1}{2} (1 - F)$$
in which P = percentage heterozygosis and F = the inbreeding
coefficient. Inbreeding at strictly the level of first cousin only for 10 generations gives $P = 0.37$. This is equivalent to $F = 0.25$, found by solving the above formula for F,
and should be compared to $F = 0.0625$, that is the inbreeding
coefficient for first cousin matings derived directly from
randomly mated stock. So it may be misleading to assume much
about the inbreeding level in a population from observations
on consanguineous matings alone.

A major complication for determining F values of a population
is that the necessary samples of genetic data to detect inbreeding are often prohibitively large. Inbreeding produces
heterozygote deficiency at a locus, as discussed previously,

so what is done is to compare observed numbers of heterozygotes to the number expected in Hardy-Weinberg equilibrium. For the simple case of one locus with two alleles, chi-square must be 3.84 or larger for significant difference at the 5 percent level of probability. With a sample of 25 genomes, the inbreeding coefficient would have to be about 0.4 to be statistically detectable, or, equivalent to the F value of several generations of incestual mating. To detect first cousin level inbreeding, F = 0.0625, one would need a sample of 938 individuals.

CONCLUSIONS

In the limiting case of interspecific hybridization, it is clear that outbreeding is usually non-adaptive. At the other extreme, most studies of close inbreeding in captivity, starting with individuals from natural populations, suggest that inbreeding depression of fitness characters also imposes a firm limit (35, 84). There is a tendency in the literature, that follows naturally from our own anthropocentric views on incest, to assume that inbreeding is always deleterious and to interpret certain behavioral processes uncritically as adaptations to avoid incest (75, 55). Such interpretations may be premature, especially when advanced without consideration of alternative explanations.

An example of potential difficulties in the interpretation of inbreeding data may be taken from results on zoo ungulates (84). The data showed significant lowering of survival of young born to "inbred" parents as compared to "non-inbred" parents. There are, however, numerous cases of a heterotic effect on viability (33) most likely accruing from crosses between differentially coadapted genomes. Thus it is possible that greater survival of "non-inbred" ungulates is explained by heterosis and the survival of "inbred" young is normal. It is essential to know the origins of the parental stock to interpret the data. Nor should we ignore those documented instances in which inbreeding depression was not observed

(54, 49, 27). They may yield important clues to the relationship between the social and genetic structure of populations.

Between the limiting cases of interspecies hybridization on
the one hand, and incest on the other, there lies a gradient
of relatedness among individuals of a population that has
consequences for the evolution of social behavior. To this
point, field researchers have concentrated on the interactions among individuals as members of social groupings,
usually without knowledge of genetic relatedness other than as
revealed by recent genealogical history. It is appropriate at
this phase in the theoretical and empirical development of our
science to raise the issue that even when genealogical data
are available for any given social cluster, the consequences
of extra-group matings vary in important ways depending on the
relatedness of spatially adjacent clusters. For any particular subset of social groups, we may need to frame the question more broadly when asking: who are kin?

If we define evolution as a change in gene frequencies, then
events that cause such changes are by definition the most important evolutionary processes. With an eye to future research, it is useful to try to rank the behavioral processes
of inbreeding and migration for their importance in relation
to selection and drift. For instance, over the long-term inbreeding systems are not going to change gene frequencies.

Genetic drift can be an important process because in the absence of mutation, migration, and selection, it always leads
to fixation of one allele and loss of the other in any one
subpopulation. This is so even in the face of selection in
favor of heterozygotes. If the population is finite and
there is no significant mutation or migration, drift will
eventually lead to fixation of an allele, albeit more slowly.
Nevertheless, subpopulations are seldom perfectly isolated and
strong theoretical arguments have been made (62, 97) that
intrapopulation drift is seldom a cause of significant

differentiation; selective differences are mostly responsible.
Moreover, there is further reason to believe (33) that selection overrides even rather high rates of gene flow.

In the final analysis, the influences of dispersal, the spatial structure of populations, and the mating system need to
be considered jointly. It may be necessary to conduct field
experiments to gather information on these fundamental factors
and their interaction. An enlightening example is the work of
Ann Baker (2) on gene flow and social structure in house mouse
populations on poultry farms in rural New York State. Many
authors have described the society of the house mouse as
tribal/territorial and the observed microspatial heterogeneity
of gene frequencies seems also to indicate a structured social
system highly resistant to gene migration. A. Baker introduced a
new allele into a farm population and observed its spread in
space and its change in frequency with numerical changes in
the population. The spread of the allele within a single
poultry coop, for example, occurred in a regular pattern, as
though from one social group to the next at each generation.
With gene flow thus quantified, house mouse social structure
appears to present fewer obstacles to gene flow than had been
supposed. Similar experiments would seem desirable for other
vertebrates as well. The early work of Haskins et al. (43)
was a notable start on fish populations.

The most rapid progress in understanding the interactions of
these variables on the genetic structure of populations will
come when theoretical geneticists model more realistic conditions and point out the important behavioral processes for
us to consider, and when ethologists become more sensitive to the
critical parameters that need estimation.

Acknowledgements. We wish to thank many conference participants for their helpful comments, particularly F. Trillmich
for a discussion of competition, F. McKinney for information on sperm competition and sex-biased dispersal, T. Olivier
for descriptions of primate migration stochastics, P. Bateson
for discussions of imprinting, and P. Harvey for serving so
effectively as a beneficent skeptic. Research was supported
by grants NSF DEB 782-2657, NSF BNS 77-16894T, and PHS MH 14651-12.

REFERENCES

(1)   Abbott, I.; Abbott, L.K.; and Grant, P.R. 1977.
      Comparative ecology of Galapagos ground finches
      (Geospiza Gould): Evaluation of the importance of flor-
      istic diversity and interspecific competition. Ecol.
      Monogr. 47: 151-184.

(2)   Baker, A.E.M. 1979. Social and ecological correlates
      of gene flow in house mice: I. Introduction of a new
      allele into free-living populations. Ph.D. thesis,
      State University of New York, Stony Brook.

(3)   Baker, M.C. 1975. Song dialects and genetic differ-
      ences in white-crowned sparrows (Zonotrichia leucophrys).
      Evolution 29: 226-241.

(4)   Baker, M.C., and Mewaldt, L.R. 1978. Song dialects as
      barriers to dispersal in white-crowned sparrows, Zono-
      trichia leucophrys nuttalli. Evolution 32: 712-722.

(5)   Baker, M.C., and Mewaldt, L.R. 1979. The use of space
      by white-crowned sparrows: Juvenile and adult ranging
      patterns and home range versus body size comparisons in
      an avian granivore community. Behav. Ecol. Sociobiol.
      6: 45-52.

(6)   Barash, D.P. 1974. The evolution of marmot societies.
      Science 185: 415-420.

(7)   Bartholomew, G.A. 1970. A model for the evolution of
      pinniped polygyny. Evolution 24: 546-559.

(8)   Bateson, P. 1979. How do sensitive periods arise and
      what are they for? Anim. Behav. 27: 470-486.

(9)   Bischoff, N. 1975. Comparative ethology of incest
      avoidance. In Biosocial Anthropology, ed. R. Fox, pp.
      37-67. New York: John Wiley and Sons.

(10) Blair, W.F. 1960. The Rusty Lizard, A Population
      Study. Austin: University of Texas Press.

(11) Boag, P.T., and Grant, P.R. 1978. Heritability of ex-
      ternal morphology in Darwin's finches. Nature 274:
      793-794.

(12) Bradbury, J.W., and Vehrencamp, S.L. 1976. Social or-
      ganization and foraging in emballonurid bats. II. A
      model for the determination of group size. Behav. Ecol.
      Sociobiol. 1: 383-404.

(13) Bradbury, J.W., and Vehrencamp, S.L. 1977. Social or-
      ganization and foraging in emballonurid bats. III.
      Mating systems. Behav. Ecol. Sociobiol. 2: 1-17.

(14) Bray, O.; Kennelly, J.; and Guarino, J. 1975. Fertil-
      ity of eggs produced on territories of vasectomized red-
      winged blackbirds. Wil. Bull. 87: 187-195.

(15) Brown, J.L. 1978. Avian communal breeding systems.
      Ann. Rev. Ecol. Syst. 9: 123-155.

(16) Bulmer, M.G. 1973. Inbreeding in the great tit.
      Heredity 30: 313-325.

(17) Catchpole, C.K. 1972. A comparative study of territory
      in the reed warbler (Acrocephalus scirpuceus) and sedge
      warbler (A. schoenobaenus). J. Zool., Lond. 166:
      213-231.

(18) Chakraborty, R., and Nei, M. 1974. Dynamics of gene
      differentiation between incompletely isolated popula-
      tions of unequal sizes. Theor. Pop. Biol. 5: 460-469.

(19) Chepko-Sade, B.D., and Sade, D.S. 1979. Patterns of
      group splitting within matrilineal kinship groups.
      Behav. Ecol. Sociobiol. 5: 61-86.

(20) Clutton-Brock, T.H., and Harvey, P. H. 1977. Primate
      ecology and social organization. J. Zool., Lond. 183:
      1-39.

(21) Compton, M.M.; Van Krey, H.P.; and Siegel, P.B. 1978.
      The filling and emptying of the uterovaginal sperm-host
      glands in the domestic hen. Poultry Sci. 57: 1696-1700.

(22) Cooke, F.; MacInnes, D.C.; and Previtt, J.P. 1975.
      Gene flow between breeding populations of lesser snow
      geese. Auk 92: 493-510.

(23) Cox, C.A., and LeBoeuf, B.J. 1977. Female incitation
      of male competition: a mechanism in sexual selection.
      Amer. Nat. 111: 317-335.

(24) Crook, J.H. 1965. The adaptive significance of avian
      social organizations. Symp. Zool. Soc. Lond. 14: 181-
      218.

(25) Crook, J.H., and Gartlan, J.S. 1966. Evolution in pri-
      mate societies. Nature 210: 1200-1203.

(26) Dice, L.R., and Howard, W.E. 1951. Distance of disper-
      sal by Prairie Deermice. Contr. Lab. Vert. Biol. Univ.
      Mich. 50: 1-15.

(27) Dobzhansky, T. 1970. Genetics of the Evolutionary
      Process. New York: Columbia University Press.

(28) Dunford, C. 1977. Kin selection for ground squirrel
      alarm calls. Amer. Natur. 111: 782-785.

(29) Eisenberg, J.F., and Kleiman, D.G. 1972. Olfactory
      communication in mammals. Ann. Rev. Ecol. Syst. 3:
      1-32.

(30) Eisenberg, J.F.; Muckenhirn, N.A.; and Rudran, R. 1972.
      The relation between ecology and social structure in
      primates. Science 176: 863-874.

(31) Emlen, S.T. 1972. An experimental analysis of the
      parameters of bird song eliciting species recognition.
      Behaviour 41: 130-171.

(32) Emlen, S.T., and Oring, L.W. 1977. Ecology, sexual
      selection, and the evolution of mating systems. Science
      197: 215-223.

(33) Endler, J.A. 1973. Gene flow and population differen-
      tiation. Science 174: 243-250.

(34) Endler, J.A. 1977. Geographic Variation, Speciation,
      and Clines. Princeton: University Press.

(35) Falconer, D.S. 1960. Introduction to Quantitative
      Genetics. New York: The Ronald Press.

(36) Falls, J.B. 1969. Functions of territorial song in the
      white-throated sparrow. In Bird Vocalizations, ed. R.A.
      Hinde, pp. 207-232. Cambridge: University Press.

(37) Fix, A.G. 1978. The role of kin-structured migration
      in genetic microdifferentiation. Ann. Hum. Genet.,
      Lond. 41: 329-339.

(38) Gilder, P.M., and Slater, P.J.L. 1978. Interest of
      mice in conspecific male odours is influenced by degree
      of kinship. Nature 274: 364-365.

(39) Gillespie, J.H. 1974. Polymorphism in patchy environ-
      ments. Amer. Natur. 108: 145-151.

(40) Graul, W.D.; Derrickson, S.R.; and Mock, D.W. 1977.
      The evolution of avian polyandry. Amer. Natur. 111:
      812-816.

(41) Green, S. 1975. Dialects in Japanese Monkeys: Vocal
      learning and cultural transmission of locale-specific
      vocal behavior? Z. Tierpsychol. 38: 304-314.

(42) Harvey, P.H.; Greenwood, P.J.; and Perrins, C.M. 1979.
      Breeding area fidelity of great tits (Parus major).
      Journal Anim. Ecol. 48: 305-313.

(43) Haskins, C.P.; Haskins, E.R.; McLaughlan, J.J.A.; and
      Hewitt, R.E. 1961. Polymorphism and population struc-
      ture in Lebistes reticulatus, an ecological study. In
      Vertebrate Speciation, ed. W.F. Blair, pp. 320-395.
      Austin: University of Texas Press.

(44) Hausfater, G. 1975. Dominance and reproduction in baboons (Papio cynocephalus): a quantitative analysis. Contrib. Primatol. 7. Basel: Karger.

(45) Hedrick, P.W.; Ginevan, M.E.; and Ewing, E.P. 1976. Genetic polymorphism in heterogeneous environments. Ann. Rev. Ecol. Syst. 7: 1-32.

(46) Hilborn, R. 1975. Similarities in dispersal tendency among siblings in four species of voles (Microtus). Ecology 56: 1221-1225.

(47) Hilden, O. 1975. Habitat selection in birds. Annales Zoologici Fennici 2: 53-75.

(48) Holm, C.H. 1973. Breeding sex ratios, territoriality, and reproductive success in the red-winged blackbird (Agelaius phoeniceus). Ecology 54: 356-365.

(49) Hyde, R.R. 1924. Inbreeding, outbreeding, and selection with Drosophila melanogaster. J. Exp. Zool. 40: 181-215.

(50) Johnston, R.F. 1956. Population structure in salt marsh song sparrows. Part I. Environment and annual cycle. Condor 58: 24-44.

(51) Kendeigh, S.C. 1941. Territorial and mating behavior of the house wren. III. Biol. Monogr. 18: 1-120.

(52) Kerster, H.W. 1964. Neighborhood size in the rusty lizard, Sceloporus olivaceus. Evolution 18: 445-457.

(53) Kimura, M., and Ohta, T. 1969. The average number of generations until fixation of a mutant gene in a finite population. Genetics 61: 763-771.

(54) King, H.O. 1918-1921. Studies on inbreeding. I-IV. J. Exp. Zool. 26: 1-54, 29: 71-112.

(55) Koenig, W.D., and Pitelka, F.A. 1979. Relatedness and inbreeding avoidance: counterploys in the communally nesting acorn woodpecker. Science 206: 1103-1105.

(56) LeBoeuf, B.J., and Peterson, R.S. 1969. Dialects in elephant seals. Science 166: 1654-1656.

(57) Levene, H. 1953. Genetic equilibrium when more than one ecological niche is available. Amer. Natur. 87: 331-333.

(58) Lill, A. 1974. Sexual behavior of the lek-forming white-bearded manakin (Manacus manacus trinitatis Hartert). Z. Tierpsychol. 36: 1-36.

(59) Löhrl, H. 1959. Zur Frage des Zeitpunktes einer
      Prägung auf die Heimatregion beim Halsbandschnäpper
      (Ficedula albicollis). J. Ornithol. 100: 132-140.

(60) MacRoberts, M.H., and MacRoberts, B.R. 1976. Social
      organization and behavior of the acorn woodpecker in
      central coastal California. Orn. Monogr. 21. Amer. Orn.
      Union, p. 115.

(61) Marler, P. 1976. On animal aggression. The roles of
      strangeness and familiarity. Amer. Psychol. 31: 239-246.

(62) Maynard-Smith, J. 1970. Population size, polymorphism,
      and the rate of non-Darwinian evolution. Amer. Natur.
      104: 231-237.

(63) Maynard-Smith, J. 1970. Genetic polymorphism in a
      varied environment. Amer. Natur. 104: 487-490.

(64) Maynard-Smith, J. 1976. The Evolution of Sex, p. 222.
      Cambridge: Cambridge University Press.

(65) Maynard-Smith, J. 1976. What determines the rate of
      evolution? Amer. Natur. 110: 331-338.

(66) McDonald, J.R., and Ayala, F.J. 1974. Genetic response
      to environmental heterogeneity. Nature 250: 572-574.

(67) Mickevich, M.F., and Johnson, M.S. 1976. Congruence
      between morphological and allozyme data in evolutionary
      inference and character evolution. Syst. Zool. 25: 260-
      270.

(68) Miller, A.H. 1947. Panmixia and population size with
      reference to birds. Evolution 1: 186-190.

(69) Nagylaki, T. 1976. Clines with variable migration.
      Genetics 83: 867-886.

(70) Nagylaki, T. 1977. Decay of genetic variability in
      geographically structured populations. Proc. Natl. Acad.
      Sci. U.S.A. 74: 2523-2525.

(71) Nei, M. 1975. Molecular population genetics and evolu-
      tion. Frontiers of Biology 40: 1-285.

(72) Nevo, E. 1979. Mole rat Spalax ehrenbergi: Mating be-
      havior and its evolutionary significance. Science 163:
      484-456.

(73) Nice, M.M. 1937. Studies in the life history of the
      song sparrow. I. A population study of the song sparrow.
      Trans. Linn. Soc. New York 4: 1-247.

(74) Orians, G.H. 1969. On the evolution of mating systems
      in birds and mammals. Amer. Natur. 103: 589-603.

(75) Packer, C. 1979. Inter-troop transfer and inbreeding
      avoidance in Papio anubis. Anim. Behav. 27: 1-36.

(76) Packer, C. 1979. Male dominance and reproductive
      activity in Papio anubis. Anim. Behav. 27: 37-45.

(77) Payne, R.B. 1973. Behavior, mimetic songs and song
      dialects, and relationships of the parasitic indigo-
      birds (Vidua) of Africa. Ornithological Monogr. 11:
      1-333.

(78) Peters, S.; Searcy, W.; and Marler, P. In press.
      Species song discrimination in choice experiments with
      territorial male swamp and song sparrows. Anim. Behav.

(79) Petrinovich, L.; and Patterson, T.L. 1978. Polygyny in
      the white-crowned sparrow (Zonotrichia leucophrys).
      Condor 80: 99-100.

(80) Pitelka, F.A.; Holmes, R.T.; and MacLean, S.F. Jr. 1974.
      Ecology and evolution of social organization of arctic
      sandpipers. Amer. Zool. 14: 185-204.

(81) Porter, R.H., and Wyrick, M. 1979. Sibling recognition
      in spiny mice (Acomys cahirinus): Influence of age and
      isolation. Anim. Behav. 27: 761-766.

(82) Powell, J.R. 1971. Genetic polymorphisms in varied en-
      vironments. Science 174: 1035-1036.

(83) Prout, T. 1968. Sufficient conditions for multiple
      niche polymorphism. Amer. Natur. 102: 493-496.

(84) Ralls, K.; Brugger, K.; and Ballou, J. 1979. Inbreed-
      ing and juvenile mortality in small populations of ungu-
      lates. Science 206: 1101-1103.

(85) Ralph, C.J., and Mewaldt, L.R. 1975. Timing of site
      fixation upon the wintering grounds of sparrows. Auk
      92: 698-705.

(86) Rasmussen, D.I. 1964. Blood group polymorphism and in-
      breeding in natural populations of the deer mouse
      Peromyscus maniculatus. Evolution 18: 219-229.

(87) Rasmussen, D.I. 1979. Sibling clusters and genotype
      frequencies. Amer. Natur. 113: 948-951.

(88) Rohlf, F.J., and Schnell, G.D. 1971. An investigation
      of the isolation-by-distance model. Amer. Natur. 105:
      295-324.

(89) Selander, R.K., and Kaufman, D.W. 1975. Genetic
      structure of populations of the brown snail (Helix
      aspersa). I. Microgeographic variation. Evolution 29:
      385-401.

(90) Sherman, P.W. 1977. Nepotism and the evolution of
      alarm calls. Science 197: 1246-1253.

(91) Slatkin, M. 1973. Gene flow and selection in a cline.
      Genetics 75: 773-756.

(92) Slatkin, M. 1976. The rate of spread of an advanta-
      geous allele in a subdivided population. In Population
      Genetics and Ecology, eds. S. Karlin and E. Nevo, pp. 767-
      780. New York: Academic Press.

(93) Smith, S.M. 1978. The "underworld" in a territorial
      sparrow: adaptive strategy for floaters. Amer. Natur.
      112: 571-582.

(94) Sokal, R.R., and Oden, N.L. 1978. Spatial autocorrela-
      tion in biology. 2. Some biological implications and
      four applications of evolutionary and ecological inter-
      est. Biol. J. Linnean Soc. 10: 229-249.

(95) Somers, P. 1973. Dialects in southern Rocky Mountain
      pikas (Ochotona princeps Lagomorpha). Anim. Behav. 21:
      124-137.

(96) Sowls, L.I. 1955. Prairie Ducks. Harrisburg, PA:
      Stackpole.

(97) Spieth, P.T. 1974. Gene flow and genetic differentia-
      tion. Genetics 78: 961-965.

(98) Struhsaker, T.T. 1969. Correlates of ecology and so-
      cial organisation among African cercopithecines. Folia
      Primatol. 11: 80-118.

(99) Tannenbaum, B. 1975. Reproductive strategies in the
      white-lined bat (Saccopteryx bilineata). Ph.D. Thesis,
      Cornell University, Ithaca, NY.

(100) Tinkle, D.W. 1965. Population structure and effective
      size of a lizard population. Evolution 19: 569-573.

(101) Vehrencamp, S.L. 1976. The evolution of communal nest-
      ing in groove-billed anis. Ph.D. dissertation, Cornell
      University, Ithaca, NY.

(102) Verner, J., and Willson, M.F. 1966. The influence of
      habitats on mating systems of North American passerine
      birds. Ecology 47: 143-147.

(103) von Haartman, L. 1951. Successive polygamy. Behaviour
      3: 256-274.

(104) Wecker, S.C. 1963. The role of early experience in
      habitat selection by the Prairie Deer Mouse, Peromyscus
      maniculatus bairdi. Ecol. Monog. 33: 307-325.

(105) Welsh, D.A. 1975. Savannah sparrow breeding and terri-
      toriality on a Nova Scotia dune beach. Auk 92: 235-251.

(106) White, M.J.D. 1978. Modes of Speciation. San
      Francisco: W.H. Freeman and Co.

(107) Wiens, J.A. 1976. Population responses to patchy envi-
      ronments. Ann. Rev. Ecol. Syst. 7: 81-120.

(108) Wiley, R.H. 1973. Territoriality and non-random mating
      in sage grouse, Centrocercus urophasianus. Anim. Behav.
      Monog. 6: 87-169.

(109) Wittenberger, J.F. 1976. The ecological factors se-
      lecting for polygyny in altricial birds. Amer. Natur.
      110: 779-799.

(110) Wittenberger, J.F. 1978. The evolution of mating
      systems in grouse. Condor 80: 126-137.

(111) Woolfenden, G.E., and Fitzpatrick, J.R. 1978. The in-
      heritance of territory in group-breeding birds. Bio-
      Science 28: 104-108.

(112) Wright, S. 1921. Systems of mating. I-V. Genetics 6:
      111-178.

(113) Wright, S. 1943. Isolation by distance. Genetics 28:
      114-138.

Evolution of Social Behavior: Hypotheses and Empirical Tests, ed. H. Markl,
pp. 81-96. Dahlem Konferenzen 1980. Weinheim: Verlag Chemie GmbH.

Measuring Fitness in Social Insects

R. A. Metcalf
Department of Zoology, University, of California
Davis, CA 95616, USA

Abstract. The key test of sociobiology today is its ability to
explain altruism. Three classes of theories have been advanced
in this regard: (a) kin selection, or the theory of inclusive
fitness, in which altruism results from the interactions of related individuals; (b) mutualism, in which altruism results from
benefits to individual fitness irrespective of relatedness; and
(c) individual recognition. Current progress in testing these
theories is evaluated.

INTRODUCTION

Social species are differentiated from solitary species upon
interactions between individuals. Chief among these special
interactions is the occurrence of apparently altruistic behavior,
i.e., behavior which appears harmful to the actor and beneficial
to the recipient. Sociobiology is based upon the hypothesis that
sociality is the expression of the results of natural selection.
Thus foremost among its empirical goals is the determination of
the mechanism by which altruism is adaptive. It is the goal of
this paper to review the problems associated with testing evolutionary theories explaining altruism, especially as they apply
to the social insects.

The social insects are of particular interest because of the frequency of evolution of eusociality in the Hymenoptera. The Hymenoptera have evolved eusociality independently at least eleven
times. This figure is in contrast to only a single occurrence in

all other insects, the termites (23). As the Hymenoptera are
the only haplodiploid social insects known, emphasis has been
placed upon the way in which this variable is reflected in
social structure.

KIN SELECTION BY INCLUSIVE FITNESS

In W.D. Hamilton's theory of kin selection, altruists propagate
their genes into subsequent generations by aiding individuals
sharing alleles by common descent, i.e., relatives. Hamilton's
rule describing the condition for the spread of an altruistic
allele is that $C/B < 1/r$, where C is the cost to the actor's fitness, B is the benefit to the recipient's fitness, and r is the
relatedness (the probability that an allele in one individual is
present in a second individual by common descent (11)).

Selection acting with respect to Hamilton's rule is said to be
maximizing the inclusive fitness. The inclusive fitness considers
both the fitness derived from an individual's own reproduction
and also his fitness through that of relatives valued in proportion to relatedness (11,21).

Hamilton's rule can be restated in terms of inclusive fitness
since an allele for altruism is predicted to spread in a population when the inclusive fitness of the individual as an altruist
is greater than its inclusive fitness as a nonaltruist.

A test of the theory of kin selection has three components.
First, relatedness between concerned individuals must be measured. Second, the individual fitness or, as an approximation,
the reproductive success of concerned individuals must be measured. From these two parameters inclusive fitness can be measured. Third, inclusive fitness must be calculated both for the
altruistic and nonaltruistic strategies.

The fact that the theory involves a comparison of alternate strategies results in considerable problems. If one strategy, altruistic or selfish, is in fact superior, then the allele causing

that result is expected to go to fixation. Thus the common expectation is that only one strategy will be expressed in nature.
How then is a valid comparison to be made? For example, sterile
worker ants invariably are altruistic in helping their mother to
produce reproductives. It is futile to compare the strategy performed to the inclusive fitness of such an individual founding
its own nest. If a comparison is to be made to a strategy that
is not in fact observed, it is a considerable problem to the investigator to justify the value of inclusive fitness calculated
for the nonobserved strategy.

An alternate approach is to consider species which are polymorphic for altruists and nonaltruists. In this case, a direct
measure of the inclusive fitnesses of the alternate strategies
is possible (16). For example, in the primitively social Polistine wasps, colonies are initiated both by single foundresses
and by multiple foundresses (sisters). In multifoundress nests,
the subordinate foundress can be considered an altruist since
most reproduction is done by the dominant foundress and the more
dangerous activities are carried out disproportionately by the
subordinate foundresses. However, subordinate foundresses appear capable of founding their own nests in that they commonly,
without obvious problems, carry on a jointly founded nest if the
dominant foundress dies or is removed (13,15,16,20). Data on
Polistes metricus show the relative inclusive fitness as 1.39,
SE=0.22 (15,16).

The advantages of such systems are that both strategies can be
observed and that the problems associated with further evolution
(such as the evolution of sterility) after an absolute commitment
to sociality has occurred are minimized.

However, such systems assume, probably falsely, that altruists
and nonaltruists (subordinate foundresses and solitary foundresses) are equal in potential. West-Eberhard has suggested that
those of least potential as solitary foundresses would gain most
by joining (21). Gibo has argued that, since a foundress has

more grandchildren when her offspring pair up in multifoundress
nests, she will be selected to cause this to occur by manipulation (9).

Consideration of these various complications reveals another
strength of polymorphic systems. In the Polistes wasp case described, assuming subordinate and solitary foundresses are equal
in potential and drawn from the same pool, the relative inclusive
fitness is predicted to be one. Relative inclusive fitness takes
on an absolute value as opposed to the inequality of Hamilton's
rule. The special considerations posed by West-Eberhard and Gibo
can be used to predict specific values for relative inclusive
fitness and thus generate additional tests.

RELATEDNESS

Relatedness can be measured in two basic ways, from pedigrees
and from correlation analysis (see also Crozier, this volume).
The construction of pedigrees can be difficult or simple depending upon the number of breeding individuals in a family unit
and the number of types of family units. For example, colonies
in several ant species have been found to consist of the offspring of a single female and male (6). In contrast, for Polistes
metricus, a social wasp of relative simplicity, it was necessary
to analyze six distinct family units derived from one or two
twice-mated foundresses (15).

The combination of genetic analysis and observation is the most
accurate way to determine pedigrees. It would be impossible to
determine from observation alone that sperm from two matings was
used in a 9:1 ratio as occurred in P. metricus (15). Also, after
an intensive observational study, egg-laying by subordinate foundresses was not thought to occur in Polistes (20). However, it
has since been shown to occur genetically (15), and more recently
has been observed occurring at night (Joan Strassman, personal
communication). It is perhaps not surprising that events such
as egg-laying by subordinate foundresses, over which conflict in
the colony is expected, are hard for observers to discern as

selection presumably is acting to cause them to be hidden from
other members of the colony. Fortunately, the techniques of
isozyme analysis by electrophoresis make genetic studies relatively tractable.

It is possible to evaluate inbreeding by constructing a multi-
generational pedigree, however, this is usually impractical.
More simply, inbreeding can be calculated as the correlation
coefficient of uniting gametes (f). Theoretical problems with
the interpretation of f will be discussed in the following
section. From data so far gathered, inbreeding seems to be
uncommon among social insects ((6,13,15,20), and Metcalf and
Finer, in preparation).

Whereas inbreeding can be calculated as the correlation between
uniting gametes, relatedness can be considered the correlation
between paired zygotes. Genetic data, particularly that from
isozyme analysis, can be used to calculate f and r.

The calculation of a significant f (and hence r) cannot be taken
as direct evidence of inbreeding. Several genetic processes,
e.g., selection, null alleles, subdivided populations, as well
as inbreeding, can cause the inference of excess homozygotes
over random mating frequencies (7).

Selection
If selection occurs against heterozygotes, then a positive f
will be observed. However, selection is unlikely to act equally
on different loci. Thus examination of f for multiple loci from
the same population can be used to exclude loci at which selection may be occurring (13).

Null Alleles
Null or unexpressed alleles can lead to positive f by the mis-
interpretation of heterozygotes (null plus an expressed allele)
as homozygotes. Again as with selection, null alleles are most
unlikely to act identically at multiple loci (7).

Subdivided Populations

Perhaps of greatest interest are the still unresolved problems
associated with population structure. Of particular concern
are cases of subdivided populations. Consider for the sake of
argument two extreme cases of subdivided populations. First,
consider the colonization and subsequent isolation of a sub-
population on an island. In this case, suppose that random
mating occurs within the parental population and on the island.
(In humans, a situation approximating that described might be
Pitcairn Island in the South Pacific, colonized by mutineers
from the H.M.S. Bounty in 1790, pop. 310.) If f is measured
from the genotypes of a sample of individuals drawn from both
the parental population and the isolated daughter population, f
is expected to be positive and to increase with time. I would
note that an isolated colony of a few individuals, such as
occurred on Pitcairn Island, is usually thought of as being inbred. However, if f is computed only from individuals found
on the island, f would equal zero.

Second, consider two reproductively isolated panmictic subpopulations occurring in the same space at the same time (an example
approximating this case is the Dunker religious sect of the
U.S.A.). As in the first example, f measured by sampling over
both subpopulations would be positive and if measured only
within one subpopulation, it would be zero. Again, it would be
usual to state that the Dunkers are inbred.

From an empirical point of view, it is important to note that
the f and r obtained by correlation analysis of data from a subdivided population would depend upon the location and dispersion
of the individuals sampled. Without a study of the genetic population structure, it is not possible to determine whether a
positive f or an f of zero results from arbitrary sampling procedures.

From a theoretical point of view, it is unresolved as to what
f would be proper to use in calculating r for the measurement

of inclusive fitness. I would suggest that in the extreme case
of no contact between subpopulations, Pitcairn Island, the
proper f would result from intrapopulation sampling. In the
case of the Dunkers, the fact that they are in competition with
non-Dunkers would indicate that the populations would behave as
if inbred, i.e., would be expected to show increased altruism
towards members of their respective subpopulations.

HAPLODIPLOID SEX RATIOS

In the analysis of conflict of the sex ratio in social haplo-
diploids, Trivers and Hare have devised the most precise testable prediction yet produced from kin selection theory (19).
Their argument briefly stated is that, in haplodiploid systems,
the queen is equally related to her male and female offspring
(r=1/2), while her daughter-workers are 3/4 related to full
sisters and 1/4 to brothers. Thus workers would maximize their
inclusive fitness by skewing the colony's parental investment
(PI) towards female reproductives in a 3:1 ratio. On the other
hand, the queen is selected to invest equally in male and
female reproductives.

The models presented by Trivers and Hare show that, depending
on factors affecting relatedness, e.g., multiple mating, polygyny, and male production from worker eggs, the queen's optimal
ratio of PI (female:male) varies from 1:1 to $0.93\overline{3}$:1, the non-
laying worker's ratio varies from 3:1 to 1:1, and the laying
worker's from 4:3 to 3:1 (19).

The theoretical analysis of Trivers and Hare has been verified
using alternate models by several authors (4,5).

Trivers and Hare tested their theory by comparing the ratio of
PI in the sexes in monogynous ants to solitary Hymenoptera using
sex ratios from the literature and weights of males and females
from museum collections as a measure of PI. They found significantly higher estimated ratios of PI (females:males) in social
than in nonsocial species.

Alexander and Sherman (1) have been critical of Trivers and Hare's interpretation of data. Alexander and Sherman argue that Hamilton's theory of local competition for mates (LMC), which also predicts female-biased investment ratios, provides a better explanation of Trivers and Hare's data. LMC occurs when sons compete with related males for matings. A son that excludes an individual that shares the same alleles is of decreased value in terms of fitness to its parents.

Resolution of these opposing views is difficult because there is no quantitative theory of LMC stated in terms that can be empirically evaluated. It can be stated from Hamilton's derivation that LMC is expected in low density viscous populations. In general, these are conditions that lead to inbreeding. Data from several genetic studies of social Hymenoptera have yet to show evidence of inbreeding ((6,13,15), and Metcalf and Finer, in preparation). It should be noted that it is possible to have LMC without inbreeding, but the necessary conditions seem likely to be rare in nature.

Several sibling species of wasps of the Polistes fuscatus species complex have been examined with the view of testing the Trivers and Hare hypothesis. P. metricus, P. fuscatus, and P. variatus found in the upper Midwest have all been shown to have close to a 1:1 ratio of PI in the sexes (13,17). In the cases of P. metricus and P. variatus, genetic data on relatedness and laying worker frequency show that, according to the Trivers and Hare theory, preferred worker PI in females is greater than twice that in males. Also genetic analysis of the population structure of P. metricus and P. variatus shows an absence of inbreeding and high male and low female dispersal. It is argued that these factors make LMC unlikely (13).

A fourth sibling species studied in California, P. apachus, has been shown to have a 2.1:1 female-biased PI ratio. Data on inbreeding from the Texas population of P. apachus show no evidence of inbreeding (Metcalf and Finer, in preparation).

P. apachus occurs at higher densities in California than in
Texas and P. apachus in California occurs at higher densities
than P. metricus which shows no evidence of LMC. Thus the
female-biased investment ratios of P. apachus appear to be a
case of worker control of the allocation of colony PI. The
reasons for the different investment patterns in these biologically similar species are unclear. It seems possible that the
extended breeding season in California leads to the opportunity
for greater worker control.

PARENTAL MANIPULATION
Kin selection as originally formulated treats the actor as the
sole individual upon which selection acts. The potential recipients, parents and other individuals whose inclusive fitness is
affected by the actor's behavior, are passive with respect to
selection (11).

Alexander has stressed the role of the actor's parents, suggesting that they control or manipulate the actor's behavior (1).
Charlesworth has admirably modeled this dichotomy considering
kin selection the case where alleles at a locus in the actor
control the behavior and considering parental manipulation the
case where alleles at a locus in the parents control offspring
behavior (4). Several studies have attempted to distinguish
between these as alternate hypotheses (9,14,22).

I suggest that it is unrealistic to consider any participant,
actor or recipient, as evolutionarily passive. Each individual
will be selected to affect its relatives by altering the environment in such a way as to maximize its own inclusive fitness.
Similar to Maynard Smith's game theory models (8), the fitness
of an actor (recipient) resulting from a specific genotype will
be determined by the phenotype of the recipient (actor). Manipulation in the sense of Alexander's parental manipulation is
then expected to occur among parents, offspring, siblings, and
other interested relatives simultaneously.

For example, in my own work on Polistes metricus, the dominant foundress was found to have an inclusive fitness of 1.83, SE=0.29, relative to a solitary foundress. The dominant foundress or recipient of the benefits of a subordinate foundress would then be expected to be selected to give up sufficient fitness components to make joining the strategy with the highest inclusive fitness for a potential joiner. Evidence for this statement is provided by the 17% reproduction carried out by the subordinate foundress when she lives through the reproductive period.

MUTUALISM

It has been argued that, if the individual fitness of two parties alone is less than their individual fitnesses when socially associated, then selection will favor the formation of the association. Such a society with its attendant apparent altruism would be based upon mutualism (12,21). A mutualistic society as opposed to a society resulting from kin selection does not require that its members be related (21).

Mutualistic societies seem most likely to be found among the semisocial bees. As noted by Lin and Michener, the best proof of this theory would be the discovery of a society where individuals are unrelated. Such a test is well within the technological capabilities of isozyme genetics but has not yet been performed.

West-Eberhard has suggested that social behavior in the wasp Metapolybia aztecoides can be explained as mutualism (22). In this case, a group of sisters found a nest and mutually produce worker-daughters. However, all but a single foundress are excluded by competition from producing the colony's reproductives. Thus the question raised is how is it adaptive for foundresses that are later excluded from reproduction to join such a colony. According to West-Eberhard, the multifoundress origin of the colony is adaptive in that it increases the colony's probability of survival until worker emergence. Nests founded by solitary foundresses are unknown in this species.

Clearly, in that the labor of sisters excluded from production
of reproductives aids nieces and nephews (r=3/8), substantial
inclusive fitness is achieved by subordinate foundresses. It is
not surprising that the sisters compete for the position of
dominant foundress, where r=1/2 to reproductives. Thus a kin
selection hypothesis does not appear to be unreasonable.

West-Eberhard argues ingeniously that the association could be
mutualistic if the foundresses initiate the nest on the prospect
of being the successful foundress. If the fitness of the dominant foundress devalued by the probability of being excluded is
greater than the individual fitness of the foundress following
alternate strategies, then selection would favor the association
based on mutualism.

The available data do not allow a determination between the two
hypotheses to be made. However, if such an association evolved
mutualistically among nonrelatives and relatives, kin selection
would favor individuals who, upon exclusion from reproduction,
had already been directing their efforts towards relatives.

Another consideration is the designation of an appropriate reference population. It may be that substantial evolution has
occurred since M. aztecoides changed from solitary to social,
therefore a comparison to the failure of present day solitary
nest formation may be invalid.

GREEN BEARD EFFECT

An intriguing third category of theories besides kin selection
and mutualism has arisen. In this case, individuals are postulated to utilize the phenotypes of, for example, full siblings
to determine whether an allele is shared and hence the appropri-
ateness of altruistic behavior.

The simplest case of this phenomenon, termed by Dawkins the
'green beard effect,' involves a pleiotropic allele causing
both a green beard phenotype and altruism towards green bearded

individuals (8). Clearly such an allele would spread in a population (a single locus genetic model of a similar case in
parent-offspring conflict has been presented (14)). Dawkins
states, and I concur, that such a mechanism seems unlikely to
be common in nature.

Alternatively, an individual could in theory compare his own
phenotype to that of another individual for several traits
resulting from alleles at independently segregating loci. From
this comparison, the individual could in effect calculate relatedness just as an investigator would from the same data. That
individual could then act according to the rules of kin selection. It is important to note that no identification of the
mutual possession of an allele for altruism occurs in this
mechanism. In other words, a mechanism would not lead to identification of full siblings with higher than average probability
of sharing the allele for altruism.

If, however, an individual could compare itself phenotypically
to another individual for one or more traits controlled by loci
linked to alleles for altruism, then full siblings with increased probability of sharing the allele for altruism could be
identified. This would be in effect a calculation of relatedness, defined as the probability that an allele at a single
locus in two individuals is identical by descent. This definition is in contrast to relatedness defined as the percentage of
alleles identical by descent shared by two individuals as was
used in the previous example. I would note that there seems to
be some confusion in the literature concerning this distinction
(3,18).

It has long been known that many social insects can distinguish
between members and nonmembers of their colonies, usually by
olfaction (23). Recently, Greenberg has presented evidence that
in the bee, Lasioglossum zephyrum, workers can distinguish between more and less related individuals (10). This fact was
established by observing differential tendencies of a nest

entrance guard bee in allowing individuals of varying degrees
of relatedness into the nest. It is not possible to determine
from the data presented whether individuals with specific
chromosome segments are being identified or whether percent
alleles shared in common is being identified. Also, it cannot
be evaluated whether this mechanism operates in wild nests (see
also Hölldobler and Michener, this volume).

CONCLUDING REMARKS

Sociobiology is in its infancy as a distinct discipline. An
assessment of its status must be considered in that light.
Three classes of theories are currently with us. First, there
are the verbal nonquantitative explanations of data constructed
after the fact, sometimes referred to by the infidel as "just-so
stories." We must admit that these are more evidence of the
flexibility of sociobiologic theory than proof of its correctness.

Second, there is the accelerating mass of models couched in untestable parameters which are, however, valuable in the clari-
fication of thinking.

Finally, there are the theories from which testable predictions
result. Foremost among these are Trivers and Hare's sex ratio
theory and, to a lesser extent, relative inclusive fitness. It
is my belief that the integrity of sociobiology as a discipline
depends on an increased and successful emphasis on predictive
theory and empirical test.

REFERENCES

(1)   Alexander, R.D.   1974.   The evolution of social behavior.
       Ann. Rev. Sys. Ecol. 5: 325-383.

(2)   Alexander, R.D., and Sherman, P.W.   1977.   Local mate
       competition and parental investment in social insects.
       Science 196: 494-500.

(3)   Barash, D.P.; Holmes, W.G.; and Greene, P.J.   1978.   Exact
       versus probabilistic coefficients of relationship: some
       implications for sociobiology. Am. Nat. 112: 355-363.

(4)   Charlesworth, B.   1978.   Some models of the evolution of
       altruistic behavior between siblings. J. Theor. Biol. 72:
       297-319.

(5)   Charnov, E.L.   1978.   Sex ratio selection in eusocial
       Hymenoptera. Am. Nat. 112: 317-326.

(6)   Crozier, R.H.   1977.   Evolutionary genetics of Hymenoptera.
       Ann. Rev. Entomol. 22: 263-288.

(7)   Crow, J.F., and Kimura, M.   1970.   An Introduction to Popu-
       lation Genetics Theory. New York: Harper and Row.

(8)   Dawkins, R.   1976.   The Selfish Gene. New York: Oxford
       University Press.

(9)   Gibo, D.L.   1978.   The selective advantage of foundress
       associations in Polistes fuscatus (Hymenoptera:Vespidae):
       a field study of the effects of predation on productivity.
       Can. Ent. 110: 519-540.

(10)   Greenberg, L.   1979.   Genetic component of kin recognition
       in primitively social bee. Science 206: 1095-1097.

(11)   Hamilton, W.D.   1972.   Altruism and related phenomena, mainly
       in social insects. Ann. Rev. Ecol. Sys. 3: 193-232.

(12)   Lin, N., and Michener, C.D.   1972.   Evolution of sociality
       in insects. Q. Rev. Biol. 47: 131-159.

(13)   Metcalf, R.A.   1980.   Sex ratios, parent-offspring conflict,
       and local competition for mates in the social wasps Polistes
       metricus and Polistes variatus. Am. Nat., in press.

(14)   Metcalf, R.A. ; Stamps, J.A.; and Krishnan, V.V.   1979.
       Parent-offspring conflict which is not limited by degree
       of kinship. J. Theor. Biol. 76: 99-107.

(15)   Metcalf, R.A., and Whitt, G.S.   1977a.   Intra-nest relatedness
       in the social wasp Polistes metricus. A genetic analysis
       Behav. Ecol. Sociobiol. 2: 339-351.

(16)   Metcalf, R.A., and Whitt, G.S.   1977b.   Relative inclusive
       fitness in the social wasp Polistes metricus.   Behav. Ecol.
       Sociobiol. 2: 353-360.

(17)   Noonan, K.M.   1978.   Sex ratio of parental investment in
       colonies of the social wasp Polistes fuscatus.   Science
       199: 1354-1356.

(18)   Sherman, P.W.   1979.   Insect chromosome numbers and eu-
       sociality.   Am. Nat. 113: 925-935.

(19)   Trivers, R.L., and Hare, H.   1976.   Haplodiploidy and the
       evolution of social insects.   Science 191: 249-263.

(20)   West-Eberhard, M.J.   1969.   The social biology of Polistine
       wasps.   Misc. Publ., Mus. Zool., University of Michigan 140:
       1-101.

(21)   West-Eberhard, M.J.   1975.   The evolution of social behavior
       by kin selection.   Q. Rev. Biol. 50: 1-33.

(22)   West-Eberhard, M.J.   1978.   Temporary queens in Metapolybia
       wasps: nonreproductive helpers without altruism?   Science
       200: 441-443.

(23)   Wilson, E.O.   1971.   The Insect Societies.   Cambridge, MA:
       Belknap Press of Harvard University Press.

Evolution of Social Behavior: Hypotheses and Empirical Tests, ed. H. Markl,
pp. 97-114. Dahlem Konferenzen 1980. Weinheim: Verlag Chemie GmbH.

Can "Fitness" Be Measured in Primate Populations?

D. S. Sade
Department of Anthropology, Northwestern University
Evanston, IL 60201, USA

Abstract. Longitudinal observations on individually recognized
animals are necessary to measure fitness and test sociobiological
hypotheses on primate populations.

INTRODUCTION

Cactus-loving Drosophila may be ideal subjects for the study of
natural selection (2) but their populations lack the social dimension on which this workshop focuses. Populations of higher
primates are organized primarily by social interaction and might
be ideal subjects for testing theories regarding the relative
importance of individual, kin, and group selection, but how can
these theories be approached empirically?

Evolution should produce optimal behaviors, statuses, strategies,
or other characteristics that maximize the fitness of the individual, family, or group that displays the optimum. Proof that a
social characteristic is optimal requires:
1) Correlational evidence that fitness is maximized,
2) Causal analysis of the mechanisms linking the social characteristic with fitness.

In addition, to show that the optimum is maintained through competition, we need:
3) Determination of the heritability of the social features.

Among primates this requires also distinguishing genetic from
cultural heritability.

If heritability is not zero, there is genetical variance associated with the variance in the behavioral trait, and genetical
selection may be occurring through competition among individuals.
If heritability is zero, genetical competition cannot be occurring and some other explanation for the observed variance in behavior is required. In this case, does variance between social
groups become an important consideration in evolutionary theory?

Points 1 and 3 require knowing the number of offspring of an individual and the similarity between offspring and parents, or at
least the similarity between siblings. Point 2 requires experimentation. Kummer's (13) experiments confirm the possibility of
causal analysis of the motivational factors underlying social
relations in primates.

Experiments on factors affecting reproductive success, however,
require manipulation of whole breeding colonies, as has been done
repeatedly with small mammals (3). The difficulties with similar
experiments on primates are not technical, as the Cayo Santiago
work shows, but financial and administrative.

The essential questions are:
1) At what levels of organization should fitness be measured?
2) To what degree of accuracy can fitness be measured?
3) Can the factors affecting fitness be identified?
4) Can the heritability of fitness or the factors affecting it be
determined?

DEFINITION
"Fitness" is a measure of the relative number of offspring that
members of a parental generation contribute to a descendent
generation. The parental generation may be partitioned into
classes whose members share sets of characteristics. Reproductive rates of classes of individuals can be determined from

combined observations on individuals and relative rates used to
indicate fitness. Authors may speak of the fitness of the characteristic itself, especially when it is one of the alternate
alleles at a chromosomal locus or a larger chromosomal segment
that replicates as a unit. It may be useful on occasion to apply
the concept of fitness to levels of organization other than the
locus or individual, such as the family, social group, or species
population. In any case, whatever level of organization is of
interest, "fitness" means the differential reproduction or replication of those units, especially when they interact in such a
way that one might eventually replace another.

Williams (26) suggests that fitness might also refer to the per-
fection of an adaptation as judged by a competent biologist
irregardless of information on whether the units in nature possess-
ing the adaptation were increasing at the expense of competing
units that lacked it. This sense will not be used in this paper
because it leads to circular reasoning. In studies on primates
there is a history of interpreting characteristics or events that
are spectacular, awesome, or merely esthetic as indicating fitness in the Darwinian sense irregardless of the lack of any
measurement of differential reproduction. This is particularly
true in regard to the evolutionary interpretation of dominance
relations, especially among males.

COMPONENTS
There are three components of reproduction that, while varying
somewhat independently of each other, contribute to a net or overall measure of fitness (15):
1) fecundity: the number of offspring produced during an individual's lifetime,
2) viability: the ability of individuals to survive,
3) rate of development: the age at which first reproduction occurs.

These are the life history characteristics that are combined in the
columns of life tables and from which the "Malthusian parameter"

or "intrinsic rate of increase" are calculated for a population or subdivision of a population. Other aspects of the individual, population, or environment that influence these three components will be called "characteristics" or "factors."

MEASURING "FITNESS" AT THE GENETIC LEVEL

The most common discussions of fitness refer to the competition of alternate alleles at a single locus. Much of sociobiological theory is derived from single-locus models: evolution occurs through the replacement of one allele by another according to the mathematical predictions and proofs of Fisher, Wright, Haldane, and others. Our information on the genetics of primate populations comes from surveys in which blood samples are taken from all or most of the individuals in social groups and the frequencies of alleles at polymorphic loci obtained. Even if a locus had a definite relation to a behavioral characteristic, could the fitnesses of its alleles be determined from their frequencies?

The procedures Prout (18,19) proposes to overcome the difficulties in estimating fitness from genotypic frequencies (19) cannot be applied in field studies of primates. Even if Prout's methods extend to the case of continuous breeding animals in populations containing overlapping generations, and if the required minimum of four successive generations could be sampled in sufficient numbers, the method could not apply to social animals. Constructing an artificial population of mixed genotypes at predetermined frequencies would mean removing the individuals from the social network, which is the object of study. Furthermore, Lewontin (15) argues that the fitness of alternate alleles at a single locus can never be measured because of the impossibility, even in experimental Drosophila populations, of randomizing the genetic background within which the alleles in question occur.

Sociobiological hypotheses based on single-locus genetical models cannot be tested empirically on primate populations.

MEASURING FITNESS AT HIGHER LEVELS OF ORGANIZATION
Most authors concede that the individual phenotype is the level
at which selection acts and therefore the proper level at which
to measure fitness.

Kin groups are considered units of evolution in many sociobiological models. Is there evidence of differential reproduction
between groups of related individuals? Sade et al. (22) show
that higher ranking families of monkeys within social groups show
higher rates of increase than families of lower ranking females.

Social groups, each composed of several unrelated families, may
compete, indicating the possibility of group selection. Populations of social groups of primates may illustrate the patterns of
growth and extinction Maynard-Smith (16) considers essential to
group selection. Southwick's (23) long-term census of rhesus
groups in India and Nepal show that over about 16 years some dis-
appeared, some declined, and some increased. Human intervention
cannot be excluded, however. Dittus (6) reports a similar pattern
in a toque macaque population in Ceylon. There was no trapping,
but modification of the habitat by extensive development may have
been a factor. Sade et al. (22), however, report considerable
differential in reproductive rates of groups of rhesus monkeys at
Cayo Santiago, uninfluenced by harvesting and in a constant
environment.

Critics of group selection have relied on single-locus genetical
models, which may be unrealistically pessimistic regarding the
importance of the process, as Wade (25) has argued on both theoretical and experimental grounds. He suggests that models based
on quantitative (polygenic) inheritance may be more favorable to
group selection.

THE INDIVIDUAL IS THE UNIT OF OBSERVATION
The units of the higher levels of organization can be studied
directly, but observations are always made on individuals. The
fitnesses of individual phenotypes are of course always measured

directly by observations on individuals. The observation of
different fitnesses of social classes referred to above depended
upon the observation of characteristics of individual monkeys who
were then classed together according to details of their social
interactions. Observation of the differential reproduction of
social groups likewise depends upon measurement of the reproductive parameters of the individuals who are members of the
groups. Even when only census information on numbers of individuals present in a group is used, the recognition of the continuity of the group over time depends upon the continuity of association of individually recognized members.

Howard (9) outlines the information needed to estimate individual
reproductive success with increasing degree of confidence. The
higher order estimates, requiring life history information on
offspring as well as parents, are the most difficult to obtain.
Before lower order estimates can be accepted as substitutes for
the more desirable higher order ones, however, some proof, now
lacking, of predictability from lower to higher should be demonstrated.

What are the requirements for measuring the components of fitness
in primate species? The life history characteristics of the
primates indicate the answer. The following discussion refers to
the so-called higher primates, that is, the Old World monkeys,
the New World monkeys, and the apes. The following figures are
intended to indicate orders of magnitude. There is little precise
information on these values for any but a very few species.

Maximum longevity approaches 30 years for monkeys and perhaps 50
years for the larger apes. Litter size, or number of young born
to a female at each birth, is better known. The figures range
from a usual one among most of the Old World monkeys, the apes,
and the larger New World monkeys, to a usual two or rarely three
among the smaller New World monkeys. Average life expectancy is
known only for Japanese macaques and for rhesus monkeys kept
under colony conditions and can be guessed at for chimpanzees.

Following the period of high infant mortality, life expectancy
for monkeys may be approximately 10 years (22), and 16 years for
chimpanzees (24). The length of the reproductive span of the
life cycle is presumed to be a large part of the total longevity
for monkeys and perhaps to a somewhat lesser extent for apes.
Rhesus monkeys may reproduce at 3 to 4 years of age and continue
producing offspring into their 20's, if they survive. The average
length of generation, as calculated from life tables, and indicating the average number of years between the birth of a female
and the birth of her first female offspring, is known only for
rhesus monkeys from an artificial colony and varies between about
5 and 10 years (22).

These estimates indicate that a very long-term effort is required
to measure the lifetime fitness of individuals. A 20-year program
of continuous observation is necessary to measure the basic components of fitness for a cohort of monkeys. Since heritability
of fitness is an important question, the program must be twice
as long. As 20 years (or 40 years) is a very significant portion
of the career of most investigators, one immediately asks: Can
the components of fitness among primates be measured by cross-
sectional samples?

A curve based on the mean values of a series of cross-sectional
samples ordered by age does not resemble the progression of an
individual in physical growth, social status, or reproductive
value. It might more adequately represent the progression of a
set of individuals. If one assumes that a cross-section of individuals of all ages sampled from a population during a reasonably
short period of time is representative of a single cohort followed
through the entire life span, one can construct time-specific
life tables and calculate reproductive parameters for the entire
population or subclassifications of the population according to
genetical or social criteria and draw conclusions regarding the
relative fitnesses of the classes so constructed. There are
advantages to the cross-sectional sample: over the 20-year period
suggested for a longitudinal study of primate reproduction, there

may be considerable haphazard environmental fluctuation which will
add statistical noise to the sample. It may be that the cross-
sectional sample might more clearly represent differences in fitness due to social or genetical criteria than would information
derived from following a single cohort through its entire life
history.

However, in order to construct a time-specific life table for
these long-lived animals, ages of the individuals must be known.
Measures of survivorship and fertility are age-specific values.
Enough is known to indicate that these measures change significantly with age. The next question is: Can ages be determined
for primates?

ESTIMATING AGE
If birth dates within some reasonably small interval are not
known by observation of mothers shortly after an infant's birth,
then the age of an animal must be estimated by comparing some
dependable feature of morphological change with standards pre-
pared by examination of animals of known age. There is no way
to escape longitudinal observation on at least some animals if
only to prepare aging standards to be used for acquiring cross-
sectional samples. Methods that have been used or might be used
can be classified according to the method of observation, the
kind of equipment necessary, and the upper limit of reliability
of the technique. Methods currently available to the field
worker, in contrast to the highly-equipped laboratory researcher,
do not allow estimates of age of primates past the very early
portion of the reproductive span. Only longitudinal observation
of individuals from a very young age will suffice to provide the
data required for measuring the components of fitness in primate
populations. This means that even cross-sectional measurements
of fitness require long-term and longitudinal base-line observations.

RELATEDNESS OF INDIVIDUALS
Many of the interesting problems in sociobiology regard the degree
of relatedness of the individuals. One might say that kinship is

the central concept in most sociobiological models. If these
models are to be tested against measurements of actual systems,
kinship relationships must be known. Kinship as a component of
social organization has been best measured among primates for
Japanese macaques (14) and for the rhesus monkeys at the Cayo
Santiago colony. Even in these two species, however, where kinship relations among females in particular play a very important
role in the organization of the social group and in the origin
of new groups (4), there are also important alliances and associations between females who are certainly not closely related
(20). Kinship relations have been inferred from interactions in
some short-term field studies. My feeling is that these attempts
are spurious, because the logic of the technique is circular.

The social groups at Cayo Santiago, which contain large numbers
of closely related animals, may not be good models for wild
groups. They may be typical only of rapidly expanding populations, which may not be common in the wild (1). The average
degree of relatedness of monkeys in groups at Cayo Santiago may
be greater than the average degree of relatedness of baboons at
Amroseli or at other locations. The only reliable way to determine kinship relations within monkey groups is to conduct long-
term, longitudinal observations of individuals from very early on
in life.

FITNESSES OF MALES

Suppose that the long-term, longitudinal observations were carried
out on a significant number of individuals and that the parameters
of reproduction were measured sufficiently to construct life
tables and to estimate the fitnesses of individuals of different
classifications within a population. The direct measures apply
only to females. Can fitnesses of males be measured in primate
populations? The answer depends on whether the paternity of a
female's offspring can be determined, and this will vary with the
mating system of the species. The higher primates include species
that are presumed to form monogamous mating pairs, one-male harems,
and promiscuous groups containing several adult males and females.

MONOGAMOUS SPECIES

Among the Callithrichidae and a few of the Cebidae (Aotus,
Callicebus) and among the Hylobatidae, the breeding unit is a
territorial male-female pair associating with their immature offspring who disperse at adolescence. It seems likely that the
paternity of an infant can be assigned precisely to the male who
shares the territorial unit with the infant's mother, particularly
among the Callithrichidae, where the male participates directly
in the care of his mate's offspring by carrying them on his back.
Nevertheless, these conclusions have been derived primarily from
laboratory and zoo studies. More recent field work indicates that
the social unit in the wild is more variable in size among some
marmosets.

I know of no long-term information at all indicating the stability
of the mated pair over a period of several years, and it is at
least possible that the monogamy of the species is less than has
been assumed. Are the older offspring associating with the female marmoset truly the offspring of the male who is currently
associating with the female? The question can be reversed: Is
the female currently associating with the male truly the mother
of the older offspring associating with him? One presumes that
the answer is yes in each case, but a presumption is not a measurement, and a measurement requires longitudinal observations of
recognizable individuals.

A serious gap in our knowledge regards the dispersal of the young
and the events that occur when a new pair is formed. This is an
important point for current sociobiological theory. The degree
of relatedness of the offspring of the monogamous pairs will
average .5. In contrast, female half-siblings among rhesus monkeys will undoubtedly average between .25 and .5: it is likely
that not all sisters among rhesus monkeys have the same father
but some might. Among the promiscuous Cercopithecidae (such as
the rhesus monkey) the female half-sibs show clearly cooperative
and mutually supportive behaviors (11), but in the monogamous
species of the Hylobatidae, Callithrichidae, and Cebidae, it is

likely that territorial conflict and competition is the rule
among dispersed full-sibs. In any case, only longitudinal studies
on individually recognized individuals will provide the information on the details of kinship relations among these neighboring, monogamous, territorial pairs of primates.

HAREM SYSTEMS

A harem system, in which a number of females mate exclusively with
one male, has been described for the Hamadryas baboon (12). Less
extreme but similar systems, from the point of view of determining paternity, are found among the one-male units of gelada monkeys, among the one-male groups of patas monkeys, and perhaps
among some African and Asiatic colobines.

One might assume that the male of the one-male unit of Hamadryas
baboons is the true father of the infants of the females maintained in his harem. However, the same qualifications that were
stated regarding the monogamously mated pairs must be applied to
these harem-breeders. We do not know the stability of these
harems over long periods of time through longitudinal observations. In the case of the monogamously mated pairs, presumably
both the male and the female are active in maintaining the pair
bond. However, among the Hamadryas it appears that only the male
plays a serious role in maintaining the continuity of the breeding
unit (12), and it is at least possible that his control may be
incomplete so that some of the offspring in his unit have been
fathered by males other than himself.

PROMISCUOUS SYSTEMS

Promiscuous systems, in which both males and females may have
several mates during a single mating season, are found among the
Cercopithecoidea and the Cebidae as well as among the great apes.
Most of the detailed information about mating behavior from these
groups comes from two related species, Macaca mulatta and Papio
cynocephalus. Most attempts for estimating the fitness of males
among primates have been made on these species. Among both
species, a female may exhibit a fairly well-defined period of

estrus, during which she will copulate, followed by a period of
diestrus, during which copulation is less frequent or absent.
In both species a female may form a consortship exclusively with
one male during her estrous period, but this usually does not
last during diestrus. The extreme or idealized consortship,
however, may not be the most frequent type. It may be more
common for a female to mate with several males during her estrous
cycle with perhaps one particular male mating with her most frequently or exclusively during the few days of the cycle on which
she is most likely to ovulate. Some females, however, may mate
with several males at any time during the cycle. In order to
estimate paternity from observations of the mating behavior, one
must draw inferences from the frequency of copulation and the
most likely time of conception.

DO DOMINANCE HIERARCHIES COME FROM INDIVIDUAL OR BIOTIC ADAPTATION?

The importance of these observations should be emphasized however,
because they have been used to test two competing hypotheses
about the role of dominance relations among males in multimale
groups of monkeys. One hypothesis is that dominance results from
interindividual competition for reproductive success among males.
If true, this would support the view of some sociobiologists that
complex social relationships are really effects of individuals
striving to maximize their own fitness. A competing hypothesis
is that the dominance relations act to favor the group by controlling aggression irrespective of the reproductive advantage that
the individual acquires.

If it were to be shown through measurement of paternity that there
is no relationship between the dominance rank of a male and his
individual fitness, then one might be led to examine his role in
maintaining or increasing the overall reproduction of the group
irrespective of the paternity of offspring within it. This would
support arguments for group selection. Very careful sampling of
frequency of mating by males with females at the most likely time
of conception show a low positive correlation between dominance

rank of male and likelihood of fathering infants (7). The ambiguity inherent in a low correlation is unsatisfying given the importance of the question under investigation. It would be highly desirable if a more direct measurement of male fitness could be used. Several workers have attempted to use genetical markers and the logic of paternal exclusions based on the techniques developed in human medical-legal practice (21).

The results also remain ambiguous and unsatisfying. They neither provide us with a clear-cut measure of reproductive success in relation to dominance rank, nor do they prove that there is no correlation. The most clear-cut conclusion that one can draw is that males other than the dominant are also fathering offspring. Even this conclusion is not as definite as would be desirable because it comes primarily from the work at Cayo Santiago. The population during the study years was characterized by an excess of males of breeding age compared to what might be expected in the wild. This and the unsatisfactory level of genetic polymorphism may mask the role of the dominant male in producing offspring. The issue remains unresolved even under what might be the best of all likely conditions.

FITNESS OF GROUPS
Suppose for the sake of speculation and argument that the role of the dominant or high ranking males is not to maximize their own inclusive fitness within the social group but to maximize the reproductive rate of the group as a whole, irrespective of their individual contribution to paternity, and to aid the group in competition with neighboring groups. What might one expect to find in the wild that would tend to support such a group selectionist point of view? One might find that there would be considerable variance in the rate of increase or decrease of local social groups, as we have already seen. How would such rates be determined?

Ideally, one would monitor a system of many social groups over a number of years to measure the actual increase or decrease both of the individual groups and of the population as a whole. Alternatively, one might calculate the rate of reproduction for each group based on short-term census data such as one might collect in a year's time. In the latter case, however, caution would be required in comparing crude rates of increase from one group to another. The crude growth rate is only comparable between two populations if the age profiles of the populations are identical. We have already seen that age estimation of primates in the wild is unreliable. The longitudinal observations that we have seen to be essential to all of the problems discussed are necessary for comparing the relative reproductive rates of different social groups.

ORIGIN OR NEW GROUPS

Differential production of new groups by fissioning might favor a group selection hypothesis. A group that shows a high rate of increase might be more likely to fission. The facts, such as we have them, unfortunately come primarily from Cayo Santiago (4,5) and can be used as anecdotal support of hypotheses favoring individual selection, kin selection, or group selection as the primary mode of evolutionary mechanisms involving sociality among rhesus monkeys.

The larger, therefore successful, groups tend to be the ones that divide (group selection?), but groups divide along genealogical lines, thus increasing the degree of relatedness among the daughter groups (kin selection?). However, the individuals that disperse tend to be those who are low ranking both in the group as a whole and within their own genealogies. They may be bettering their reproductive potential by moving to a new social circumstance (individual selection?), but this requires establishing closer cooperative relationships with non-relatives than with kin (group selection?). The males who become the core of the new groups cooperate with one another although they are unrelated (group selection?). Perhaps as individuals they are bettering their reproductive potential by achieving high rank in a way which would not be easy for them in the original group (individual selection?). The facts do not clearly point to one or another mode of selection as having been the most important.

One is left with the impression that even when with great difficulty one measures the parameters of fitness in a primate population at the various levels of organization that are important to current theory, one is left with results which are inconclusive in regard to the central theories that have been proposed to explain them.

CONCLUSIONS

Any attempt to test sociobiological hypotheses requires measures or reliable estimates of the fitnesses of individuals, families, or groups. If this is to be done on primate populations, the necessary data can only be acquired through long-term, longitudinal observations on recognizable individuals. The results that can be derived from such studies based on the few such that have yet been done may be inadequate for genuine test of hypotheses even after years of effort. It might be that many more longitudinal studies or more precise ones will solve the ambiguities that currently persist.

Humans may be better subjects than non-human primates for studies on fitness, because life histories can be obtained from interviews in relatively short periods of time (10).

Much attention is being directed towards other highly social, yet shorter-lived mammals, with higher absolute rates of reproduction, especially ground-living Sciuridae (8). Do the primates offer unique opportunities for sociobiologists or can all problems be researched on more tractable species? Much of the earlier impetus for research on primates came from hopes of finding homologues for human behavior. The chimpanzee alone has failed to disappoint these hopes. Social carnivores may provide better analogues for early human groups. Ground squirrels may provide better models of kin-related adaptations. Could not the effort being expended on primates be better directed towards other orders?

It might be that the fault lies not with the observational studies
nor the details that are currently available, but rather with the
hypotheses themselves. If they are not genuine alternatives,
then no amount of measurement or testing will distinguish between
them, no matter however favorable a species is chosen.

Acknowledgements. This work was supported by NSF grant BNS77-
14882. The author is grateful to A. Wasserman for preparing the
manuscript. The author is grateful to B.D. Chepko-Sade,
J. Cheverud, J. Hewitt, W. Irons, T.J. Olivier, and D. Rhodes
for comments.

REFERENCES

(1) Altmann, J.; Altmann, S.A.; Hausfater, G.; and McCuskey, S.A. 1977. Life history of yellow baboons: Physical development, reproductive parameters, and infant mortality. Primates 18: 315-330.

(2) Barker, J.S.F. 1977. Cactus-breeding Drosophila: A system for the measurement of natural selection. In Measuring Selection in Natural Populations. Lecture Notes in Biomathematics 19, eds. F.B. Christiansen and T.M. Fenchel. Berlin: Springer-Verlag.

(3) Batzli, G.O.; Getz, L.L.; and Hurley, S.S. 1977. Suppression of growth and reproduction of microtine rodents by social factors. J. Mammal. 58: 583-591.

(4) Chepko-Sade, B.D., and Olivier, T.J. 1979. Coefficient of genetic relationship and the probability of intra-genealogical fission in Macaca mulatta. Behav. Ecol. Sociobiol. 5: 263-298.

(5) Chepko-Sade, B.D., and Sade, D.S. 1979. Patterns of group splitting within matrilineal kinship groups. A study of social group structure in Macaca mulatta (Cercopithecidae: Primates). Behav. Ecol. Sociobiol. 5: 67-86.

(6) Dittus, W.P.J. 1977. The social regulation of population density and age-sex distribution in the toque monkey. Behaviour 63: 281-322.

(7) Hausfater, G. 1975. Dominance and reproduction in baboons (Papio cynocephalus). Contrib. Primatol. 7. Basel: S. Karger.

(8) Hoogland, J.L. 1980. Nepotism and cooperative breeding in the black-tailed prairie dog (Scuiridae: Cynonys ludovicianus). In Natural Selection and Social Behavior: Recent Research and New Theory, eds. R.D. Alexander and D.W. Tinkle. New York: Chiron Press, in press.

(9) Howard, R.D. 1979. Estimating reproductive success in natural populations. Amer. Naturalist 114: 221-231.

(10) Irons, W. 1979. Cultural and biological success. In Evolutionary Biology and Human Social Behavior: An Anthropological Perspective, eds. N. Chagnon and W.A. Irons. North Scituate, MA: Duxbury Press.

(11) Kaplan, J.R. 1978. Fight interference and altruism in rhesus monkeys. Amer. J. phys. Anthrop. 49: 214-250.

(12) Kummer, H. 1968. Social Organization of Hamadryas Baboons. A Field Study. Chicago: University of Chicago Press.

(13)   Kummer, H.   1971.   Primate Societies: Group Techniques
       of Ecological Adaptation.   Chicago: Aldine-Atherton.

(14)   Kurland, J.A.   1977.   Kin selection in the Japanese
       monkey.   Contrib. Primatol. 12. Basel: S. Karger.

(15)   Lewontin, R.C.   1974.   The Genetic Basis of Evolutionary
       Change.   New York: Columbia University Press.

(16)   Maynard Smith, J.   1976.   Group selection.   Quart. Rev.
       Biol. 51: 277-283.

(17)   Prout, T.   1965.   The estimation of fitnesses from
       genotypic frequencies.   Evolution 19: 546-551.

(18)   Prout, T.   1969.   The estimation of fitnesses from
       population data.   Genetics 63: 949-967.

(19)   Prout, T.   1971.   The relation between fitness components
       and population prediction in Drosophila.   I: The estimation
       of fitness components.   Genetics 68: 127-149.

(20)   Sade, D.S.   1972.   Sociometrics of Macaca mulatta.   I.
       Linkages and cliques in grooming matrices.   Folia primat.
       18: 196-223.

(21)   Sade, D.S.   1980. Population biology of free-ranging
       rhesus monkeys on Cayo Santiago, Puerto Rico.   In Bio-
       social Mechanisms of Population Regulation, ed. M. Cohen
       New Haven: Yale University Press, in press.

(22)   Sade, D.S.; Cushing, K.; Cushing, P.; Dunaif, J.;
       Figueroa, A.; Kaplan, J.R.; Lauer, C.; Rhodes, D.; and
       Schneider, J.   1976.   Population dynamics in relation to
       social structures on Cayo Santiago.   Yearb. phys. Anthrop.
       20: 253-262.

(23)   Southwick, C.H.; Teas, H.J.; and Siddiqi, M.F.   1980.
       Rhesus monkey populations in India and Nepal: Patterns
       of growth, decline, and natural regulation.   In Biosocial
       Mechanisms of Population Regulation, ed. M. Cohen.   New Haven:
       Yale University Press, in press.

(24)   Teleki, G.; Hunt, E.E., Jr.; and Pfifferling, J.H.   1976.
       Demographic observations (1963-1973) on the chimpanzees
       of Gombe National Park, Tanzania.   J. Hum. Evol. 5:
       559-598.

(25)   Wade, M.J.   1978.   A critical review of the models of
       group selection.   Quart. Rev. Biol. 53: 101-114.

(26)   Williams, G.C.   1966.   Adaptation and Natural Selection.
       Princeton: Princeton University Press.

Evolution of Social Behavior: Hypotheses and Empirical Tests, ed. H. Markl,
pp. 115-128. Dahlem Konferenzen 1980. Weinheim: Verlag Chemie GmbH.

Fitness in Complex Avian Social Systems

J. L. Brown
Department of Biological Science, State University of New York
Albany, NY 12222, USA

Abstract. Helping behavior in birds is found in a variety of
social systems. It is suitable for empirical testing of inclusive fitness theory because, by definition, the recipient
is not a descendent of the donor. Although helpers are sometimes closely related to recipients, some empiricists refused
to accept an evolutionary theory of helping that combined
benefit to the helper as an individual with benefit to non-
descendent relatives. At first, opponents claimed that
helpers did not actually raise recipients' fitness and that
helpers might actually do more harm than good to recipients.
Recent work has shown that helpers cause increased reproductive success in at least one species and that this effect can
be demonstrated even when complicating variables are
controlled experimentally. Recently, benefits to recipients
have been interpreted as byproducts of direct benefits to
donors rather than as important components of donor inclusive
fitness. No attempt is made here to debate this issue.
Instead certain improvements in terminology and concepts are
proposed which, it is hoped, should enable a more accurate and
impartial assessment of the evidence. Basic distinctions are
made between direct and indirect effects on fitness and
between present and future effects. Last, some desiderata
for future modeling and field work are listed.

INTRODUCTION

Sufficient diversity exists among avian social systems (10) to

provide fertile testing grounds for sociobiological theories.

Since 1970 attention has centered on communal birds. These

are defined primarily by the presence of helpers. The definition of a helper is operational and arbitrary. To establish
that a bird is a helper, one must a) arbitrarily designate
certain types of aid-giving behavior as criteria, b) show
that the helper performs the designated behavior, and last c)
establish that the recipient is not a descendent of the helper.
No assumptions or observations about the effect of the aid on
the fitness of the donor or recipient need be made in order
to establish that an individual is a helper. In practice the
criteria usually involve behavior that would normally be performed by a parent of the recipient. In the most frequently
studied case, a helper is identified as a bird that feeds young
that are not its own. Because of its relevance to contemporary
sociobiological theories, helping behavior will be the focus of
this review, though other kinds of aid-giving will also be included. The next two sections provide brief background material.
Following these are some suggestions for future modeling and
empirical studies.

DIVERSITY
Helpers in birds are found in a great variety of species and
social systems, many of which have little in common except the
presence of helpers. Consequently, great care must be exer-
cised in generalization; for example, communal jays are quite
unlike colonial kingfishers socially. Because these differences must be taken into account when discussing helper
systems a short classification is provided in Table 1.

A fundamental division in Table 1 is between territorial and
non-territorial species. The territorial species tend to
occur in small (2-25), tightly knit, communal units. Members
of such units tend to act together in territorial defense,
foraging, anti-predator behavior, and other behavior. The
non-territorial species are in nearly all cases colonial. The
nests of colonial species are clumped, but the pairs of most
colonial species do not usually travel together as one large,

social unit. Helpers are associated with some of the pairs,
but in many of the colonial species now being studied a large
fraction of pairs lacks helpers, and pairs with helpers have
few of them.

TABLE 1 - Classification of some avian communal breeding
systems.

Name of Category	Typical size of communal unit
All-purpose territory present	
Singular breeding - 1 pair per unit	
scrub jay, superb blue wren	2-7
Plural breeding - 2 or more pairs per unit	
Multiple nesting - Mexican jay	5-15
Joint nesting - anis, ww. chough	2-18
All-purpose territory absent	
Nests clumped (colonial)	
Nests structurally independent	
pinon jay, pied kingfisher	2-4
Lodge builders, nests connected	
sociable weaver	2-4
Nests not clumped except by habitat	
noisy miner	4-20

For further classification, references and complete names see
(2).

Among territorial species an important division occurs between
species in which each unit contains only one breeding pair
(singular breeding) and those in which units commonly or
usually have two or more breeding pairs (plural breeding). In
the latter case it is possible for individuals to be both
breeders and helpers simultaneously. This is inevitable when
the eggs of different parents become so mixed up that even
their own parents cannot tell them apart.

EARLY CONTROVERSIES
The first debate over helping behavior concerned the effect of
helping on fitness of recipients. Zahavi (26) in 1974
questioned the existing data suggesting that helpers bene-
fitted fitness of parents and suggested instead that "...non-
breeding birds may do more harm than help to the reproduction

of the breeding pair." An independent analysis of his data,
however, revealed a positive correlation ($r = 0.35$; $P = 0.09$)
(1) rather than the negative one implied by Zahavi. Following
the initial report of such a positive correlation by Rowley
(13), several other such positive findings have accumulated
(references in (2)), and this point is now rarely disputed.

Positive correlations could not be accepted as proof of a
cause-effect relationship, however, because of the possibility
of other variables being correlated positively with success
and with number of helpers (10). Field studies provided
evidence that parental experience (23) and habitat quality (3)
might be important causes of such correlations. The next step
was to hold constant such additional variables and to vary the
number of helpers independently. This was first achieved by
an experiment in which the number of helpers was manipulated
by removing all but one from some units while leaving all in
other units of comparable initial size (4). Breeding success
in the units from which helpers were removed was reduced to
the level of small control units. The reduction in success
was equal to half a fledgling for each helper removed. The
general conclusion that helpers raise the fitness of their
recipients is now widely accepted for several species.

THE ALTRUISM BOONDOGGLE
An altruist by Hamilton's definition incurs a loss in direct
fitness (see below), meaning a loss in own offspring surviving
to maturity (7). Although others exist, this is the standard
definition of altruism in sociobiology. If we could prove
such a fitness loss for helping, or for any aid-giving phenotype, we would have shown that the phenotype must have evolved
by indirect selection (see below) or interdemic selection.
Overlooked by some authors is the fact that the converse is
not true. Disproving the existence of a fitness loss in a
donor does not rule out the possibility that indirect selection is important because indirect selection may also occur in
mutualism and selfishness (7).

There is a substantial literature concerning the possible role of indirect selection ("kin selection") in altruism, but there is very little on its role in cooperative (= mutualistic) behaviors (in which the donor's direct fitness benefits). This imbalance must be corrected if we are to understand the relative roles of direct and indirect fitness in nature. (Population geneticists, such as Uyenoyama and Feldman, personal communication, realize that altruism is a worst-case model and have good reason to focus on this case. Unfortunately, this rationale is rarely stated by geneticists and its omission seems to have misled some empiricists into believing that indirect selection operates only in altruism.)

Sociobiology has passed through a period of carelessness in characterizing virtually all aid-giving behaviors as altruism. I believe that this is associated primarily with the use of effort and energy as indices of direct fitness (rather than mature offspring). Some efforts and energy expenditures lower direct fitness, but some raise it (e.g., parental care). To assume that donor efforts always lower donor fitness merely because they expend energy or incur risk is incorrect. A prime example is the tendency among a minority of sociobiologists to regard ordinary parental care as altruism (e.g., (14), discussed further in (15)), despite Hamilton's (7) caution that it is easily explained by the classical theory. Inclusive fitness theory is, of course, still useful in cost-benefit analyses of parental behavior even when Hamilton's caveat is heeded, as in Trivers' treatment (17). To deny that parental care is altruistic is not to deny that it has costs and trade-offs.

Another mistake is the tendency to regard feeding of another's young as altruism simply because food is transferred. A loss of food is not a loss of direct fitness unless the donor can utilize the food to raise its direct fitness more effectively in some other way. If it cannot, then giving it away cannot cause a loss in direct fitness. Moreover, if the consequence

of the giving also raises the giver's direct fitness, the
giving is mutualism (= cooperation), not altruism. Field
studies suggest that hungry helpers in nature do not feed
others; even parents may sometimes avoid feeding their own
offspring.

For theoretical reasons donor sacrifice is likely to be kept
as small as possible by selection (4). There are also
empirical reasons to believe that in birds any evolved
sacrifice will be so small as to be virtually undetectable.
The upper limit on evolved sacrifice is set by the genetic
gain thereby achieved. In birds this gain per helper has been
estimated as a fraction of a fledgling. It has not been possible to prove or disprove the existence of such losses with
present field techniques (2).

TYPES OF FITNESS
Some of the more basic terms in sociobiology are used differently by different workers. To establish a frame of reference
for this paper I have classified a variety of kinds or components of fitness in Table 2. The dichotomy between direct and
indirect fitness, although conceptually present in Hamilton
(7), was not explicitly and conveniently named until recently
(4). No synonym exists for indirect fitness. Existing terms
were often misused. For example, kin selection and inclusive
fitness were often used where indirect selection and indirect
fitness were intended. The dichotomy between direct and
indirect is convenient because it can be applied to fitness,
selection, reproductive value, genetic pathways, and other
contexts in which brief and explicit distinctions of this
nature are needed. For example, skeptical field workers are
wont to ask, "What facts about social behavior require or are
better explained by the addition of indirect fitness to direct
fitness"?

TABLE 2 - Components of inclusive (intrademic) fitness.

1	Direct Fitness (= classical individual fitness)
2	Self Effects - not involving others, e.g. thermoregulation
3	Social Effects - involving others
4	Parental care e.g., care of descendents
5	Other aid e.g., courtship feeding; see Table 4
6	Indirect Fitness (inclusive fitness minus direct fitness)
7	Effects on non-descendent relatives
8	Effects on non-relatives and relatives more distant than included in 7
9	Mediated by viscosity - reduced dispersal
10	Mediated by environmental sorting according to genotype
11	Mediated by stochastic effects on unit composition

For comparison: Inclusive fitness
                        Hamilton (1964): 1, 7, and 9
                        Hamilton (1975): 1, 7, 9, 10, and 11
                  Kin selection
                        Maynard Smith (1964): 4, 7, and 9
                        West-Eberhard (1975): 7
                        Wilson (1975): 7
                        Oster and Wilson (1978): 4 and 7

FITNESS NETWORKS IN AVIAN SOCIAL SYSTEMS

In a social organization of significant complexity, the actions
of one individual (the donor) may affect the fitness of others
(primary recipients), whose altered behavior or condition may
in turn have consequences for the fitness of still others (secondary recipients). Similarly, tertiary and higher order
recipients are possible. The web of all possible effects on
fitness resulting from a donor's social interactions may be
conceived as a donor fitness network. When all possible
donors are included, a comprehensive fitness network results,
possibly with emergent properties of its own.

An important property of fitness networks that has perhaps
been underappreciated is the possibility that donor behavior
can have consequences at higher levels that, by feedback, influence lower levels, especially the donor itself. An example
of this might be courtship feeding of the female by the male

in birds. Assume that courtship feeding benefits the mate
nutritionally, resulting in greater reproductive success (by
larger clutch, greater attentiveness, or both). Then the
donor's (feeder's) effect on the primary recipient (mate)
would include a positive feedback on the donor's fitness,
assuming that the donor is the parent.

Another example of fitness feedback occurs in cooperative
courtship. In promiscuous species some males who presumably
would meet with little success alone combine their display
efforts in courting females. For example, male turkeys in
sibling groups court females together under some population
conditions (20). Male pairs of manakins that are apparently
unrelated are also known to court females cooperatively (6).
A more specialized example of cooperative courtship occurs in
the ruff (18), in which color polymorphism is coupled with
behavioral polymorphism to result in a specialized form of
cooperative courtship between morphs. Cooperating males are
presumably unrelated, but this is not well documented. In
some cooperatively breeding species polyandry may be combined
with cooperative territory defense, again resulting in sharing
of a female (e.g. Todus, (9); Buteo galapogoensis (19)).

Although many examples of such fitness feedback effects can be
plucked from the descriptive literature, the phenomenon of
fitness feedback does not seem to have entered the sociobiological modeling literature except in the special case of
"reciprocal altruism" (16). Failure to model feedback in
avian systems has led, in my opinion, to great discrepancies
between predictions of the old inclusive-fitness theory and
the new empirical observations of natural populations.

THE TRADE-OFF BETWEEN PRESENT AND FUTURE
In analyzing the secondary consequences of helping behavior
for inclusive fitness, it is useful to distinguish between
effects realized during the present breeding effort (or season) and effects potentially realized in future efforts.

These will be referred to as D and d for present and future
direct effects and I and i for present and future indirect
effects, as summarized in Table 3. In deciding how to behave
so as to maximize the contribution of the present year toward
its inclusive fitness, the individual should consider the sum
of D, d, I, i for a given behavior compared to the corresponding sum for alternative behaviors. Mathematical formulations
of D, d, I, i have not been precisely defined; however, it may
be useful to think of them as being similar to the corresponding fractions of reproductive value which has been expanded
in scope to include indirect effects.

TABLE 3 - Present and future components of direct and indirect
effects on inclusive reproductive value or inclusive fitness.

	Present Reproductive Effort	Future Reproductive Effort
Direct Fitness	D	d
Indirect Fitness	I	i

Many of the possible secondary consequences of helping behavior are mediated through d and i. For example, consider one
of the primary consequences of helping behavior, namely, the
augmentation of unit size stemming from increased reproductive
success. Such augmentation might have secondary consequences
for the helper itself, for its parents, and for other relatives in the unit, particularly for sibs. These effects are
classified in Table 4. The best known of these has been described by Woolfenden (23, 24). He argued that augmentation
might increase the direct fitness of dominant male helpers by
facilitating their acquisition of a neighboring territory in
a subsequent breeding season (d). In his view, effects of
the type designated here under d are more important in
selection for helping behavior than benefits to indirect
fitness. The increase in effectiveness of territory defense

should also benefit the parents and other relatives by reducing their defense costs (i) and should also help subordinate male sibs attain territories (i), especially if the
dominant helper dies or leaves the unit. Effects of enlargement of unit size on survival of all unit members are also
possible; detection and harassment of predators may be more
effective. If the predator takes a fixed number of prey over
a certain period, then unit enlargement reduces the chance
that any one parent or relative will be taken - designated the
dilution effect in Table 4. Last, the young added to the
unit by the helper's efforts will aid the breeders in the
following breeding season, enhancing their reproductive success. These breeders will most likely include one or both of
the original parents (i), but they might include the original
helper (d) or its relatives (i).

TABLE 4 - Some secondary consequences of helping behavior in
territorial communal birds for parents, helper, and other
relatives of the helper.

Secondary Recipient	Helper's Fitness Component	Anti Predator Behavior	Dilution Effect	Defense of Natal Territory	Acquire New Territory	Feed Young
Parent	i	+	+	+	-	+
Helper	d	+	+	+	+	+
Relative	i	+	+	+	+	+

The helper is the donor and its parent is the primary recipient. The young attributable to the helper can have secondary
effects on their parent, on the original helper, and on other
unit members, presumably including other relatives, such as
sibs and half-sibs.

A NEED FOR MEASUREMENT OF EFFECTS ON FITNESS

The above examples of direct and indirect effects on fitness
and of their primary and secondary consequences are intended
to illustrate the complexity of helper systems and to raise
the possibility that fitness feedback may be significant in
communal birds. In a strict accounting of the costs and benefits of helping strategies to inclusive fitness, all of the
items in Table 4 plus many others must be included. Only

those involving d have received serious attention in the
literature; effects on i have been ignored. Since d may be
the primary or sole determinant of inclusive fitness in many
simple systems involving cooperation among unrelated individuals, it is imperative that we find ways to measure secondary
consequences to both donors and recipients. Such measurements
of future direct effects should be in terms of a currency that
allows comparison with present and future indirect effects.

The most important trade-off in the genetic economics of
social behavior is that between immediate and future payoffs.
Most, if not all, social vertebrates are iteroparous with
overlapping generations, yet where is there a model for the
genetic evolution of social behavior that incorporates these
features? Such a model must be ecological and demographic.
Part of the confusion that exists today in the study of
helping behavior stems from lack of a comprehensive theory
that takes into account the difference in value to the helper
between a young produced in the present by helping (I) and a
young produced in the future by breeding (d). Present young
are more valuable for two reasons: a) The helper may never
get a chance to breed in the future; it may die first or
remain low in status. b) As pointed out by Cole (5), putting
off young to the future increases generation time, thus
lowering fitness drastically in a growing population. In
effect, the helper shortens its inclusive, genetic generation
time by helping. Many communal species have irregular population fluctuations characterized by periods of slow decline
alternating with rapid growth, thus providing a possibility
for this type of advantage. In measuring effects of behavior
on fitness, therefore, it is essential to take into account
both reproductive value and generation time.

The above shopping list of desiderata has concentrated on
sharpening concepts and identifying new directions. Several
other outstanding problems also deserve brief mention. The
role of the environment in shaping aid-giving behavior remains

nebulous. To what extent is aid-giving favored by particular
patterns of resource use, by resource patchiness, or spatio-
temporal unpredictability of resources? Will ergonomic
approaches elucidate avian aid-giving? The merging of life-
history theory with socio-genetic theory remains in its
infancy. Mathematical formulations of D, d, I, and i are
needed. What are the population genetic consequences in
communal birds of variations in age structure, sex ratio,
age-specific patterns of reproduction, survival, and dispersal?
A greater variety of dependent variables should be examined.
What factors determine optimal unit size for males, for females, for breeders, for helpers? What factors influence the
degree of despotism or benevolence exerted by breeders on non-
breeders? What factors lead to plural breeding? To joint
nesting? To various intensities and frequencies of helping?

Summarizing, if we are to relate empirical observations of
aid-giving behavior to ecological and genetic theories, we
shall have to pay more attention to cooperation (mutualism)
and avoid the tendency to label all aid-giving as altruism.
In addition, the sloppiness in use of terms that designate
the components of inclusive fitness must be cured. The
prevalence of bad habits in use of terms is no excuse for
continuing them. Last, sociobiological modelers who wish
to be taken seriously by empiricists must deal with iteroparous animals with overlapping generations, and they must
incorporate fitness network phenomena in their models.

Acknowledgment. Supported in part by a research grant from
the U.S. Public Health Service (MH16345, MH33498).

REFERENCES

(1) Brown, J.L. 1975. Helpers among Arabian babblers,
     Turdoides squamiceps. Ibis 117: 243-244.

(2) Brown, J.L. 1978. Avian communal breeding systems.
     Ann. Rev. Ecol. Syst. 9: 123-155.

(3) Brown, J.L., and Balda, R.P. 1977. The relationship of
     habitat quality to group size in Hall's babbler
     (Pomatostomus). Condor 79: 312-320.

(4) Brown, J.L., and Brown, E.R. 1980. Kin selection and
     individual selection in babblers. In Natural Selection
     and Social Behavior: Recent Research and New Theory,
     eds. R.D. Alexander and D.W. Tinkle. New York: Chiron
     Press, in press.

(5) Cole, L.C. 1954. The population consequences of life
     history phenomena. Quart. Rev. Biol. 29: 103-137.

(6) Foster, M.S. 1977. Odd couples in manakins: a study
     of social organization and cooperative breeding in
     Chiroxiphia linearis. Amer. Natur. 111: 845-853.

(7) Hamilton, W.D. 1964. The genetical evolution of social
     behaviour. I and II. J. Theoret. Biol. 7: 1-52.

(8) Hamilton, W.D. 1975. Innate social aptitudes of man:
     An approach from evolutionary genetics. In Biosocial
     Anthropology, ed. R. Fox, pp. 133-155. New York:
     Wiley & Sons.

(9) Kepler, A.K. 1977. Comparative study of todies
     (Todidae) with emphasis on the Puerto Rican tody, Todus
     mexicanus. Publ. Nuttall Ornithol. Club 16: 1-190.

(10) Lack, D. 1968. Ecological Adaptations for Breeding in
     Birds. London: Methuen.

(11) Maynard Smith, J. 1964. Group selection and kin selec-
     tion. Nature 201: 1145-1147.

(12) Oster, G.F., and Wilson, E.O. 1978. Caste and ecology
     in the social insects. Monogr. Pop. Biol. 12: 1-352.

(13) Rowley, I. 1965. The life history of the superb blue
     wren Malurus cyaneus. Emu 64: 251-297.

(14) Sherman, P.W. 1977. Nepotism and the evolution of
     alarm calls. Science 197: 1246-1253.

(15) Shields, W. Ground squirrel alarm calls: nepotism or
     parental care? Amer. Natur, in press.

(16)   Trivers, R.L.   1971.   The evolution of reciprocal
       altruism.   Q. Rev. Biol. 46: 35-57.

(17)   Trivers, R.L.   1974.   Parent-offspring conflict.   Amer.
       Zool. 14: 249-264.

(18)   van Rhijn, J.G.   1973.   Behavioural dimorphism in male
       ruffs Philomachus pugnax (L.).   Behaviour 47: 153-229.

(19)   Vries, T. de 1973.   The Galapagos Hawk.   Amsterdam:
       Free University Press.

(20)   Watts, C.R., and Stokes, A.W.   1971.   The social order
       of turkeys.   Sci. Am. 224: 112-118.

(21)   West-Eberhard, M.J.   1975.   The evolution of social
       behavior by kin selection.   Q. Rev. Biol. 50: 1-33.

(22)   Wilson, E.O.   1975.   Sociobiology.   Cambridge: Harvard
       University Press.

(23)   Woolfenden, G.E.   1975.   Florida scrub jay helpers at the
       nest.   Auk 92: 1-15.

(24)   Woolfenden, G.E.   1976.   Co-operative breeding in
       American birds.   In Proceedings 16th Int. Ornithol.
       Congr., eds. H.J. Frith and H. Calaby, pp. 674-684.

(25)   Woolfenden, G.E., and Fitzpatrick, J.W.   1978.   The
       inheritance of territory in group-breeding birds.
       BioScience 28: 104-108.

(26)   Zahavi, A.   1974.   Communal nesting by the Arabian
       babbler: a case of individual selection.   Ibis 116:
       84-87.

Evolution of Social Behavior: Hypotheses and Empirical Tests, ed. H. Markl,
pp. 129-146. Dahlem Konferenzen 1980. Weinheim: Verlag Chemie GmbH.

Genetical Structure of Social Insect Populations

R. H. Crozier
School of Zoology, University of New South Wales
Kensington, N.S.W. 2033, Australia

Abstract. Many features of the genetics of social insects
have the potential to influence the original likelihood of
eusociality evolving, or to influence their present
population and colony structures in terms of characteristics
such as degree of female dominance, population size, colony
distinctness, and caste determination. Such features
include the general nature of their sex-determination (i.e.,
male haploid or male diploid), the genic-level mechanism
involved, and chromosome number. Mode of sex-determination
may also affect levels of genic variation, but it is
uncertain at present that there is, in fact, any systematic
difference in such levels between male haploids and other
bisexual insects to explain. Both local mate competition
and inbreeding have been suggested to be common in social
Hymenoptera but have yet to be demonstrated, although this
may be an artefact of the range of species examined so far.
Even though effective population size estimates are only so
far available for common species, these are rather low
compared with Drosophila species, even rare ones, reflecting
the effects of restricting reproduction to a small segment
of the adult population. Such estimates are rendered less
useful by the complex hierarchical subdivision possible
within social insect populations; possible levels are those
of the family, nest, and colony. This subdivision leads to
a consideration of relatedness between individuals in
definable groups at these various levels as a vital factor
in understanding social insects, both in games-theoretic
terms and as a necessary aid in constructing more realistic
exact models. Three methods, each with its own strengths
and weaknesses, exist for estimating relatedness in natural
populations of social insects: the pedigree, electrophoretic
identity, and regression methods. Application of these
methods shows that nestmates of social Hymenoptera can be
related as full sisters, but that in many species their level
of relatedness falls markedly below this. Practically all
these considerations apply only to Hymenoptera; data from
termites are almost totally lacking and are badly needed.

INTRODUCTION

In this paper, I will use a broad definition of the genetical structure of populations, but a narrow one of social insect: I will discuss only ants, termites, and eusocial bees and wasps, and ignore those spiders and other arthropods that sometimes show concerted group action. The rationale for including topics will be their relevance to the general conference theme, and the recent invoking of matters such as chromosome number in sociobiological thinking leads me to present a broad genetical background.

SEX-DETERMINATION

Hymenopteran females are diploid and normal males haploid, except in secondarily thelytokous species. The genic-level mechanism behind the cytological observations is well understood in only two species: the honeybee Apis mellifera and the parasitoid Bracon hebetor, in which heterozygotes at a single sex locus become females while homozygotes and hemizygotes become males. That diploid males sometimes occur in various other species, including wasps, ants, bees, and sawflies, suggests that the general sex-determination mechanism in Hymenoptera involves one or more sex loci, with individuals heterozygous at one or more of these becoming female (8).

Such a method of sex-determination imposes a genetic load, so that in the case of a single sex-locus with n alleles, at least $1/n$ of the diploids will not be workers or potentially queens but rather diploid males and hence either inviable or effectively sterile under normal conditions. Robert E. Page (unpublished) has shown that this load provides a plausible explanation for multiple-mating in honeybees, a phenomenon previously interpreted as a group-selected adaptation to increase effective population size. Page found that in species such as the honeybee, with colony reproduction occurring near the upper asymptote of colony size, the reduction in variance of diploid male production due to multiple-mating is expected to increase

the mean fitness of multiple-maters compared with single-maters.
On the other hand, mean fitness is increased by single-mating
if colony reproduction occurs during exponential colony growth -
as it does in many other social species. Page's work provides
a possible explanation for the wide interspecific variation in
how often females of eusocial Hymenoptera mate.

In termites, both sexes are diploid. Males, but not females,
show multivalents at meiosis I, which suggests a multi-X,
multi-Y system.

KARYOTYPE

Hymenopteran chromosome numbers have a wide spread (n = 3-46),
this breadth being due entirely to one group, the ants (8, 9).
Polyploidy may have given rise to one sawfly karyotype, and
has been suggested for some bees, but it does not seem to
have been important in hymenopteran evolution. Robertsonian
polymorphisms for chromosome number occur in a number of
species of ants, the best-studied group, and this mode of
numerical change has probably been the chief one in the
karyotype evolution of ants and possibly other Hymenoptera.

Termites have a more restricted range of chromosome numbers,
with $\underline{n}$ = 16-26 for female gametes (25). Most species have
$X_1X_2Y_1Y_2$ sex-chromosome systems, and some have $X_{1-7}Y_{1-7}$
systems (suggesting that perhaps 44% of their genes are effectively sex-linked). But the Y chromosomes are not cytologically distinct from the Xs, leading Luykx and Syren (unpublished) to suggest that all loci on them are functional. Luykx
and Syren further suggest that the reduction in genetic
variability between termite siblings due to extensive sex-
chromosome systems may have played a part in the evolution of
eusociality in termites similar to that widely assumed for
male haploidy in the Hymenoptera, but such systems are unknown
in cockroaches (the closest relatives to termites), although
some species have autosomal interchange complexes (4).

Sherman (22) and Templeton (23) have pointed out that increasing the chromosome number raises the chance of evolving eusociality by reducing the genetic variance between
siblings. Sherman's analysis shows that the chromosome numbers of social Hymenoptera probably do average higher than
those of nonsocial Hymenoptera, and termites have significantly higher numbers than do related insects. The increase
in number may, of course, have followed rather than precipi-
tated the evolution of sociality, as Sherman acknowledges,
but his results are suggestive. Ants present a complicating
factor, in that present data indicate a negative correlation
between mean chromosome number and geographic range of genus
(9); but this correlation probably arose after eusociality
evolved.

CASTE DETERMINATION
Reproductive division of labor is the hallmark of insect
sociality, and it is expressed in caste differences. Sex
(hence genetic) divisions dominate hymenopteran societies,
in that females alone perform all non-reproductive roles,
but sexual division of labor is weakly developed in termites.
Environmental influences have a very strong role in determining the various female castes of social Hymenoptera, but in
two cases a significant role has been claimed for genetic
factors.

Kerr, long ago, claimed that in various Melipona species,
only females heterozygous at each of two postulated caste-
determining loci could become queens, basing this view
on an apparent upper limit of 25% of females becoming queens
even under optimal conditions. We now know that underfeeding
results in all females becoming workers (3) and, conversely,
that treatment with juvenile hormone leads to all well-fed
female larvae becoming queens (24), supporting a strong
trophogenic role for caste determination in these bees, in
addition to the suggested genetic one. In fact, the overall
data collected under the genetic hypothesis remain only

suggestive rather than compelling in support of it. Linkage
tests of the postulated loci are impractical now, but a
simple test is now possible using the hormonally-determined
queens: their female progeny, unlike those of "natural" queens
should range from 0% to 100% queens under optimal conditions.

A general but weaker role for heterozygosity in caste determination is plausible: the more heterozygous larvae should be more
likely to reach queen-ness or similar thresholds, and hence
queens should be more heterozygous than workers. Single-locus
tests have, however, shown no differences between queen and
work heterozygosities in the ants Rhytidoponera chalybaea, R.
metallica, Pheidole sp., (6), Aphaenogaster rudis (n = 20 species (8)), and Formica sanguinea (21).

While heterozygosity has not yet been shown to have a role
in Rhytidoponera caste determination, these species may have
a mechanism of the Harpagoxenus type. Buschinger (2) gives
compelling evidence that a single locus strongly influences
caste determination in H. sublaevis, with well-fed ee larvae
having queen potential and EE and Ee individuals not.

Various small Rhytidoponera species produce queens sporadi-
cally, and Ward (26) found recently that polymorphism for the
presence or absence of queens occurs in the R. impressa group,
rainforest-dwellers regarded as primitive. Inseminated workers,
or ergatomorphs, perform the egg-laying role in colonies of
Harpagoxenus and Rhytidoponera lacking true queens. In
Buschinger's model for Harpagoxenus, queen-potential is re-
cessive, but it is dominant in Ward's tentative application
of a similar model to the R. impressa group.

LEVELS OF GENETIC VARIATION
Various authors have suggested, based on electrophoretic
data from a wide variety of social and solitary Hymenoptera,
that male haploidy leads to a reduction in genic variation.
A survey made in connection with a theoretical study of the

effects of male haploidy on genic variation (Pamilo and
Crozier, unpublished) bears out this impression, but also
indicates that most of the difference between Hymenoptera
and other bisexual insects is due to Drosophila. Rather
than Hymenoptera having unusually low levels of genic
variation, it seems likely that Drosophila has unusually
high levels and that this has biased previous surveys. The
data also indicate differences between other orders, and
between various hymenopteran groups, but the data on non-
Drosophila bisexual male diploids are too sparse to be
certain of much at present.

Whether Hymenoptera are finally thought to have reduced or
to have average levels of genic variation, there is no
shortage of theoretical explanations for either result ((8);
Pamilo and Crozier, unpublished). The more convincing
explanations would be, for reduced variability, that most
observed allozyme polymorphisms are in mutation-selection
balance or are maintained by constant-fitness balancing
selection, and for average variability, that most polymorphisms are maintained by frequency-dependent selection or that
allozyme variants are effectively neutral (and that effective
population sizes for Hymenoptera are within the normal insect
range).

Pamilo et al. (20) studied the correlation between level of
genic variability and colony structure or nest architecture
in European Formica ant species. Their data suggest that
gene diversity is lower in mound-nesting species than in
ground-nesting ones. This result, if confirmed, could indicate that some of the allozyme variation is associated with
environmental heterogeneity, because ground nests are less
homeostatic than mounds and hence impose greater environmental
fluctuations on the ants, other things being equal. Pamilo
et al. also found an increase in genic variation with increasing number of queens in the ground-nesting species, which
could reflect a probable larger effective population size.

Genic variation has not been studied in termites. If termites
are found to have low levels of genic variation, this may not
reflect any effect of sociality, because Orthoptera (the
order closest to termites) average low levels (17).

Chromosomal variation is known in various ant species, but not
in any other social insects (8, 25), with one possible exception: the termite Incisitermes schwarzi varies geographically in
the number of chromosomes involved in multivalent formation in
male meiosis (Luykx and Syren, unpublished). This apparent
difference of ants probably reflects their being karyotypically
by far the best-known social insects. Some of the chromosom-
ally-variable ant species could be suitable for studies on the
modes of natural selection acting on ants.

INBREEDING AND LOCAL MATE COMPETITION
Observers of social insects have often been impressed with features of their social organization that should be effective in
promoting outbreeding. In particular, many ant and termite
species stage widespread mating flights in which winged males
and females emerge from many nests simultaneously. These expectations seem to have been borne out by the allozyme studies
made so far on ants (Aphaenogaster rudis, Pogonomyrmex spp.,
Formica spp., Rhytidoponera spp., Myrmecia pilosula (7, 8, 21,
26); Ward, unpublished), bees (Apis mellifera, Melipona subnit-
ida (5, 15), and wasps (Polistes metricus (16)), with genotype
frequencies close to expectation within the limits of analyses
dealing with social insects. These limits arise especially
when, as is often unavoidable, workers alone are analysed.
Consider a sample of ten colonies of a species with a single,
once-mated queen in each. Such a sample will often by chance
have a slight excess of, say, homogametic matings (AA x A);
this excess would be recognized as statistically insignificant
when the ten queens are considered, but may not be when 100 of
their worker progeny determine the apparent degrees of freedom.
Analysis should therefore be restricted to the queen level, but

in large studies spurious excesses of heterozygotes can result
through the exclusion of samples because some matings can be
classified only as AA x B or BB x A.

The Polistes and Rhytidoponera data included cases where a significant inbreeding coefficient was found for one locus but not
for others in the same population. It is unlikely that insects
adjust their mating preferences differently from one locus to
the next, and the authors concerned plausibly suggest that the
significant values reflect the influence of selection ((16, 26);
Ward, unpublished).

Actual inbreeding levels in termites are unknown: noone has
studied them.

Despite the genetic evidence for outbreeding in some social
Hymenoptera, much natural history evidence suggests extensive
inbreeding in others, as Alexander and Sherman (1) perhaps
overemphasize. Sib-sib mating has long been held to be frequent in many ants, especially rare ones, and yet such intra-
nest, or apparently intranest, mating may not reflect strong
inbreeding, as has often been supposed. Matings "within the
family" (1) are well-known in unicolonial species (species
with no evident hostility between colonies), but in such species the number of queens is often very great, and they are
transferred readily when "colonies" come into contact. Furthermore, outbreeding is favored in many ants with flightless
queens through their pheromonal "calling" of flying males
from other nests (11). Another point is that "inbreeding" can
refer to either the preferential mating of relatives or to the
effects of population isolation. Perhaps the "colonies" of
unicolonial species are better regarded as being semi-isolated
populations rather than as analogs of the family-based colonies
of multicolonial species.

The various gleanings above all suggest that inbreeding may be
much less common in social insects than is often thought, but

there is an obvious need for more genetic data. Data are especially needed for termites, which combine mating flights (promoting outbreeding) with, in many species, replacement of dead primary reproductives from within the colony (promoting inbreeding). But termite reproductives, especially queens, can live for a long time so that the actual extent of replacement in nature is uncertain. Termite mating flights may be less effective than those of ants in promoting outbreeding, because they usually cover only short distances: although the large alates of Macrotermes may fly "a few kilometers," flights of other genera may be as short as "a few dozen meters" (19). Nutting (19) notes a further bar to long-distance dispersal in most termites: a pair is needed to found a colony, whereas in the Hymenoptera a female can fly on after mating.

Local mate competition, the competition between sibs or other relatives for mates, has been suggested to be possibly widespread in social Hymenoptera (1). The detection of inbreeding indicates likely local mate competition, but the absence of inbreeding is not compelling evidence for a lack of local mate competition because, for example, colonies often release only males (or only females) at one time, which alates could then compete with each other for mates from other colonies. Males of many social Hymenoptera form aggregations, or leks, to which females fly to mate; these leks could be dominated by males from one colony. But Apis mellifera males at leks are drawn from a wide area, so that the dominance of the lek by males from any one colony seems unlikely. Males of the ant Pheidole sitarches continually arrive at swarms "from various directions" (27), again suggesting that no one colony dominates the lek. Marking showed that male aggregations of the wasp Polistes fuscatus (18) and the bee Scaptotrigona postica (13) are drawn from several nests. While these data suggest that local mate competition is rare in social Hymenoptera, this conclusion will remain tentative until many more species have been examined.

EFFECTIVE POPULATION SIZE

At first sight, effective population size should be relatively easy to determine in social insects. After all, the number of nests in many species can easily be counted. But the complexity of the hierarchical subdivisions of many social insect populations will often make the estimation of N_e rather difficult. These possible subdivisions are those at the level of the family (single queen plus offspring), the nest (individuals living in the same set of galleries), the colony (set of nests integrated through exchanging individuals), the local aggregation of colonies, and the local population, or deme. Various of these levels coincide in many species, such as the family, nest, and colony in ants such as Aphaenogaster rudis, but in other species each level can be important in population structure. The number of times a queen mates, and, especially, the number of laying queens in a colony, are of particular importance in estimating N_e. Cases of true polygyny must be distinguished from those where the extra queens are non-laying "understudies" ready to take over when the true queen dies.

Honeybee populations sometimes occur as isolated groups of hives. Queens mate 5 - 17 times, depending on the area, but there is almost always only one per nest, allowing the estimation of N_e. Yokoyama and Nei (29) give 428 and 1093 as the estimated effective sizes of two isolated populations.

Many other eusocial bees also have one queen per colony, who mates but once. However, a new complication often emerges, one true also for many ants: some or all of the males arise from worker-laid eggs. Paradoxically, this increase in the number of egg-laying females lowers N_e, although this is not well understood quantitatively, because the laying workers interpose an additional source of sampling error (8).

Ward (unpublished) estimates N_e to be "of the order of" 10^3 to 10^5 in populations of the Rhytidoponera impressa group. These

ants are restricted to rainforest stands, usually of limited
extent, so that it is feasible to try estimating the total
number of ests forming a panmictic unit.

Many species, however, occupy large continuous areas, with discrete populations likely to be the exception rather than the
rule. Isolation-by-distance models are appropriate in such
cases. The mean flight distances of alates could be used to
determine the neighborhood size (area within which mating is
effectively at random) and hence, given the colony density, the
number of colonies in a panmictic unit. In this way, Kerr (12)
estimated that panmictic units of Scaptotrigona postica in one
area of Brazil contain an average of 150.2 colonies. Given
that colonies of this bee are headed by a single, once-mated
queen, this yields an N_e of 225, but this is an overestimate
because workers of this species join in male-production. Kerr
also estimated that honeybees in the same area have an N_e of
4,524. While this approach may not be easily applied to species with complex colony makeups, it should be applicable to
many termite species, for example, some in parts of northern
Australia where colony density is very high (a mound every 5
m or less).

LEVELS OF ORGANIZATION

The Australian meat ants (Iridomyrmex purpureus group),
recently studied by Halliday (10), bring out some of the
complexities possible in the hierarchical subdivision of
social insect populations. This group occurs throughout
the Australian mainland and comprises a cluster of sibling
species differing in nest-form, worker color, allozyme
frequencies, and minor chromosomal features. Colonies arise
from single founding queens. Young colonies have single
nests but tend to expand in territory and number of nests
as they mature. Colonies are mutually hostile, competing
for Eucalyptus and other trees supporting important food
insects. Many colonies lose this competition. Halliday
found that the allozyme genotypes of workers in a group of

small colonies of the "red" species were consistent with
each colony being headed by a single, once-mated queen.
Multinest colonies of the same form had a range of worker
genotypes, strongly suggesting that mature colonies have a
number of laying queens.

In the "red" and some other meat ant species, nests have low,
gravel-topped mounds with up to several hundred entrance holes.
Castings indicate that each hole opens into a separate gallery
system from the rest, which is also indicated by the failure of
marked ants to reemerge from a different hole to the one they
have entered (even when starved). Workers also have a strong
tendency to return to the same hole after foraging. Consistent
with these observations, Halliday found significant heterogeneity for worker allozyme genotypes between nests of the same
large colony.

Meat ant populations are thus divided at both the nest and colony levels. They may be divided at the family level as well,
if each gallery system can hold only one queen, but this has
not been tested for. Mature colonies can be large (the one
Halliday surveyed for heterogeneity had 86 nests and a territory of 10 hectares), so that on occasion the colony and the
local aggregation could become the same thing. This is likely
to be rare, as it would require discontinuities in distribution
rare for meat ants.

While even mature and multinested meat ant colonies are hostile to each other, various unicolonial ants are known in which
intercolony hostility is either absent or is insufficient to
prevent the substantial interchange of workers between colonies. This phenomenon also occurs in the wasp Vespula maculi-
frons (14) and can happen if honeybee colonies are placed close
together. Such cases pose methodological, theoretical, and
conceptual problems, such as one reminiscent of the gene-flow
question in speciation theory: how much worker exchange is
necessary before two nests are classified as belonging to the
same colony?

RELATEDNESS

Three methods have been used to estimate relatedness in social insects using genetic data. In the pedigree method, such data are used to infer the family structure of colonies, and relatedness is then estimated from appropriate weightings of known pedigree values. Ward's (26) electrophoretic identity method compares individuals for the electromorphs shared, and the resulting average electrophoretic identity of the population is converted to a relatedness estimate using a conversion based on the population gene frequencies. The regression method ((6); Pamilo and Crozier, unpublished) compares the allele frequencies of individuals with those of their colonies, and the relatedness estimate is given by the regression coefficient between the two.

Each relatedness estimator has its own strengths and weaknesses. The pedigree method is exact (within the limits of the actual variation between siblings) in cases of simple and invariant colony structures but cannot be used at all when the situation is too complex for pedigrees to be determined, and it is extremely laborious in complex situations and will yield a serious underestimate if significant inbreeding in previous generations goes undetected. However, the pedigree method can be used with a single colony, whereas the other two require population data. Both the pedigree and electrophoretic identity methods can use multi-allelic data, but the regression method is restricted to biallelic data. On the other hand, the regression method can yield a standard error estimate from a single population, whereas the electrophoretic identity method cannot. The electrophoretic identity method depends critically on accurate allele frequency estimates, which is not so for the regression method. But Ward (26) obtained a narrower range of relatedness estimates using the electrophoretic identity than the regression method for populations suspected from pedigree data of having all worker nestmates full sibs, although the two approaches gave very similar mean estimates.

Social insect species have a wide spread of intracolony relatedness. Worker nestmates are full sisters in the ants
Aphaenogaster rudis (8), Iridomyrmex purpureus (young "red"
form colonies (10)), Rhytidoponera chalybaea and R. sp. (monogynous colonies (26)), and in meliponid bees such as Scaptotrigona postica (12). But worker nestmates have relatedness
values slightly below 0.5 in Formica sanguinea (21), in polygynous Rhytidoponera impressa group colonies (26), and in
Polistes wasps ((16); Lester and Selander, unpublished). Nestmate workers in the ant Myrmecia pilosula are only distantly
related ($\underline{b}$ ≈ 0.17 (7)). Associating Polistes queens are less
related than full sisters (16), and such queens in M. pilosula
are only about as related as cousins. Relatedness in honeybee
colonies must be low, probably around 0.30, but remains to be
determined and will probably be found to vary between populations depending on the local levels of polyandry.

The spread of relatedness estimates is striking, and a broader
survey would be worthwhile. Future studies should routinely
measure relatedness between colony members and the brood, as
variations in parental contributions over time may lead to a
lower such relatedness than between adults. Studies on termites are especially needed, as none have yet been done.

A final complication is the likely greater relatedness between
adjacent colonies in many species, especially in those in which
new colonies are produced by fission of preexisting ones.
Formica sanguinea is such a species, and in a single-locus
study the relatedness between neighboring nests was found to
be 0.25 (21).

CONCLUDING REMARKS
Social insect populations often have an unusually complex hierarchical organization that makes standard population genetic
studies difficult, but progress is possible in many species.
In particular, estimates of relatedness between various categories can and should be made in a wide array of species. The

present broad spread of estimates may support the parental
manipulation model for the evolution of social behavior or
focus attention on K in Hamilton's Rule, according to one's
personal inclination, but more data are needed.

The greatest lack is the absence of data from termites.

Acknowledgements. Supported by grants from the USNSF, the
Australian Research Grants Committee, and the Ian Potter
Foundation. I thank E. Charnov, R. Craig, P.I. Dixon,
R.B. Halliday, R.M. May, A. Mazanov, P. Pamilo, A. Stark,
P.S. Ward, D. Wiernasz and G.C. Williams for comments on
various drafts of this paper, but they should not be held
responsible for its content as I did not always follow
their advice.

REFERENCES

(1) Alexander, R.D., and Sherman, P.W. 1977. Local mate com-
     petition and parental investment in social insects. Science
     196: 494-500.

(2) Buschinger, A. 1978. Genetisch bedingte Entstehung ge-
     flügelter Weibchen bei der sklavenhaltenden Ameise Harp-
     agoxenus sublaevis (Nyl.) (Hym., Form.). Insectes Soc.
     25: 163-172.

(3) Carmargo, C.A. de; Almeida, M.G. de; Parra, M.G.N.; and
     Kerr, W.E. 1976. Genetics of sex determination in bees.
     IX. Frequencies of queens and workers from larvae under
     controlled conditions. (Hymenoptera: Apoidea). J. Kansas
     Entomol. Soc. 49: 120-125.

(4) Cochrane, D.G., and Ross, M.H. 1967. Preliminary studies
     of twelve cockroach species (Blattaria: Blattidae, Blatelli-
     dae, Blateridae). Ann. Entomol. Soc. Am. 60: 1265-1272.

(5) Contel, E.P.B., and Mestriner, M.A. 1974. Esterase poly-
     morphisms at two loci in the social bee. J. Hered. 65:
     349-352.

(6) Craig, R., and Crozier, R.H. 1978. No evidence for role
     of heterozygosity in ant caste determination. Isozyme Bull.
     11: 66-67.

(7) Craig, R., and Crozier, R.H. 1979. Relatedness in the poly-
     gynous ant Myrmecia pilosula. Evolution 33: 335-341.

(8)   Crozier, R.H. 1977. Evolutionary genetics of the Hymen-
      optera. Ann. Rev. Entomol. 22: 263-288.

(9)   Crozier, R.H. 1980. Genetic aspects of ant evolution.
      In Essays on Evolution and Speciation in Honor of M.J.D.
      White, eds. W.R. Atchley and D.S. Woodruff. Cambridge:
      University Press.

(10) Halliday, R.B. 1978. Genetic studies of meat ants (Iri-
      domyrmex purpureus). Unpublished Ph.D. thesis, University
      of Adelaide, Adelaide, Australia.

(11) Hölldobler, B. 1978. Ethological aspects of chemical com-
      munication in ants. Adv. Stud. Behav. 8: 75-115.

(12) Kerr, W.E. 1974. Genetik des Polymorphismus bei Bienen.
      In Sozialpolymorphismus bei Insekten, ed. G.H. Schmidt, pp.
      94-109. Stuttgart: Wissenschaftliche Verlagsgesellschaft
      GmbH.

(13) Kerr, W.E.; Zucchi, R.; Nakadaira, J.T.; and Butolo, J.E.
      1962. Reproduction in the social bees (Hymenoptera: Aphi-
      dae). J. NY Entomol. Soc. 70: 265-276.

(14) Lord, W.D.; Nicolson, D.A.; and Roth, R.R. 1977. Foraging
      behavior and colony drift in Vespula maculifrons (Buysson)
      (Hymenoptera: Vespidae). J. NY Entomol. Soc. 85: 186.

(15) Mestriner, M.A., and Contel, E.P.B. 1972. The P-3 and
      Est loci in the honeybee Apis mellifera. Genetics 72: 733-
      738.

(16) Metcalf, R.A., and Whitt, G.S. 1977. Intra-nest relatedness
      in the social wasp Polistes metricus. A genetic analysis.
      Behav. Ecol. Sociobiol. 2: 339-351

(17) Nevo, E. 1978. Genetic variation in natural populations:
      patterns and theory. Theoret. Popul. Biol. 13: 121-177.

(18) Noonan, K.M. 1978. Sex ratio of parental investment in
      colonies of the social wasp Polistes fuscatus. Science
      199: 1354-1356.

(19) Nutting, W.L. 1969. Flight and colony foundation. In
      Biology of Termites, eds. K. Krishna and F.M. Weesner, vol. 1,
      pp. 233-282. New York: Academic Press.

(20) Pamilo, P.; Rosengresn, R.; Vepsalainen, K.; Varvio-Aho,
      S.-L.; and Pisarski, B. 1978. Population genetics of
      Formica ants. I. Patterns of enzyme gene variation.
      Hereditas. 89: 233-248.

(21) Pamilo, P., and Varvio-Aho, S.-L. 1979. Genetic structure
      of the nests in the ant Formica sanguinea. Behav. Ecol.
      Sociobiol. 6, in press.

(22)   Sherman, P.W.   1979.   Insect chromosome numbers and euso-
       ciality.   Am. Nat. 113: 925-935.

(23)   Templeton, A.R.   1979.   Chromosome number, quantitative gene-
       tics, and eusociality.   Am. Nat. 113: 937-941.

(24)   Velthuis, H.H.W., and Velthuis-Kluppell, F.M.   1975.   Caste
       differentiation in a stingless bee, Melipona quadrifasciata
       Lep., influenced by juvenile hormone application.   Proc. K.
       Ned. Akad. Wet. Ser. C Biol. Med. Sci. 78: 81-94.

(25)   Vincke, P.P., and Tilquin, J.P.   1978.   A sex-linked ring
       quadrivalent in Termitidae (Isoptera).   Chromosoma 67: 515-516.

(26)   Ward, P.S.   1978.   Genetic variation, colony structure, and
       social behaviour in the Rhytidoponera impressa group, a spe-
       cies complex of ponerine ants.   Unpublished Ph.D. thesis,
       University of Sydney, Sydney, Australia.

(27)   Wilson, E.O.   1957.   The organization of a nuptial flight of
       the ant Pheidole sitarches Wheeler.   Psyche 64: 46-50.

(28)   Wilson, E.O.   1971.   The Insect Societies.   Cambridge: Harvard
       University Press.

(29)   Yokoyama, S., and Nei, M.   1979.   Population dynamics of
       sex-determining alleles in honey bees and self-incompatibil-
       ity alleles in plants.   Genetics 91: 609-626.

Evolution of Social Behavior: Hypotheses and Empirical Tests, ed. H. Markl,
pp. 147-162. Dahlem Konferenzen 1980. Weinheim: Verlag Chemie GmbH.

Genetic and Evolutionary Relationships of Apes and Humans

F. J. Ayala
Department of Genetics, University of California
Davis, CA 95616, USA

Abstract. Informational macromolecules have, in recent years,
provided considerable information concerning the evolutionary
history of humans and apes. This evidence is not always consistent with the phylogenies proposed by paleontologists and
anatomists. Consideration of all the evidence presently
available suggests that the hylobatids (gibbon and siamang)
separated first from a lineage leading to the great apes and
humans; next, the orangutan lineage separated from the other
apes and humans. The chimpanzee, gorilla, and human lineages
separated from each other at about the same time. The degree
of genetic differentiation between humans and the great apes
is similar to that observed between species of the same genus
in other groups of organisms. The amount of genetic variation
in the apes as well as in other primates is considerably lower
than the genetic variation present in humans and in nonprimate
mammals.

INTRODUCTION

The study of proteins and nucleic acids has recently provided
considerable information concerning the evolutionary relationships among the living hominoids (humans and apes). The
emerging evidence is not always consistent with the phylogeny
traditionally proposed by comparative anatomists and paleontologists. I shall briefly evaluate the various sources of
evidence and suggest a phylogeny of the hominoids based on all
the existing information. I shall also present data

concerning the levels of genetic variation observed in the hominoids as well as in other primate species. This evolutionary and genetic information might serve as background knowledge for a discussion of the genetics and social behavior of the primates.

HOMINOID PHYLOGENY

Our closest living relatives are the apes. There are five genera of living apes; three of them Asiatic, the other two African. The Asiatic apes are the relatively small gibbon (Hylobates) and siamang (Symphalangus) and the larger orangutan (Pongo). The two genera of African apes are the gorilla (Gorilla) and the chimpanzee (Pan). The two smaller Asian apes are classified in the family Hylobatidae; the three larger apes are classified in the family Pongidae. Homo sapiens is the only living species of the family Hominidae. The Hominidae, Pongidae, and Hylobatidae are all included in the superfamily Hominoidea (Table 1).

TABLE 1 - Taxonomic classification of the living apes and humans, which are all included in the superfamily Hominoidea (hominoids) within the order Primates. Vernacular names are given in parentheses.

Family	Genus	Species
Hylobatidae (gibbons)	Hylobates (gibbon)	H. agilis H. concolor H. lar H. pileatus
	Symphalangus (siamang)	S. syndactylus
Pongidae (pongids)	Pongo (orangutan) Pan (chimpanzee)	P. pygmaeus P. troglodytes P. paniscus (pygmy chimpanzee)
	Gorilla (gorilla)	G. gorilla
Hominidae (hominids)	Homo (man)	H. sapiens

Phylogeny was traditionally the subject matter of paleontology and comparative anatomy. However, in recent years it has become apparent that proteins and nucleic acids (the so-called "informational" macromolecules) store a wealth of information concerning evolutionary history. Protein sequencing, immunology, electrophoresis, and DNA hybridization are among the molecular techniques used in phylogenetic studies. These techniques have generally confirmed previously established evolutionary relationships, and in many cases have provided information where little or none was available from the fossil record. There are instances, nevertheless, when molecular studies lead to conclusions contrary to those reached by paleontologists or comparative anatomists.

One case of disagreement concerns the evolutionary history of the hominoids. Paleontologists and comparative morphologists place the Asiatic orangutan much closer to the African apes (the gorilla and the chimpanzee) and to man than to the two other genera of Asiatic hominoids, the siamang and the gibbon. Some molecular evolutionists have proposed that the orangutan is much less closely related to the African apes and man and may be as removed from these as the siamang and gibbon.

Disagreement also exists with respect to the phylogenetic propinquity of the chimpanzee, the gorilla, and man. Paleontologists and comparative morphologists generally propose that the gorilla and the chimpanzee are more closely related to each other than to man, while some molecular studies suggest that the chimpanzee is at least as closely related to man as to the gorilla.

Informational macromolecules document evolutionary history. Degrees of similarity in such macromolecules reflect, on the whole, degrees of phylogenetic propinquity. But the phylogenetic information obtained by protein sequencing, immunology, electrophoresis, and nucleic acid annealing should be seen as complementary to that obtained by such "classical" methods as comparative anatomy and the study of the fossil record. Both macromolecular evolution and morphological evolution reflect the same evolutionary history. The information gained from the study of macromolecules must be weighed together with that derived from comparative anatomy and paleontology in order to ascertain phylogenetic relationships among organisms.

Among the methods employed in the study of a single gene or protein, the most phylogenetic information is gained from the nucleotide sequencing of genes, a technique that has only very recently become available. The amino acid sequence provides the second highest amount of information per gene locus concerning phylogeny, followed successively by immunological methods that evaluate the number of amino acid differences between proteins, and by electrophoresis. Protein sequencing is a rather laborious technique, and thus only a limited number of proteins, if any at all, have usually been sequenced in any given organism or group of organisms. Such techniques as microcomplement fixation involve considerably less work, but require that antibodies specific for a given protein be developed. Electrophoresis has the advantage of being a simple technique that makes possible to study a fairly large number of proteins with a moderate amount of cost and work. DNA hybridization of single-copy sequences is a method by which the overall amount of genetic divergence between living species can be estimated, although it requires obtaining radioactively labeled DNA from one or more reference species, a far from simple procedure.

Figure 1 gives a simplified view of the phylogeny of the hominoids, according to different sources of evidence. Although not all scholars in any given discipline agree, the phylogenies given may be taken as representative of the prevailing views. The phylogenies given are based on the following works: a) Fossil record (24); comparative anatomy (22, 23). b) Immunology (17); protein sequencing, a reconstruction based jointly on (16-18) and (26); DNA hybridization

(10, 12). c) Immunology (6, 8, 20); DNA hybridization (3); chromosome banding (7, 14). d) Electrophoresis (5).

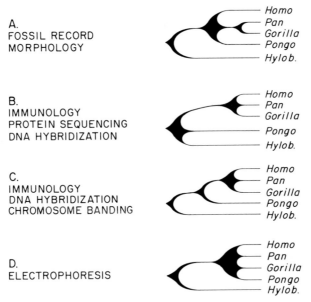

A.
FOSSIL RECORD
MORPHOLOGY

Homo
Pan
Gorilla
Pongo
Hylob.

B.
IMMUNOLOGY
PROTEIN SEQUENCING
DNA HYBRIDIZATION

Homo
Pan
Gorilla
Pongo
Hylob.

C.
IMMUNOLOGY
DNA HYBRIDIZATION
CHROMOSOME BANDING

Homo
Pan
Gorilla
Pongo
Hylob.

D.
ELECTROPHORESIS

Homo
Pan
Gorilla
Pongo
Hylob.

FIG. 1 - Phylogeny of the hominoids according to various sources of evidence. The dark zones covering the precise position of branching points suggest degrees of uncertainty concerning phylogenetic events.

One major discrepancy apparent in Figure 1 concerns the phylogenetic position of the orangutan (Pongo) relative to the other hominoids. The fossil record (24) and comparative anatomy (22, 23) - A in Figure 1 - support an early divergence between the lineage leading to the Hylobatidae (gibbons and siamang) and the great apes; a divergence which, according to Simons (21) and Tuttle (23), occurred about 27 or more million years ago. The lineage leading to Pongo would have split from the human, chimpanzee, and gorilla lineages much later (about 17 million years ago, according to the authors quoted). Immunological studies through microcomplement fixation (20), DNA annealing (10), and the amino acid sequences of globins (16-18) and

fibrinopeptides (25) - B in Figure 1 - are, however, consistent
with a phylogenetic split of the Hylobatidae and Pongo lineages both at about the same time from the Gorilla-Pan-Homo
lineage and from each other. Immunodiffusion with antiserum
against whole plasma (6, 8) supports an intermediate phylogeny -
the Hylobatidae lineage would have separated first from the
pongid-human lineage, but the orangutan lineage would branch
off from the lineage leading to the other great apes and man
before these separate from each other - C in Figure 1. The
DNA hybridization data of Benveniste and Todaro (3) also support the phylogeny shown in Figure 1C. The banding patterns
of the chromosomes (7, 14) support a phylogeny similar, but
not identical, to that shown in Figure 1C - the orangutan
would branch from the man-chimpanzee-gorilla lineage before
these branch from each other, but much later than the branching of the hylobatids; thus, the split of the Pongo lineage
should be placed somewhat closer to the human-African apes
lineage than appears in the figure.

The electrophoretic data (5) - Figure 1D - support the phylogenetic placement of Pongo close to the African apes proposed
by paleontologists and comparative anatomists and disagree
with the molecular phylogenies which place Pongo as distant
from man and the African apes as the hylobatids. The average
genetic distance between Pongo on the one side and Homo, Pan,
and Gorilla on the other is $\bar{D}$ = 0.343, which is not significantly different from the average distance between pairs of
the latter three species ($\bar{D}$ = 0.367).

In my opinion, the evidence cited, together with recent data
on the amino acid sequence of orangutan hemoglobin (13), supports on the whole a phylogeny with the same topology as that
shown in Figure 1C, although perhaps with Pongo somewhat
closer to the African apes and man than appears in the figure.
Additional evidence will be required before deciding the
approximate point at which the Pongo lineage splits from the
human-African apes lineage.

The phylogenies shown in Figure 1 also disagree concerning the phylogenetic propinquity of Gorilla, Pan, and Homo. Paleontologists and comparative anatomists propose a closer relationship between the gorilla and the chimpanzee than between these and man; the immunological and protein-sequence phylogenies data support an equal distance among the three taxa (25); while chromosome banding (14) suggests a somewhat closer relationship between man and the gorilla than between these and the chimpanzee.

With respect to paleontological data, the proposed greater similarity between the gorilla and the chimpanzee is hardly based on any substantial evidence: the last fossil ancestral remains of the Pan and Gorilla lineages are the Dryopithecines, which lived about 13 and 22 million years ago; but the Dryopithecus is also the presumed last common ancestral stock to Homo, Pan, Gorilla, and Pongo. It seems that the most reasonable conclusion is to state that, at present, the molecular and paleontological evidence is on the whole consistent with the notion that Gorilla, Pan, and Homo are approximately equally distant phylogenetically from each other. The chromosome banding data indicating a closer relationship between Gorilla and Homo is not sufficiently weighty to depart from the phylogeny suggested by the molecular data.

GENETIC DIFFERENTIATION AMONG THE HOMINOIDS

The basic morphological similarities between humans and apes were already recognized by Linnaeus in his classification of living beings (first published in 1735) by placing them together in the order of primates (Anthropomorpha), although in separate genera. (No taxonomic category between "genus" and "order" was recognized by Linnaeus; the category "family" was introduced later.) Linnaeus would later (1978) muse that he perhaps should have classified men and apes in a single genus: "I demand of you, and of the whole world that you show me a generic character ... by which to distinguish between man and ape. I myself most assuredly know of none. I wish

TABLE 2 - Genetic identify, $\underline{I}$ (above diagonal) and genetic distance, $\underline{D}$ (below diagonal) between pairs of nine taxa representing all six extant genera of hominoids. Data from (5).

	1	2	3	4	5	6	7	8	9
1 Homo sapiens		.680	.732	.689	.707	.705	.489	.429	.333
2 Pan troglodytes	.386		.902	.688	.738	.800	.510	.446	.452
3 Pan paniscus	.312	.103		.680	.789	.892	.489	.429	.333
4 Gorilla gorilla	.373	.373	.385		.617	.646	.618	.537	.447
5 Pongo p. abelii	.347	.304	.238	.484		.878	.550	.553	.469
6 Pongo p. pygmaeus	.350	.223	.115	.437	.130		.583	.532	.425
7 Hylobates lar	.716	.673	.716	.482	.598	.540		.878	.714
8 Hylobates concolor	.847	.807	.847	.622	.592	.632	.130		.810
9 Symphalangus syndactylus	1.099	.793	1.099	.806	.756	.856	.337	.211	

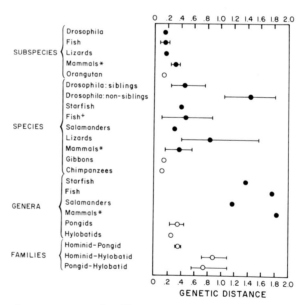

FIG. 2 - Average genetic distance (circles) and range (lines) for various groups of organisms at various levels of taxonomic separation.

somebody would indicate one to me. But, if I had called man
an ape, or vice versa, I would have fallen under the ban of
the ecclesiastics. It may be that as a naturalist I ought to
have done so." The general view of today's taxonomists is,
however, that Linnaeus was correct in his original classification, and hence they place humans and apes in different genera
(and indeed in different families after the introduction of
the "family" category).

Molecular studies lend some support to Linnaeus' perception
that humans and apes may be biologically no more different
than some congeneric species are. Bruce and Ayala (5) have
surveyed by electrophoresis 23 gene loci coding for red-cell
and plasma proteins in all extant species of hominoids. The
genetic identity and genetic distance (calculated according to
(15)) between all pairs of taxa are given in Table 2. The genetic distance may be interpreted as the number of electrophore-
tically detectable amino acid substitutions that have taken
place in the populations being compared since their divergence
from a common ancestor. The significance of these results is
enhanced by comparing them with the average genetic distances
obtained by similar electrophoretic studies in other organisms
(Figure 2). The nonprimate data are taken from the Ayala review
(1) and give the ranges and (unweighted) mean values.

The primate data involve an intersubspecific comparison,
namely, between Pongo pygmaeus pygmaeus and P. p. abelii, the
Bornean and Sumatran orangutans. On the basis of 21 proteins,
the genetic distance between these two subspecies is D =
0.130, a value comparable to those found between subspecies
in other organisms.

Two comparisons between congeneric species exist for the hominoid data. The genetic distance is D = 0.103 between the
chimpanzees, Pan troglodytes and P. paniscus, and D = 0.130
between the gibbons, Hylobates lar and H. concolor (Table 2).
These distances are at the lower end of the range of values

found between congeneric species in other organisms and are
similar to typical distances found between subspecies. Even
within the hominoids, the distance between the two orangutan
subspecies is equal to that between the two gibbons and
larger than the distance between the two chimpanzees.

The average genetic distance between the three pongid genera
(Pan, Gorilla, Pongo) is $\bar{D}$ = 0.353 $\pm$ 0.071, and between the
two hylobatid genera (Hylobates and Symphalangus) is even
smaller, $\bar{D}$ = 0.274 $\pm$ 0.063. These intergeneric differences
are typical of the values observed for comparisons between
congeneric species, rather than those typically found between
confamilial genera (see Figure 2 and (1)). The same is
true of the genetic distance between Homo and the three pongid
genera, $\bar{D}$ = 0.357 $\pm$ 0.008; although this involves interfamilial comparisons, the genetic distance observed is within the
typical range observed for comparisons between congeneric species in most types of organisms studied. King and Wilson (11)
compared humans and chimpanzees (Pan troglodytes) on the basis
of 44 gene loci and also estimated a small genetic distance
between them (although somewhat larger than the value given
in Table 2). The average genetic distances for the other two
interfamilial comparisons ($\bar{D}$ = 0.887 for Homo versus the
Hylobatidae and $\bar{D}$ = 0.721 for the Pongidae versus the
Hylobatidae) are somewhat higher than most average values
observed between congeneric species, but somewhat lower than
the genetic distances observed between confamilial genera in
other groups of organisms.

If differentiation at structural gene loci as observed in
electrophoretic studies would be used as the criterion for
taxonomic classification, it would seem appropriate to classify
men, chimpanzees, gorillas, and orangutans all in a single
genus, and the hylobatids in a separate genus but in the same
family as the pongids and humans. King and Wilson (11) and
others have argued that the evolution biologically most
significant - i.e., affecting morphology, reproductive

incompatibility, and behavior - may not be accurately reflected
by changes in structural gene loci, because it involves primarily changes in genetic regulation. This is an intriguing,
albeit as yet far from substantiated, hypothesis. The notable
differences in morphology and behavior between humans and pongid are apparent, and this can hardly be exclusively attributed to the fact that we are more likely to notice differences
that involve us than differences between other organisms.

GENETIC POLYMORPHISM

Using electrophoretic techniques, Bruce and Ayala (5) have
studied genetic variation in the hominoids. Of the 23 gene
loci sampled, 16 code for red-cell proteins and the other 7
for plasma proteins. The results are summarized in Table 3.

TABLE 3 - Genetic variation in the hominoids. After (5).

Genus	No. of species	No. of individuals	No. of loci*	Frequency of polymorphic loci*	Hetero-zygosity* Obs.	Exp.
Homo**	1	--	71	.282	.067	--
Pan	2	27	23	.044	.005	.014
Gorilla	1	10	22	.090	.036	.046
Pongo***	2	15	23	.130	.022	.058
Hylobates	2	6	21	.048	.030	.022
Symphalangus	1	1	21	.000	.000	.000
All nonhuman species	8	59	22.1	.051	.017	.023

*When several species are involved, the values given are the
 averages among the species.
**Data from (9).
***Two subspecies (P. p. pygmeus and P. p. abelii) rather
   than two species are involved.

In humans, the average frequency of heterozygous individuals per locus
is $\bar{H}$ = 0.067 and the frequency of polymorphic loci is $\underline{P}$ = 0.282 (9).
Similar values have been obtained, on the average, for mammals ($\bar{H}$ =
0.051, $\underline{P}$ = 0.206, for 30 species) and for vertebrates in general ($\bar{H}$ =
0.060, $\underline{P}$ = 0.247, for 68 species) ((2), p. 81). The values

observed for the ape species are lower: $\bar{H}$ = 0.017 (or 0.023, for the expected frequencies calculated according to the Hardy-Weinberg formula as if all sampled individuals of the same species belonged to a single random-mating population) and $\bar{P}$ = 0.051.

Electrophoretic estimates of genetic variation are potentially subject to large sampling errors. The number of individuals sampled in the hominoid species is low, which makes the estimated frequency of polymorphic loci unreliable. (A locus is considered polymorphic in these studies when more than one allele is found in the sample; hence the greater the number of individuals examined, the larger the probability that a locus will be found polymorphic.)

Estimates of heterozygosity, however, are not correlated with the number of individuals sampled and their accuracy depends less on the number of individuals than on the number of loci sampled (because average heterozygosity is normally distributed among individuals but not among loci). The number of loci surveyed in the hominoids is moderately large (21 to 23 per species) and similar to the number examined in other mammals. In general, a sample of 20 loci is sufficient, so that electrophoretic estimates usually do not change significantly as the number of loci is increased beyond 20. Hence, the heterozygosity estimates given in Table 3 for the hominoids are likely to be reliable (with the exception of Symphalangus syndactylus of which only one individual was sampled).

The reason why the nonhuman hominoids are genetically less variable than humans and other mammals remains conjectural. One possible factor could be population size that is much greater for humans than for the other hominoids. However, other mammal species that exhibit considerably more genetic variation than the apes are no more numerous than some of the ape species.

TABLE 4 - Genetic variation in primates. After (4).

Genus	No. of species	No. of individuals	No. of loci*	Frequency of polymor- phic loci*	Hetero- zygosity* Obs.	Exp.
		Prosimii				
Lemur	3	13	21	.063	.005	.013
	Ceboidea (New World Monkeys)					
Callithrix	1	6	19	.158	.011	.053
Saguinus	2	11	19	.105	.000	.036
Aotus	1	16	20	.250	.053	.101
Ateles	1	9	20	.200	.038	.087
Cebus	1	15	19	.053	.000	.012
Saimiri	1	11	21	.095	.024	.039
All Ceboidea species	7	68	19.6	.138	.018	.052
	Cercopithecoidea (Old World Monkeys)					
Cynopithecus	3	7	16	.078	.017	.027
Macaca	7	91	18	.102	.007	.027
Papio	2	18	20	.175	.025	.051
Presbytis	3	5	18	.071	.038	.027
All Cercopi- thecoidea species	15	121	17.9	.091	.018	.030

*When several species are involved, the values given are the averages among the species.

It seems likely that primates, in general, have less genetic variation than most other mammals. Table 4 summarizes the results of Bruce's study (4) for 25 other species of primates. On the aver- age, the heterozygosities of the Old World monkeys ($\bar{H}$ = 0.018) as well as the New World monkeys ($\bar{H}$ = 0.018) and the prosim- ians ($\bar{H}$ = 0.005) are less than half the heterozygosities observed in humans and most other mammals.

160   F.J. Ayala

REFERENCES

(1) Ayala, F.J. 1975. Genetic differentiation during the speciation process. Evolutionary Biology 8: 1-78.

(2) Ayala, F.J., and Valentine, J.W. 1979. Evolving. The Theory and Processes of Organic Evolution. Menlo Park: Benjamin.

(3) Benveniste, R.E., and Todaro, B.J. 1976. Evolution of type c viral genes: evidence for an Asian origin of man. Nature 261: 101.

(4) Bruce, E.J. 1977. A study of the molecular evolution of primates using the techniques of amino acid sequencing and electrophoresis. Ph.D. Thesis. University of California, Davis.

(5) Bruce, E.J., and Ayala, F.J. 1979. Phylogenetic relationships between man and the apes: Electrophoretic evidence. Evolution 33: 1040-1056.

(6) Dene, H.T.; Goodman, M.; and Prychodko, W. 1976. Immunodiffusion evidence on the phylogeny of the primates. In Molecular Anthropology, Genes and Proteins in the Evolutionary Ascent of the Primates, eds. M. Goodman and R.E. Tashian. New York: Plenum Press.

(7) Dutrillaux, B. 1979. Chromosomal evolution in primates: Tentative phylogeny from Microcebus murinus (Prosimian) to man. Human Genetics 48: 251-314.

(8) Goodman, M. 1976. Toward a genealogical description of the primates. In Molecular Anthropology, Genes and Proteins in the Evolutionary Ascent of Primates, eds. M. Goodman and R.E. Tashian. New York: Plenum Press.

(9) Harris, H., and D.A. Hopkinson. 1972. Average heterozygosity per locus in man: an estimate based on the incidence of enzyme polymorphism. Ann. Hum. Genet. Lond. 36: 9-20.

(10) Hoyer, B.H.; van de Velde, N.W.; Goodman, M.; and Roberts, R.B. 1972. Examination of hominid evolution by DNA sequence homology. J. Human Evol. 1: 645-649.

(11) King, M.C., and Wilson, A.C. 1975. Evolution at two levels. Molecular similarities and biological differences between humans and chimpanzees. Science 188: 107-116.

(12) Kohne, D.E.; Chiscon, J.A.; and Hoyer, B.H. 1972. Evolution of primate DNA sequences. J. Human Evol. 1: 627-645.

(13) Maita, T.; Araya, A.; Goodman, M.; and Matsuda, G.
     1978. The amino acid sequence of two main components of
     adult hemoglobin from orangutan (Pongo pygmaeus) in
     Hoppe-Seyler's Z. Physiol. Chem. 359: 124-132.

(14) Miller, D.A. 1977. Evolution of primate chromosomes.
     Science 198: 1116-1124.

(15) Nei, M. 1972. Genetic distance between populations.
     Amer. Nat. 106: 283-292.

(16) Romero-Herrera, A.E.; Lehmann, H.; Joysey, K.A.; and
     Friday, A.E. 1973. Molecular evolution of myoglobin
     and the fossil record: a phylogenetic synthesis. Nature
     246: 389-395.

(17) Romero-Herrera, A.E.; Lehmann, H.; Joysey, K.A.; and
     Friday, A.E. 1976. Evolution of myoglobin amino acid
     sequences in primates and other vertebrates. In
     Molecular Anthropology, Genes and Proteins in the
     Evolutionary Ascent of the Primates, eds. M. Goodman and
     R.E. Tashian. New York: Plenum Press.

(18) Romero-Herrera, A.E.; Lehmann, H.; Joysey, K.A., and
     Friday, A.E. 1976. Myoglobin of the orangutan as a
     phylogenetic enigma. Nature 261: 389-395.

(19) Sarich, V.M., and Cronin, J.E. 1976. Molecular system-
     atics of the primates. In Molecular Anthropology, Genes
     and Proteins in the Evolutionary Ascent of the Primates,
     eds. M. Goodman and R.E. Tashian. New York: Plenum
     Press.

(20) Sarich, V.M., and Wilson, A.C. 1967. Immunological
     time scale for hominid evolution. Science 158: 1200-
     1203.

(21) Simons, E.L. 1976. The fossil record of primate
     phylogeny. In Molecular Anthropology, Genes and Proteins
     in the Evolutionary Ascent of the Primates, eds. M.
     Goodman and R.E. Tashian. New York: Plenum Press.

(22) Simpson, G.G. 1945. The principles of classification
     and a classification of mammals. Bull. Amer. Mus. Nat.
     Hist. 85: 1-350.

(23) Tuttle, R. 1975. Parallelism, brachiation and hominoid
     phylogeny. In Phylogeny of the Primates, A
     Multidisciplinary Approach, eds. W.P. Luckett and F.S.
     Szalay. New York: Plenum Press.

(24) Walker, A. 1976. Splitting times among hominoids
     deduced from the fossil record. In Molecular
     Anthropology, Genes and Proteins in the Evolutionary
     Ascent of the Primates, eds. M. Goodman and R.E. Tashian.
     New York: Plenum Press.

F.J. Ayala

(25) Wilson, A.C.; Carlson, S.S.; and White, T.J. 1977. Biochemical evolution. Ann. Rev. Biochem. **46**: 573-639.

(26) Wooding, G.L., and Doolittle, R.F. 1972. Primate fibrinopeptides: evolutionary significance. J. Human Evol. **1**: 553-563.

Group on <u>Methodology and Sociobiology Modeling</u> - Seated, left to right: Brian Charlesworth, Charles Lumsden, Eberhard Curio, John Maynard Smith, Marc Feldman. Standing: Rolf Heller, Peter Hammerstein, George Oster, Jack Bradbury, Wolfgang Wickler, Paul Sherman, Bob May, Glenn Hausfater.

Evolution of Social Behavior: Hypotheses and Empirical Tests, ed. H. Markl,
pp. 165-180. Dahlem Konferenzen 1980. Weinheim: Verlag Chemie GmbH.

Methodology and Sociobiology Modeling Group Report

G. F. Oster, Rapporteur
J. W. Bradbury, B. Charlesworth, E. Curio, M. W. Feldman,
P. Hammerstein, G. Hausfater, R. Heller, C. J. Lumsden,
R. M. May, J. Maynard Smith, P. W. Sherman, W. Wickler

INTRODUCTION

Interest in the puzzle of the evolution of social behavior traces
back to Darwin's perplexity concerning sterile castes in the social
insects. However, it was not until Hamilton's now classic 1964
paper (20) that the evolution of altruism was attacked from a quantitative perspective. Hamilton reasoned that an altruistic act
would be selectively advantageous for providing the fitness cost,
c, accruing to the performer was less than its fitness benefit,
b, to the recipient of the act, discounted by the "degree of relatedness" between them:

$$c < rb$$

or

$$\frac{c}{b} < r \qquad (1)$$

Since that time, theoretical work on the evolution of social behavior has developed in two main directions. First, attempts
have been made to incorporate Hamilton's ideas into the corpus

of classical population genetics and to determine the validity of
his concept of inclusive fitness.   Second, other processes, e.g.,
parental manipulation, reciprocal altruism, mutualism, theories
of sexual selection, foraging, and dispersal strategies which do
not depend on kin-directed altruism have been proposed and in-
vestigated as mechanisms for the evolution of social behavior.
And third, field work has begun examining whether animals behave
according to the kin selection model.

WHAT ARE THE SELECTIVE MECHANISMS THAT MIGHT HAVE GIVEN RISE TO SOCIAL BEHAVIOR?

A.   Certain types of social behavior can be rationalized without
explicit reference to hypothesized genes affecting altruistic
behavior.   Examples are:

1.   Parental manipulation theory (1).   Here the power of parents
to control the behavior of their offspring can be used to produce
sterile castes in social insects and to foster other types of
"apparently" altruistic behavior by the subordination of offspring.
However, models of this process should also take into account selection acting on the offspring (15), for in such cases kin selection
is also relevant.

2.   The "selfish herd" notion of Hamilton (22), wherein each member of the herd, acting on its own behalf to avoid predation,
nevertheless creates collective behavior that may actually increase the rate of predation on the group as a whole.

3. The phenomenon of "spite" is a theoretical possibility, i.e.,
an individual may increase its fitness relative to nearby neighbors by preferring acts which, while they reduce its own personal
fitness, nevertheless reduce the fitness of its neighbors even
more (21,24,42).   An interesting example of this is given by
Arnold (3).   These situations generally require an extremely
"viscous" (low mobility) population.   (From the viewpoint of
modeling "spite" and "altruistic" models differ only by a sign
change.)

B. <u>Interdemic Selection or Group Selection</u> can act if the population is subdivided into groups, "demes," between which there is
little migration (54). Selection for altruism can act in several
ways:

1. <u>Differential production of migrants among the demes</u> (55).

2. <u>Differential extinction and colonization of the subgroups</u>.
This is group selection as originally conceived (56).

The former has received little theoretical attention, while the
latter has been addressed by numerous authors (5,17,19,26,32).
Wade (49) has shown experimentally that group selection can affect group fitness, but the experiments required a high degree
of reproductive isolation between the demes. These processes may
have been important in the evolution of diseases, thus indirectly
may have modified group behavior, but it is unlikely that they
have played a direct role in evolving altruistic or other social
behavior.

C. <u>Selection for Altruism</u> can occur due to interaction between
neighbors or within temporary groups which need not be reproductively isolated. This can come about in several ways:

1. <u>Randomly formed groups</u> can engender selection under various
circumstances (50):
a) If there are mutualistic (or synergistic) interactions among
the group members.

If fitnesses are determined by simply summing costs and benefits,
genes causing altruism cannot spread. However, such genes can
spread if the advantages of cooperation are high enough; for example, the fitness of each of a pair of interacting altruists
must be higher than would be predicted from interactions between
a selfish and an altruistic individual. The term "synergistic"
is suggested to indicate the need for such a non-additive effect.
Interacting groups must be small or must be exposed to different

selective regimes. Even when these conditions are met, it is difficult for altruistic genes to invade a population deme when ini-
tially rare. Several models address this situation (14,31,36,
47,52).

"Conditioned altruism," in which an individual acts cooperatively
only if those with which it interacts do likewise, can be selected
for. In such cases it is difficult to "cheat" because the cooperative act is performed only if others reciprocate simultaneously.
This is to be distinguished from "reciprocal altruism," discussed
next.

b) Reciprocal altruism refers to cases in which an altruistic act
by one individual is reciprocated on a later occasion. It requires
long-term learning/memory on the part of the recipient of the altruistic act. Thus it may be restricted to higher animals. The
original treatment by Trivers (44) was qualitative; analytical
(e.g., game theoretic) models would help to evaluate its role in
social evolution. It appears likely that there may be difficulty
in establishing altruistic genes by this mechanism.

c) Rousseau's notion of the Social Contract, in which cheating is
prevented by collective action, may be a force for social evolution
in humans. The economic literature concerns itself with models of
this sort (e.g., "team theory"). It is worth asking whether an
analogous behavior occurs in animals, especially the primates.

2. If, in addition, the groups, or neighbors, are genetically
similar then other selective forces may come into play.

a) Kin selection is currently the predominant selective mechanism
in the sociobiological literature. This stems from Hamilton's (20)
classic paper on the evolution of eusociality in hymenoptera. There
are currently two types of models which treat kin selection from
the genetical viewpoint:

i) <u>Neighbor-modulated or personal fitness</u> models approach the problem from the standpoint of classical population genetics (7,37). Only the direct progeny of an individual are counted, but allowance is made for the effects on the individual of the altruistic acts of its relatives.

ii) <u>Inclusive fitness</u> models (11,15,38,51) calculate the effects of altruistic or selfish acts on the fitness of the individual performing them and on the fitness of its relatives.

The former is the most formally correct approach since it focuses on the evolution of genotype frequencies. However, it is mathematically less tractable and intuitively less appealing. The inclusive fitness approach focuses on genes for altruism and on cost-benefit bookkeeping. While it appears to have a greater intuitive appeal to many, it is precise only when selection is weak, and has been applied only when the effects on fitness are additive. These differences will be discussed further in the section "What are the uses and limitations of optimization models?"

b) <u>Assortative settlement</u>. It may be that interacting individuals are genetically similar, not because they are related, but because of genetically determined habitat choice (52). This process requires that the same genes which determine altruism also determine habitat choice, i.e., an extreme form of pleiotropism. It can also be shown that a rare gene causing altruism will not be able to spread through the population (12).

The above catalog of processes related to social evolution is surely not complete, and theorists will undoubtedly concoct other possibilities. Moreover, it is likely that, in nature, more than one of these mechanisms operates in any given situation. Models combining these processes are needed and methods required to discriminate between the theoretical possibilities before definitive statements can be made about how social evolution actually proceeds. Finally, it should be noted that certain of the above mechanisms are relevant for studying the maintenance of altruism

but are not likely candidates for its initiation (e.g., mutualism, reciprocal altruism, assortative settlement).

POPULATION GENETICS AND THE INCLUSIVE FITNESS CONCEPT
A. What is the Relevance of Single Locus Models to the Study of Behavioral Evolution?

Altruistic or other social behaviors, if they have any genetic
component at all, are likely to be affected by a large number of
loci. Therefore, one might question the relevance of single
locus models in addressing any behavioral trait. Apart from the
fact that a relatively complete theory of selection dynamics exists
only for the single locus case, there are several reasons for having some confidence in the utility of single locus models. In the
first place, the main requirement for such models to be relevant
is that the crossing of "adaptive valleys" (i.e., the transition
from the two locus genotype ab to the better adapted AB, via the
less fit genotypes aB and Ab) should not have been important in
evolution. Theory suggests that such transitions can occur only
as a result of drift in small populations (54). Second, strong
non-random associations between alleles at different loci have
been detected only in the highly exceptional cases known as "supergenes." Even when supergenes occur, it has been possible to explain their evolution by selection causing one gene substitution
at a time (see, for example, (46) for a discussion of mimicry
supergenes). Third, when examining modifications of polygenet-
ically inherited behavioral traits, the selective change in the
mean value of the character can be viewed as arising from the sum
of the effects of the changes contributed by the individual loci.

Hence, although there is certainly scope for more theoretical and
experimental work on genes with interacting effects on fitness,
it is reasonable to ask whether a behavioral trait is stable
against deviant strategies by examining the conditions for spread
of a single gene affecting the trait. This implicitly assumes
that the genes controlling the trait are loosely linked and have
small and approximately additive effects. (In fact, even if
significant linkage disequilibrium between polygenic loci is built

up by selection, this will affect only the rate, not the direction, of change in the population mean of the character, as discussed by Bulmer (6) and Lande (25)). The assumption of approximate additivity of gene effects and loose linkage for most metric
characters seems to be upheld by experiments in quantitative
genetics (18).

B.   How Valid is the Inclusive Fitness Concept?
In order to use Hamilton's cost-benefit analysis (Eq. 1), we must
ask whether his notion of "inclusive fitness" makes good sense
from a genetical viewpoint. Several authors have examined this
issue using somewhat different genetical models (7,12,48).

A detailed treatment reveals that inclusive fitness predictions
are exact only when selection on each locus is weak, and the costs
of an individual's altruistic behavior can be combined linearly
with the benefits it receives from other altruists. The "coefficients of relatedness" that enter into Eq. 1 were first derived
correctly by Crozier (16) and are exact only in the case of genetically symmetrical relationships, and approximate in the case of
brother-sister interactions in haplodiploidy or sex-linkage
with diploidy.

Nevertheless, while a complete one-locus treatment of altruistic
traits is available based on classical population genetics, the
models are probably too involved mathematically to be intuitive
to most behavioral biologists. Moreover, it turns out that in
many cases, the deviations of the rigorous treatments from the
approximate inclusive fitness analysis are small. Thus, it is
likely that empiricists will continue to think in terms of inclusive fitness when examining social behavior. However, they
should beware of some hidden assumptions and logical inconsis-
tencies contained in such a view (e.g., weak selection). In particular, if one attempts to examine problems of kin selection
using Eq. 1, the assumption that relatedness-discounted benefits
and costs can be simply subtracted is only approximately true in
certain cases (cf. (48)).

Finally, there is the practical problem of accurately measuring
the fitness costs and benefits resulting from altruistic or
other social behaviors. The uncertainties in assessing b and
c in Eq. 1 can easily swamp the above considerations of formal
rigor. Theory can offer no general principles here, and one is
ultimately left with the judgement and resourcefulness of the
field investigator.

WHAT ARE THE USES AND LIMITATIONS OF OPTIMIZATION MODELS?

A. Optimization Models have been, and are likely to remain, the
principal conceptual framework for thinking about evolutionary
trends at the phenotypic level. Their uses and pitfalls have
been dealt with at length in a number of recent reviews and so
there is little point in recapitulating those descriptions here
(27,34,39,40). For the most part optimization models are employed as a guide for guessing how natural selection might have
culled specific adaptations in the absence of any detailed knowledge about the underlying genetic processes. The models may
be static or dynamic, linear or nonlinear, deterministic or stochastic, depending on the specific application and the mathematical sophistication warranted by the available data (or the ex-
pertise of the modeler). It is easy to construct examples of
genetic models whose evolution does not coincide with any optimization criterion. Thus the most important caveat to the unwary
empiricist is to eschew the naive view that nature always op-
timizes, or that every behavioral or anatomical feature of an
animal is optimally designed. ⌈Optimization is a subjective tool
for rating the relative merits of a set of strategies selected
a priori by the modeler according to criteria.⌉Thus we should
always view the results of such models as guides to the possible,
not deductions about the actual. ⌉In particular, if the model is
contradicted by the data, it may mean that the behavior being modeled is not optimal, or that the fitness functions and/or constraints may have been guessed incorrectly (29). Conversely,
if the model is consistent with the data, the behavior may be,
provisionally, regarded as optimal according to the specified
criteria (30).

B. Game Theory Models are simply optimization models with the
added feature that there are two or more "players," each trying
to optimize its own fitness (or "payoff") by manipulating its
own set of strategies. Thus the payoff accruing to a player
adopting a particular strategy depends on the actions of the
other players. The same caveats concerning optimization models
certainly apply to game theory models; however, there are certain features unique to "evolutionary games" that require special comments.

In a game situation neither player can optimize its fitness, so
one must devise a sensible notion of how a game should be resolved. The generally accepted definition is Maynard Smith's
notion of an "evolutionarily stable strategy," or ESS (cf.
Maynard Smith, this volume, for formal definition). An ESS is a
strategy (pure or mixed) that ensures that deviators, or inva-
ders, with a different strategy will always receive a smaller
fitness reward. There are various ways of representing this
mathematically depending on the type of model under consideration; thus one should be aware of semantic confusion (cf. the
technical comment at the end of this section). Strictly speak-
ing, one would like to formulate equations for gene frequencies
governing the evolution of each trait. Unfortunately, this is
seldom possible. Thus one is forced to resort to reasoning on
phenotypes, and implicitly assuming simply that strategies are
heritable to some extent and follow, on the average, haploid or
parthenogenetic inheritance rules. Thus we nimbly sidestep the
imponderables and deal directly with strategies.

Unfortunately, as in optimization theory, it is easy to construct
examples wherein the game-theoretic ESS is unobtainable, that
is, the ESS is not consistent with the constraints of Mendelian
inheritance (4,43). In this connection, one situation in particular deserves special caution. That is, an ESS may be a
"mixed strategy" in two ways: the population can consist of (a)
individuals who play a mixed strategy (e.g., play strategy 1
with frequency p_1 and strategy 2 with frequency $1-p_1$), and (b)

a fraction p_1 of individuals who play exclusively strategy 1
and the rest play strategy 2. The latter case may run afoul of
Mendelian constraints unless the trait is controlled by a large
number of loci; for example, in the "war of attrition" game (35)
the ESS is an exponential frequency distribution, which could not
be produced by a few loci. Finally, a mixture of strategies in
the ESS proportions can arise by learning in a population of
individuals which play the same game repeatedly against different opponents.

There are a number of directions that need further investigation.
For example, under the assumption that population structure and
dynamics can influence selection (e.g., population "bottlenecks"
and founder groups), one is tempted to incorporate population
models into the game situation. Unfortunately this added touch
of realism may lead to situations where there is no dynamically
stable ESS or to situations which are "chaotic" (i.e., apparently random) and difficult to interpret in a sensible way (4,39).
Finally, models with age structure and/or explicit consideration
of dispersal mechanisms are probably important in many situations;
Charnov (13) and Hamilton and May (23), respectively, have taken
some initial steps in this direction.

Technical Remark
As originally conceived by Maynard Smith an ESS was a purely
game-theoretic notion, which could be computed with reference
to the payoff matrix only. The underlying hereditary dynamical
equations governing the inheritance of the strategies was implicitly parthenogenetic. The notion of "noninvasibility" in
classical population genetics refers to the stability of the
boundaries of the frequency simplex (i.e., will a rare allele
spread?). Various authors (e.g., (10,13)) have studied the evolution of the sex ratio in explicitly genetic models by param-
eterizing the fitnesses by a strategy parameter and seeking a
value of the parameter which is non-invasible. Feldman and his
colleagues, in their work on modifier loci and sex ratio problems, use the boundary stability criterion for noninvasibility.

Finally, Oster and Rocklin (39) and Mirmirani and Oster (36)
used both the game-theoretic and genetic framework to locate
"unbeatable" strategies. Thus the reader is warned that the
generic term "ESS" has been used to refer to quite distinct
mathematical criteria for "unbeatable strategies," or "noninvasibility."

WHAT ARE THE MOST PROMISING DIRECTIONS FOR FUTURE WORK?
It is a truism that evolution is largely a historical process.
Different social groups arise and persist for different combinations of reasons, and no general theory is possible which
will ever satisfactorily explain every case. Indeed, it is
doubtful whether unequivocal explanations are in principle ob-
tainable, and we will always have to be satisfied with a set of
"most plausible" stories. Theory provides a shopping list of
mechanisms and modeling techniques which can be applied to individual cases and which have provided qualitative insights into
one of the major mysteries of social behavior: the origin and
maintenance of altruism. However, no longer are imaginative
and plausible sounding theories sufficient to carry the day.
Quantitative empirical tests must be carried out to sort out
the theorist's list of possibilities. The models must be applied
to a great number of specific systems before general principles
are likely to emerge. This means closer collaboration between
theoreticians and experimentalists so that strong-inference
tests can be devised to decide between alternative mechanisms.
Whether or not field workers can gather data of sufficient resolution to discriminate between theories remains to be demonstrated.

To date, one of the most ambitious and sensible attempts to resolve a sociobiological issue is the Trivers and Hare (45) paper
on worker-queen conflict in the social insects. Unfortunately,
this pioneering attempt was statistically flawed and failed to
consider important alternative models (2). One hopes that this
is not to be the fate of all tests of theories concerning the
evolution of behavior - plausible stories reposing in eternal
ambiguity.

FUTURE RESEARCH

As the emphasis in sociobiological research shifts from the obsession with kin-related phenomena, greater attention will be
focused on alternatives, such as mutualism and reciprocal altruism, and on behavioral phenomena which may not require a
genetic explanation. To this end models to incorporate learning
and "cultural" (vs. genetic) transmission of traits need to be
developed. There already exists a substantial body of models in
mathematical psychology, sociology, and economics that can be
adapted with profit to problems of learning, small group dynamic,
parent-offspring interactions, nonverbal communication, and other
ethological processes. One of the most interesting recent efforts to unite genetic and cultural modes of transmission is the
work of Feldman and Cavalli-Sforza (7). Their formalism extends
the structure of classical genetic and epidemiological models
to behavioral traits which are influenced by genetic, cultural,
and environmental factors. A somewhat different approach to the
problem of gene-culture coevolution is being pursued by Lumsden
and Wilson (28). Other models are needed which address the
puzzles of infanticide (9), alarm calls, cooperative hunting
and breeding tradeoffs between risk and return in foraging and
parental care, and kin selection in structured populations. In
each instance, specific models will have to be constructed and
suitable organisms selected whose special properties make testing of models feasible.

Finally, at various times throughout the conference, some concern
was expressed that the subject may be evolving two separate cultures - "theorists" and "empiricists" - whose activities are
becoming mutually incomprehensible. There are, of course, not
simply two groups, but rather a great range of personal interests,
and many different styles of, and approaches to, research. Nevertheless, it remains true that as the discipline develops it
runs the risk of fragmenting. One solution is to encourage individuals with the gift for lucid review and interpretive synthesis, for only through such reviews can the study of the evolution
of social behavior remain a unified endeavor.

REFERENCES

(1) Alexander, R.D. 1974. The evolution of social behaviour. Ann. Rev. Ecol. Syst. 5: 325-383.

(2) Alexander, R.D., and Sherman, P.W. 1977. Local mate competition and parental investment in social insects. Science 196: 494-500.

(3) Arnold, S. 1977. Polymorphism and geographic variation in the feeding behavior of the garter snake Thamnophis elegans. Science 197: 676-678.

(4) Auslander, D.; Guckenheimer, J.; and Oster, G. 1978. Random Evolutionarily Stable Strategies. Theor. Pop. Biol. 13: 276-293.

(5) Boorman, S.A., and Levitt, P.R. 1973. Group selection at the boundary of a stable population. Theor. Pop. Biol. 4: 85-128.

(6) Bulmer, M.G. 1980. Introduction to the Mathematical Theory of Quantitative Genetics. Oxford: Oxford University Press.

(7) Cavalli-Sforza, L., and Feldman, M.W. 1978. Towards a theory of cultural evolution. Interdisc. Sci. Rev. 3: 99-107.

(8) Cavalli-Sforza, L., and Feldman, M.W. 1978. Darwinian selection and "altruism." Theor. Pop. Biol. 14: 268-280.

(9) Chapman, M., and Hausfater, G. 1979. The reproductive consequences of infanticide in langurs: a mathematical model. Behav. Evol. Sociobiol. 5: 227-240.

(10) Charlesworth, B. 1977. Population genetics, demography and the sex ratio. In Measuring Selection in Natural Populations, eds. F.B. Christiansen and T.M. Fenchel, pp. 346-363. Berlin: Springer-Verlag.

(11) Charlesworth, B. 1978. Some models of the evolution of altruistic behaviour between siblings. J. Theor. Biol. 72: 297-319.

(12) Charlesworth, B. 1979. A note on the evolution of altruism in structured devices. Am. Nat. 113: 601-605.

(13) Charnov, E.L. 1978. Sex-ratio selection in eusocial hymenoptera. Am. Nat. 112: 317-326.

(14) Cohen, D., and Eshel, I. 1976. On the founder effect and the evolution of altruistic traits. Theor. Pop. Biol. 10: 276-302.

(15) Craig, R. 1979. Parental manipulation, kin selection, and the evolution of altruism. Evolution 33: 319-334.

(16)   Crozier, R.H.   1970.   Coefficients of relationship and the
       identity of genes by descent in the Hymenoptera.

(17)   Eshel, I.   1972.   On the neighbourhood effect and the evo-
       lution of altruistic traits.   Theor. Pop. Biol. $\underline{3}$: 258-277.

(18)   Falconer, D.S.   1960.   Introduction to Quantitative Genetics.
       Edinburgh: Oliver and Boyd.

(19)   Gilpin, M.E.   1975.   Group Selection in Predator-Prey Com-
       munities.   Princeton: Princeton University Press.

(20)   Hamilton, W.D.   1964.   The genetical evolution of social
       behaviour.   I and II.   J. Theor. Biol. $\underline{7}$: 1-16; 17-32.

(21)   Hamilton, W.D.   1970.   Selfish and spiteful behaviour in an
       evolutionary model.   Nature $\underline{228}$: 1218-1220.

(22)   Hamilton, W.D.   1971.   Geometry for the selfish herd.   J.
       Theor. Biol. $\underline{31}$: 295-311.

(23)   Hamilton, W.D., and May, R.M.   1977.   Dispersal in stable
       habitats.   Nature $\underline{269}$: 578-581.

(24)   Knowlton, N., and Parker, G.A.   1979.   An evolutionarily
       stable strategy appropriate to indiscriminate spite.   Nature
       $\underline{279}$: 419-421.

(25)   Lande, R.   1976.   The maintenance of genetic variability by
       mutation in a polygenic character with linked loci.   Genet.
       Res. $\underline{26}$: 221-235.

(26)   Levins, R.   1970.   Extinction.   In Some Mathematical Prob-
       lems in Biology, eds. M. Gersterheber.   Providence, RI:
       The American Mathematical Society.

(27)   Lewontin, R.C.   1979.   Fitness survival and optimality.   In
       Analysis of Ecosystems, eds. D. Horn, R. Mitchell, and G.
       Stairs.   Columbus, OH: Ohio State University Press.

(28)   Lumsden, C., and Wilson, E.O.   1981.   Gene-Culture Coevolu-
       tion, in preparation.

(29)   McCleery, R.H.   1978.   Optimal behavior sequences and de-
       cision making.   In Behavioural Ecology, eds. J.R. Krebs and
       N.B. Davies.   Oxford: Scientific Publications.

(30)   McFarland, D.J.   1977.   Decision making in animals.   Nature
       $\underline{269}$: 15-21.

(31)   Matessi, C.A., and Jayakov, S.D.   1976.   Conditions for the
       evolution of altruism under Darwinian selection.   Theor.
       Pop. Biol. $\underline{9}$: 360-387.

(32)   Maynard Smith, J.   1964.   Group selection and kin selection.
       Nature $\underline{201}$: 1145-1147.

(33) Maynard Smith, J. 1976. Group selection. Quart. Rev.
      Biol. 51: 277-283.

(34) Maynard Smith, J. 1978. Optimization theory in evolution.
      Ann. Rev. Ecol. Syst. 9: 31-56.

(35) Maynard Smith, J., and Parker, G.A. 1976. The logic of
      asymmetric contests. Anim. Behav. 24: 159-175.

(36) Mirmirani, M., and Oster, G. 1978. Competition, kin selec-
      tion and evolutionary stable strategies. Theor. Pop. Biol.
      13: 304-331.

(37) Orlove, M.J. 1975. A model of kin selection not invoking
      coefficients of relationship. J. Theor. Biol. 49: 289-310.

(38) Oster, G; Eshel, I; and Cohen, D. 1977. Worker-queen con-
      flict and the evolution of social insects. Theor. Pop.
      Biol. 12: 49-85.

(39) Oster, G, and Rocklin, S. 1979. Optimization in evolution-
      ary biology. In Lectures on Mathematics in the Life Sciences,
      ed. S. Levin, vol. II. Providence, RI: The American Mathe-
      matical Society.

(40) Oster, G., and Wilson, E.O. 1978. Caste and Ecology in the
      Social Insects. Princeton: Princeton University Press.

(41) Pohley, H.J., and Thomas, B. 1979. On Evolutionarily
      Stable Strategies in populations with subpopulations raving
      isolated strategy repertoires. Biosystems 11: 263-268.

(42) Rothstein, S.I. 1979. Am. Nat. 113: 317-331.

(43) Taylor, P., and Jonker, L. 1978. Evolutionarily stable strat-
      egies and game dynamics. Math. Biosci. 40: 145-156.

(44) Trivers, R.L. 1971. The evolution of reciprocal altruism.
      Quart. Rev. Biol. 46: 35-57.

(45) Trivers, R.L., and Hare, H. 1976. Haplodiploidy and the
      evolution of the social insects. Science 191: 249-263.

(46) Turner, J.R.G. 1977. Butterfly mimicry: the genetical evo-
      lution of an adaptation. Evol. Biol. 10: 163-206.

(47) Uyenoyama, M.K. 1979. Evolution of altruism under group
      selection in large and small populations in fluctuating
      environments. Theor. Pop. Biol. 15: 58-85.

(48) Uyenoyama, M., and Feldman, M. 1980. Theories of kin and
      group selection: a population genetics perspective. Theor.
      Pop. Biol., in press.

(49) Wade, M.J. 1977. Experimental study of group selection.
      Evolution 31: 134-153.

(50) Wade, M.J. 1978. A critical review of the models of group
      selection. Quart. Rev. Biol. 53: 101-114.

(51) West-Eberhard, M.J. 1975. The evolution of social behavior
      by kin selection. Quart. Rev. Biol. 53: 1-33.

(52) Wilson, D.S. 1975. A theory of group selection. Proc.
      Nat. Acad. Sci. 72: 143-146.

(53) Wilson, E.O. 1975. Sociobiology. Cambridge: Harvard
      University Press.

(54) Wright, S. 1931. Evolution in Mendelian populations.
      Genetics 16: 97-159.

(55) Wright, S. 1945. Tempo and mode in evolution - a critical
      review. Ecology 26: 415-419.

(56) Wynn-Edwards, V.C. 1962. Animal Behaviour in Relation to
      Social Behavior. Edinburgh: Oliver and Boyd.

Group on <u>Mechanisms of Kin-Correlated Behavior</u> - Seated, left to right: Peter Marler, Paul Harvey, Fritz Trillmich, Jim Markl, Pat Bateson, Bert Hölldobler. Standing: Manfred Milinski, Steve Emlen, Mich Michener, Eduard Linsenmair, Norbert Bischof, Bernd Kramer, Myron Baker, Emil Menzel.

Evolution of Social Behavior: Hypotheses and Empirical Tests, ed. H. Markl,
pp. 183-202. Dahlem Konferenzen 1980. Weinheim: Verlag Chemie GmbH.

Mechanisms of Kin-Correlated Behavior
Group Report

P. H. Harvey, Rapporteur
M. C. Baker, P. Bateson, N. Bischof, S. T. Emlen, B. Hölldobler,
B. Kramer, K. E. Linsenmair, H. Markl, P. Marler, E. W. Menzel, Jr.
C. D. Michener, M. Milinski, F. Trillmich

INTRODUCTION

Behavioral interactions between individuals within a population are often non-random with reference to the identities of
the participants. Frequently, kin relationships are the
source of such asymmetries. This paper discusses the mechanisms of kin-correlated behavior. We first define kinship for
operational purposes and ask whether it can be measured in
natural populations. We then discuss the relevance of various
models that either describe or invoke kin relationships when
considering population structure. Our discussion continues
with a consideration of the reasons for expecting kin-correlated behavior to evolve in natural population, followed by a
brief overview of the data base. Proximate mechanisms for
effecting kin-correlated behavior and the ecological conditions
under which it is likely to evolve comprise our closing sections. Overall, we attempt to identify areas of ignorance,
particularly those that have a strong bearing on attempts to

distinguish between various theories proposed for the evolution
of kin-correlated behavior.

DEFINITION OF KINSHIP

Kinship can be either social (see below) or genetical. The
latter can be measured over many hundreds of generations or
over few. For present purposes, a suitable operational definition of kinship is provided by the regression measure $b_{IJ}$of
genetic relatedness between recipient J and donor I. This
represents the probability that J contains a gene identical by
descent with a random gene at the same locus sampled from I.
As far as our discussion pertains to pedigree analysis for
measuring relatedness, b_{IJ} is appropriate. We stress that this
is not a correlational measure (r) so that under certain
genetic systems (e.g., haplodiploid inheritance) b_{IJ} need not
always have the same value as b_{JI}.

RELIABILITY OF KINSHIP MEASURES

Many genetic models for the spread of behavioral traits demand
accurate estimation of b_{IJ}, especially those involving altruistic behavior (behavior causing a reduction in fitness of the
donor that results in an increase in fitness of the recipient).
An important general question for the behavioral ecologist
must be: Can we draw reliable conclusions about actual kinship from apparent kinship? A knowledge of certainty of
paternity is extremely important. The Hymenoptera have been
the subject of most speculation and provide a good case study.
Among species producing monogynous colonies, repeated matings
are often reported for a single queen and we do not yet have a
good idea about the sequence in which the sperm of the different males are released. If random release occurs, then the
supposed 3/4 relationship between worker females may be a
gross overestimate. Among truly polygynous species (those
containing many, sometimes hundreds, of queens that do not
compete for egg laying), circumstantial evidence indicates a
lower frequency of multiple matings and higher inbreeding.
However, certainty of maternity now becomes a key variable.

There is very little evidence for a marked effect of sperm
clumping. This question, together with the frequency of
multiple matings, is best studied using polymorphic enzyme
loci (in the absence of suitable genetically controlled morphological variation). For instance, at the moment we depend
on inference to describe the mating structure in termite
colonies; genetic marker studies will soon provide data that
will allow us to produce a more accurate assessment of the
true picture. Recent Polistes studies indicate a b_{IJ} between
workers of about 1/2, but in other populations or other
species frequent inbreeding and single inseminations could
raise the value <u>above</u> 3/4. R. H. Crozier (this volume) reports
recent evidence that interspecific differences in average
degree of relatedness among workers in some genera may be considerable. Similarly, among congeneric species (e.g., Lasioglossum spp.) the readiness of queens to accept multiple
matings may be quite different (C. D. Michener, personal
communication), varying from those willing to mate again
within 30 minutes to others that refuse to remate after
several days.

Genetic marker studies allow us to examine both intracolony
and intercolony genetic differences among the social insects.
At present, very little is known about the latter.

Behavioral ecologists studying vertebrates have only recently
recognized that certainty of paternity is an important problem.
However, recent evidence using both vasectomized males (see
M. C. Baker and P. Marler, this volume, for a discussion of
the technique which may underestimate the extent of certainty
of paternity) and genetic markers is beginning to reveal the
extent of extra-pair-bond copulations and sperm competition in
monogamous bird species. Forced copulations have been recorded
in about 40 species of Anatidae and a genetic marker experiment
with captive mallards showed that they can be effective in
fertilizing eggs. In one polygynous bird species, vasectomy

studies indicated that harems may be infiltrated to the extent
that the harem holder may only father about 1/2 the offspring
produced during his tenure (see M. C. Baker and P. Marler, this
volume). The problem is not confined to studies of birds:
the Cayo Santiago work on rhesus monkeys used both observational and genetic marker data to suggest that perhaps 5% of
offspring are fathered by males from outside the group. And
among bats, McCracken and Bradbury's recent work (39) indicates
a certainty of paternity of between 60 and 90% in one harem
species. Sneaking copulations by extragroup males (kleptogamy)
is reported from a variety of vertebrate taxa although the genetic consequences (the likelihood that the kleptogamist actually
fathers offspring) are virtually unknown. The need for further
genetic marker work in long-term field studies is evident.

MODELS OF POPULATION STRUCTURE
Several long-term field studies are beginning to produce
detailed descriptions of population structure, including
patterns of mating success, demography, dispersion, and dispersal. There is a tendency to attempt to relate these descriptions to the population drift models of Sewall Wright and
others, and then to draw conclusions about effective population size (N_e), the spread of genes that might influence
behavior, and the accumulation of genetic variation among
demes. Several problems should be considered. First, it is
particularly difficult to apply these models to real data.
For instance, we should not take it for granted that there
will be a correspondence between population subsets in the
models and those in real populations. Second, it is important
to know who moves: stepping-stone models show that genetic
differentiation between sub-populations is rapidly reduced if
very few individuals move long distances. It is not the modal
distance moved that should concern us here, but the tail of
the dispersal curve; the 2% of animals that move the longest
distances are very important in destroying or slowing down
sub-population differentiation. Third, the importance of measuring the inbreeding coefficient in relation to a particular

population is relevant (see R. A. Metcalf, this volume). And
fourth, such models are usually based on neutral alleles;
selective pressures which may vary between sub-populations
can result in considerable genetic differentiation.

Before leaving the topic of models of population structure, it
is important to note that the inclusive fitness model, due to
Hamilton (30), postulates a gene with a particular effect.
A "rule of thumb" is used to determine the individuals to which
a particular animal should dispense altruistic acts (see below). As the gene spreads through the population, that same
rule of thumb is used. If a gene programs an animal to help
sibs under certain circumstances, even when it has reached
fixation within the population, sibs are still the only
animals helped (see Dawkins (20) for an extended discussion of
these and other fallacies). Similarly, although overall homo-
zygosity within the population (or effective population size)
may correlate with the conditions under which such a gene
might spread, it does not determine those conditions. There
is no current theory that helps us to make any predictions
about the effect of population subdivision on the dynamics of
kin selection.

WHY SHOULD WE EXPECT KIN-CORRELATED BEHAVIOR?
Kin are more likely to share genes that are identical by descent than are individuals selected at random from the population. Increasing the fitness of kin increases the inclusive
fitness of an individual so long as costs are not incurred;
if there are costs involved, then, depending on the degree of
relatedness of the kin and the cost:benefit ratio, inclusive
fitness may still be increased. This is the nub of Hamilton's
argument for the evolution of altruistic behavior by kin
selection (30).

Cooperation between kin will generally be favored over cooperation between non-kin, whether this involves mutualism, reciprocal altruism (48) or passive interactions, since additional
benefits will accrue through kin selection. In addition, kin

are likely to be associated spatially and will, therefore,
interact more frequently than will individuals taken from the
population at random. Vehrencamp (50) has argued that there
may be exceptions to this generalization when strong skew in
reproductive success among group members is possible and when
the costs of dispersing between groups are low. The conditions
under which kin might be preferentially excluded from groups
have not yet received formal attention.

There are, however, limits to cooperation between kin. These
have been discussed elsewhere - in particular the development
of parent-offspring conflict (49) and the evolution of parental manipulation (1, 19). It may be that consideration of
the effect of genes among offspring for resisting manipulation
by the parents (or even for "psychologically manipulating" the
parents: Trivers (49)) will be a profitable area of research;
that is not to say that such genes will inevitably spread, just
that they might under certain circumstances.

Nevertheless, close kin are often expected to avoid each other
as mates. The degree of inbreeding depression expected may,
to a large extent, depend on the history of inbreeding in the
population (e.g., see (44)). Although inbreeding depression
has been widely demonstrated in laboratory populations, there
are, as yet, very few field data. It is generally true that
populations appear to be structured so that close kin rarely
interbreed. However, the extent of inbreeding and its effects
in the wild (which are likely to be more striking than under
less harsh laboratory conditions) are clearly identified as
important areas of research (28).

DATA ON KIN-CORRELATED BEHAVIOR
The data base on kin-correlated behavior is large and reviews
have generally focused on apparent cases of altruism, particularly where these appear to have evolved independently among
several closely related taxa. Eusociality in the Hymenoptera
and termites (31) and cooperative breeding in birds (21) are

cases in point. In both instances, the functional significance of the described behavior or social system is still a matter for debate. Data that will allow us to distinguish between various hypotheses that postulate the spread of genes which determine changes from purely selfish to apparently altruistic behavior are not available. For example, among the social Hymenoptera, workers are female offspring of the queen who remain in the nest and help to rear reproductive siblings (full or half); kin selection and parental manipulation are competing (and to some extent complementary) hypotheses (19). Among the termites, ecological factors leading to high levels of inbreeding may be relevant to the evolution of eusociality (5).

It is often costly, in terms of survival or fitness, to initiate a breeding group or to enter one. In Polistes, sisters may cooperate to found a new colony. Even if one sister subsequently leaves the nest or acts as a subordinate (producing few or no eggs), she may gain indirectly through kin selection (reproduction by a sister) compared with the possible direct benefits resulting from attempting to set up a colony alone. Assortment of sisters is marked (N. M. Ross and G. J. Gamboa, personal communication): keeping 50 females isolated over winter and then placing them into groups of ten, consisting of five sisters from one source and five from another resulted in 44 resting associations of two or more wasps; 41 of these involved sisters only. Among mammals, it may be common for brothers (or half brothers) to help each other to gain reproductive access to groups of females. Hrdy (34) reports this among langurs (Presbytis entellus) where a group of related males may cooperate to oust the harem male, and subsequently all but one of the invading males are ejected. In lions (8, 10), brothers cooperate both to oust previous reproductive males from prides and, subsequently, to prevent takeovers. Similarly, brothers (or half brothers) may help each other to enter breeding groups of rhesus monkeys on Cayo Santiago (D. S. Sade, personal communication); sometimes an older brother who is already a member of the troop helps a younger sib to join and on other

occasions brothers migrate together. And among chimpanzees,
uterine kin often form coalitions against others in the same
group.

Group fission may also be kin-correlated in that groups may
divide along kin lines. Group fission has now been observed
in free-ranging populations of three species where individuals
were known: Japanese monkeys (24, 25, 26, 36), rhesus monkeys
(13, 16, 35, 40), and olive baboons (41). The pattern has
been similar in each: groups have split along matrilines so
that certain females and their offspring leave together. This
has the consequence that the average degree of relatedness
within new groups is higher than that between individuals in
the original troop (14, 15).

Clutton-Brock and Harvey (17) have produced simple models
that attempt to describe such group splits in functional terms.
They assume that the rate at which dominant animals direct
aggression towards subordinates depends on the degree of relatedness between the animals involved. The number of threats
received by an animal is, therefore, a consequence of the extent to which it is unrelated to dominant group members. As group
size increases, the lowest animal will, for example, suffer
such feeding interference that she will wish to leave the group.
Since daughters rank below mothers, the mother (acting in the
interests of her own inclusive fitness) might also leave in
order to protect her offspring. Groups would therefore split
along matrilines, and it would also be predicted that the
lowest ranking matrilines should be those to split away first.
This was indeed the case in each of the three species mentioned
above. Models such as these are clearly over-simplified. For
example, males are not considered, yet in Nash's (41), Furuya's
(25) and Koyama's (36) studies, group fission followed a
period of instability in the male dominance hierarchy. However, Chepko-Sade and Olivier (15) found that matrilineages
involved in group fission subdivided when the average degree of
relatedness between members fell below that of first cousins.

Whole social groups fissioned when the average degree of relatedness between members fell below the level of second cousins.
In these cases, degrees of relatedness were calculated only
through the maternal line, and therefore the types of model out-
lined above may be relevant.

Group fission has also been observed and well-documented in
the Yanamamö Indians of the Amazon Basin (11). Although the
Yanamamö did not split along matrilines, the average degree of
relatedness within the new groups was markedly higher than in
the old group. One important aspect of the Yanamamö split was
that although kinship terminology is sometimes applied to individuals who are social but not biological kin (e.g., calling a
non-relative "uncle" or "brother"), when group fission occurred
the new subgroup tended to contain biological kin. Chepko-Sade
(14) also reports that, in Chagnon's study, internal soli-
darity is higher in equal sized groups of more highly related
individuals than in groups with lower average degrees of
relatedness.

Alarm calling among a variety of vertebrate taxa is also often
kin-correlated and a review of the hypotheses and tests can be
found in Harvey and Greenwood (32).

The evidence for incest avoidance is largely (though not
wholly: (9, 43, 46)) circumstantial. For instance, sex differences in dispersal rates and distances occur among most vertebrates (42) that have been studied: in birds, females generally move longer distances than males from their natal area to the
site of first breeding, while in mammals it is the males who more
commonly move from their natal group and the females who tend to
remain (see Greenwood (27) for a review). However, among most
species of vertebrates, the distances moved are small (generally
less than 10 home ranges or territory widths), and it may be
that there exists some optimal level of outbreeding. Bateson (6)
reports that Japanese quail appear to select potential mates so

that neither close inbreeding nor maximal outbreeding would
result. More data are clearly required, but Bateson's experiments provide an important start.

MECHANISMS OF KIN-CORRELATED BEHAVIOR

If animals are to interact assortatively with kin, how do they
recognize kin? Animals do not need to be able to recognize kin
for kin-selected behavior to evolve; they may simply interact
preferentially with animals who are more likely to be kin.
There are several likely mechanisms.

It has already been pointed out that vertebrates tend to be
philopatric (although one sex more than the other). It may
be that the sex that does not disperse treats other conspecifics of the same sex in the group as though they were kin
of a particular degree of relatedness (B. Hölldobler and
C. D. Michener, this volume).

Familiarity provides a more fine-grained mechanism for kin
recognition than does simple philopatry. A well-known
example is filial imprinting. Shortly after hatching, birds
such as ducklings and chicks narrow their filial preferences
to their mother (or, in experimental conditions, some substi-
tute for her). Simultaneously the mother learns the characteristics of her young and becomes so selective in her
parental behavior that she may attack and even kill young of
other broods. Meanwhile, the young birds also learn the
characteristics of their siblings. This process of familiarization together with filial imprinting can leave a long-term
effect on the choice of a mate since the birds prefer not to
mate with their immediate kin. They do, however, prefer a
mate looking rather like the individuals to which they were
exposed when young - as can be strikingly demonstrated when
birds are reared with members of a different species. Sexual
imprinting, as it is called, is found to occur after siblings
have moulted into their adult plumage but before they have
dispersed (7).

Bateson's optimal discrepancy theory (6, 7) proposes that a single learning process sets a standard of what immediate kin look like, and the birds subsequently prefer to mate with an individual who looks slightly different. Bischof (9) proposes an alternative idea, namely, that sexual imprinting involves learning the general characteristics of the species and that, at maturity, previous attachment to mother and sibs is replaced by active detachment and exploration. The result is that, while under natural conditions the birds prefer to mate with their own species, they also prefer not to mate with close kin. Differential predictions arising from Bateson's and Bischof's theories have not yet been tested.

Familiarization required to detect kin could involve something as simple as sensory adaptation to own odor; subsequently individuals that smelled the same as self could be distinguished from those that smelled differently. However, the available evidence from invertebrates, which might be expected to employ such simple devices, suggests that they employ processes resembling, at least superficially, classical imprinting in birds. Greenberg's data (reviewed by B. Hölldobler and C. D. Michener, this volume) are of this type. Here Lasioglossum zephyrum guards are more likely to allow individuals with familiar odors into the natal burrow, but the guard does not use its own odor as a cue. There is clearly a genetical component to variation in odor production in this case (so that sibs have similar odors), though there does not appear to be innate knowledge on the receptor side.

Another example comes from Linsenmair's study of the isopod Hemilepistus ((38), and in preparation). Up to 100 offspring from a single monogamous pair live together for their first year of life in a burrow up to 1 meter deep and between 2 and 3 meters long. There is severe competition for access to burrows and associated cannibalism of conspecifics (though not of close kin). Strangers are attacked when they approach the entrance to the burrow, but members of the sibship are allowed to enter.

Since the young leave the burrow on occasion (to forage), a
clear kin recognition signal is essential. Linsenmair has
conclusively demonstrated that there is an important genetic
component to the odor or taste (so that sibs smell or taste
very much the same as each other), but that sibs do not use
their own odor as a signal for kin recognition; this must be
learned through previous association with sibs.

There are, as yet, no reported instances of innate sib-recog-
nition systems among arthropods or vertebrates.* It will be
interesting to follow the development of the work by Waldman
and Adler (51) who reported sib-association among tadpoles.
This may be determined by mechanisms similar to those described by Greenberg and Linsenmair (learning).

Kin recognition by demographic characteristics (e.g., maternity which must be certain in viviparous animals) together
with other mechanisms listed by J. L. Brown (this volume)
are, of course, also relevant.

The absence of innate kin recognition systems on the hard-
wired receptor side may be a consequence of one or more
factors. Perhaps plasticity has been selected for because
particular sensory cues may vary through an individual's
lifetime (e.g., among the social insects where colony odor
changes through time because of differences in dietary mix
(B. Hölldobler and C. D. Michener, this volume) or replacement of the queen). There may also be selection, under
certain circumstances, against genes for the reception of
kin recognition because they may be "cheated against." This
highlights the need for a whole class of formal genetic
models that examine the conditions under which genes for kin
recognition as opposed to genes for the absence of kin recognition would be selectively favored; already, several papers (2,
23, 45, 47) have considered the possibility that such genes
might exist in one form or another.

---

*Footnote added in proof: but see Wu, H.M.H.; Holmes, W.G.;
Medina, S.R.; and Sackett, G.P. 1980. Kin preference in
infant Macaca nemestrina. Nature 285: 225-227.

Various animal groups use different sensory modalities to
recognize conspecifics (and presumably, kin), as well as
combinations of different modalities during the course of a
lifetime. We assume that individuals adapt to use an optimal
combination given the species sensory capabilities and the
environmental constraints operating at a particular time.

ENVIRONMENTAL CONSTRAINTS RELEVANT TO KIN-CORRELATED BEHAVIOR
Kin-correlated behavior will evolve when kin associate (or
disperse). This section focuses on some of the environmental conditions that are likely to favor kin association.

Among the social insects, defense against predators is likely
to have been a potent force favoring cooperative behavior.
For instance, among the wasps and bees, ground nesting species
are likely to be subject to attacks by predators, parasites,
and even conspecifics. Solitary individuals are less able to
defend themselves against such attacks than groups. Note
that viral, bacterial, protozoan, and other internal parasites are more easily maintained as population density increases, so that this factor works against group formation;
some of these effects can be differentially disadvantageous
for groups of kin compared with groups of unrelated individuals - see, e.g., the reviews of Anderson and May (3, 4).
However, as group size increases in the absence of predators,
so productivity per individual decreases; the rate of decline
of productivity with increase in group size varies enormously
between species. Colony size presumably represents a balance
between defense against natural enemies and loss of productivity with increased colony size. The evolution of sociality
is, therefore, a reversible process. A possible example of
such a transition back from sociality to asociality is provided by the halictids or sweat bees (C. D. Michener, personal
communication). Augochlora contains two taxa, one of which is
ground nesting and social while the other lives in rotten logs
(where natural enemies are few) and is asocial. The close

relative, Augochlorella, is ground nesting and social. The
most parsimonious interpretation of the phylogeny of the group
would interpret asociality as having evolved once, rather
than sociality having evolved twice.

Also among the wasps, if sisters were to clump nests around that
of the mother and the mother had only been inseminated once,
then it would not matter to them if the mother placed her
eggs in their nests; each would have the same degree of
relatedness to the offspring (assuming a 50:50 sex ratio).
The mother would gain a great deal if she were able to manipulate the daughters to accept the eggs. Clearly, such a
system is fragile and open to potential exploitation but
could represent an early stage in the evolution of worker
castes. It is interesting to note that the system does not
depend on haplodiploidy and would work equally well for
diploid species: it is the life history pattern of the wasp
involved (presumably responding to environmental conditions
and clumping the nests) that would favor the evolution of the
system (12).

Why then, among the Hymenoptera, might polygyny evolve from
a monogynous system? Based on a simple classification repro-
duced in Figure 1, Hölldobler and Wilson (33) offer several
plausible explanations. When considering the adaptive significance of secondary polygyny in the ants, they argue that
two sets of ecological conditions may be relevant. "(1) The
first set is specialized on exceptionally short-lived nest
sites. Such species are opportunistic in the sense employed
by ecologists--they occupy local sites that are too small or
unstable to support entire large colonies with life cycles
and behavioral patterns dependent on monogyny. (2) The
second adaptation is specialization on habitats--entire habitats, as opposed merely to nest sites--that are long lived,
patchily distributed, and large enough to support large populations. The two forms of specialization are not mutually
exclusive; some ant species, for example Iridomyrmex humilis

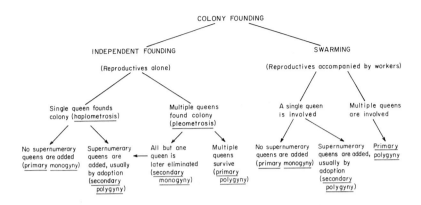

FIG. 1 - An elementary classification of colony founding and later colony composition, with reference to the number of queens.

and Pheidole megacephala, possess both." The reader is referred to Hölldobler and Wilson (33) for further elucidation of the relevant ecological parameters. Under certain circumstances (see above, as in Polistes) individuals may be unable to found colonies alone; several animals may need to cooperate and primary polygyny will evolve. An additional hymenopteran example to Polistes is provided by the honey-pot ant, Myrmecocystus mimicus, where three or four queens are necessary to produce honey storage castes within the short period of the rainy season. The queens (who are unlikely to be relatives) cooperate in this venture, each producing a supply of workers who subsequently and cooperatively eject all but one of the queens (B. Hölldobler, personal communication). An adaptive explanation for this behavior is obscure, though the rejected queens can remain near the colony and might reenter if the old queen dies.

Recently, several papers and reviews have considered the environmental conditions (and the taxonomic constraints) under which group living is favored and, as a consequence, how any one of a variety of breeding systems can evolve among vertebrates (17, 22, 52). Particularly relevant to the present discussion is Emlen and Oring's (22) distinction between resource defense and mate defense breeding systems; it has recently been argued (27) that the dispersing sex (and therefore the one that is least likely to benefit from kin associations) is likely to be the male when the breeding system is one of female defense and the female when the system is based on resource defense by the male. This fits the gross picture of female-biased movement in birds and male dispersal in mammals. Whether the exceptions are also explained is a matter for speculation at present.

We finish on a note of speculation. When considering the conditions likely to favor kin association and kin cooperation, it is important to examine the reasons for grouping in the first place. We might profitably distinguish between conditions under which mutualism does not involve costs to other conspecifics and those where it does involve such costs (R. Wrangham, personal communication and in preparation). In the latter case, kin associations will be more strongly favored. This will be especially true when the costs of migration and exclusion from group membership are high. Other relevant factors are likely to include the costs involved within particular interactive situations; for a given benefit conferred on a recipient, a donor is more likely to help when the costs are high if the recipient is related (a straightforward application of kin selection theory).

REFERENCES

(1) Alexander, R.D. 1974. The evolution of social
     behavior. Annual Review of Ecology and Systematics
     5: 325-383.

(2) Alexander, R.D., and Borgia, G. 1978. Group selection,
     altruism, and the levels of organization of life.
     Annual Review of Ecology and Systematics 9: 449-474.

(3) Anderson, R.M., and May, R.M. 1979a. Population
     biology of infectious diseases: I. Nature 280:
     361-367.

(4) Anderson, R.M., and May, R.M. 1979b. Population biology
     of infectious diseases: II. Nature 280: 455-461.

(5) Bartz, S.H. 1979. Evolution of eusociality in termites.
     Proceedings of the National Academy of Sciences, U.S.A.
     76: 5764-5768.

(6) Bateson, P.P.G. 1978. Sexual imprinting and optimal
     outbreeding. Nature 273: 659-660.

(7) Bateson, P.P.G. 1979. How do sensitive periods arise
     and what are they for? Animal Behaviour 27: 470-486.

(8) Bertram, B.C.R. 1976. Kin selection in lions and in
     evolution. In Growing Points in Ethology, eds. P.P.G.
     Bateson and R.A. Hinde, pp. 281-301. Cambridge:
     University Press.

(9) Bischof, N. 1975. Comparative ethology in incest
     avoidance. In Biosocial Anthropology, ed. R. Fox,
     pp. 37-67. London: Malaby Press.

(10) Bygott, G.D.; Bertram, B.C.R.; and Hanby, J.P. 1979.
     Male lions in large coalitions gain reproductive
     advantages. Nature 282: 839-841.

(11) Chagnon, N.A. 1979. Mate competition favoring close
     kin and village fissioning among the Yąnomamö Indians.
     In Evolutionary Biology and Human Social Behavior: An
     Anthropological Perspective, eds. N.A. Chagnon and W.
     Irons, pp. 86-132. North Scituate, Mass.: Duxbury Press.

(12) Charnov, E.L. 1978. Evolution of eusocial behavior:
     offspring choice or parental parasitism. Journal of
     Theoretical Biology 75: 451-465.

(13) Chepko-Sade, B.D. 1974. Division of group F at Cayo
     Santiago. American Journal of Physical Anthropology
     41: 472.

(14) Chepko-Sade, B.D. 1979. Monkey group splits up. New
     Scientist 82: 348-350.

(15) Chepko-Sade, B.D., and Olivier, T.J. 1979. Coefficient of genetic relationship and the probability of intra-genealogical fission in Macaca mulatta. Behavioral Ecology and Sociobiology 5: 263-278.

(16) Chepko-Sade, B.D., and Sade, D.S. 1979. Patterns of group splitting within matrilineal kinship groups: a study of social group structures in Macaca mulatta (Cercopithecidae: Primates). Behavioral Ecology and Sociobiology 5: 67-86.

(17) Clutton-Brock, T.H., and Harvey, P.H. 1976. Evolutionary rules and primate societies. In Growing Points in Ethology, eds. P.P.G. Bateson and R.A. Hinde, pp. 195-237. Cambridge: University Press.

(18) Clutton-Brock, T.H., and Harvey, P.H. 1978. Mammals, resources and reproductive strategies. Nature 273: 191-195.

(19) Craig, R. 1979. Parental manipulation, kin selection, and the evolution of altruism. Evolution 33: 319-334.

(20) Dawkins, R. 1979. Twelve misunderstandings of kin selection. Zeitschrift für Tierpsychologie 51: 184-200.

(21) Emlen, S.T. 1978. Cooperative breeding. In Behavioral Ecology: An Evolutionary Approach, eds. J.R. Krebs and N.B. Davies, pp. 245-281. Oxford: Blackwell.

(22) Emlen, S.T., and Oring, L.W. 1977. Ecology, sexual selection and the evolution of mating systems. Science 197: 215-223.

(23) Fagen, R.M. 1976. Three-generation family conflict. Animal Behaviour 24: 874-879.

(24) Furuya, Y. 1968. On the fission of troops of Japanese monkeys: 1. Five fissions and social changes between 1955 and 1966 in the Gagyusan troop. Primates 9: 323-350.

(25) Furuya, Y. 1969. On the fission of troops of Japanese monkeys: 2. General view of troop fission in Japanese monkeys. Primates 10: 47-69.

(26) Furuya, Y. 1973. Fissions in the Gagyusan colony of Japanese monkeys. In Behavioral Regulators of Behavior in Primates, ed. C. R. Carpenter, pp. 234-258. New Jersey: Bucknell University Press.

(27) Greenwood, P.J. 1980. Mating systems, philopatry and dispersal in birds and mammals. Animal Behaviour, in press.

(28) Greenwood, P.J.; Harvey, P.H.; and Perrins, C.M. 1978. Inbreeding and dispersal in the great tit. Nature 271: 52-54.

(29) Hamilton, W.D. 1963. The evolution of altruistic behavior. American Naturalist 97: 354-356.

(30) Hamilton, W.D. 1964. The genetical evolution of social behaviour, I, II. Journal of Theoretical Biology 7: 1-52.

(31) Hamilton, W.D. 1972. Altruism and related phenomena, mainly in social insects. Annual Review of Ecology and Systematics 3: 193-232.

(32) Harvey, P.H., and Greenwood, P.J. 1978. Anti-predator defence strategies: some evolutionary problems. In Behavioural Ecology: An Evolutionary Approach, eds. J.R. Krebs and N.B. Davies, pp. 129-151. Oxford: Blackwell.

(33) Hölldobler, B., and Wilson, E.O. 1977. The number of queens: an important trait in ant evolution. Naturwissenschaften 64: 8-15.

(34) Hrdy, S.B. 1977. The Langurs of Abu. Cambridge, Mass.: Harvard University Press.

(35) Koford, C. 1966. Population changes in rhesus monkeys, 1960-1965. Tulane Study of Zoology 13: 1-7.

(36) Koyama, N. 1970. Changes in dominance rank and division of a wild Japanese monkey troop in Arashiyama. Primates 11: 335-390.

(37) Krebs, J.R., and Davies, N.B. 1978. Behavioural Ecology: An Evolutionary Approach. Oxford: Blackwell.

(38) Linsenmair, K.E. 1972. Die Bedeutung familienspezifischer "Abzeichen" für den Familienzusammenhalt bei der monogamous Wüstenassel Hemilepistus reanmuri Audoin u. Savigny. Zeitschrift für Tierpsychologie 31: 131-162.

(39) McCracken, G.F., and Bradbury, J.W. 1977. Paternity and genetic heterogeneity in the polygynous bat, Phyllostomus hastatus. Science 198: 303-306.

(40) Missakian, E.A. 1973. The timing of fission among free-ranging rhesus monkeys. American Journal of Physical Anthropology 38: 621-626.

(41) Nash, L.T. 1976. Troop fission in free-ranging baboons in the Gombe Stream National Park. American Journal of Physical Anthropology 44: 63-77.

(42) Packer, C.R. 1979. Inter-troop transfer and inbreeding avoidance in Papio anubis. Animal Behaviour 27: 1-36.

(43) Pusey, A. 1979. Intercommunity transfer of chimpanzees
     in Gombe National Park. In The Great Apes, eds. D.A.
     Hamburg and E.R. McCown, pp. 465-479. Menlo Park, CA:
     Benjamin/Cummings.

(44) Ralls, K.; Brugger, K.; and Ballou, J. 1979. Inbreed-
     ing and juvenile mortality in small populations of
     ungulates. Science 206: 1101-1103.

(45) Seger, J. 1976. Evolution of responses to relative homo-
     zygosity. Nature 262: 578-580.

(46) Shepher, J. 1980. Incest: The Biosocial View. New York:
     Garland Press.

(47) Sherman, P.W. 1979. Insect chromosome numbers and eu-
     sociality. American Naturalist 113: 925-935.

(48) Trivers, R.L. 1971. The evolution of reciprocal altruism.
     Quarterly Review of Biology 46: 35-57.

(49) Trivers, R.L. 1974. Parent-offspring conflict. American
     Zoologist 14: 249-264.

(50) Vehrencamp, S. 1980. The role of individual, kin and
     group selection in the evolution of sociality. In Handbook
     of Behavioral Neurobiology, Social Behavior and Communica-
     tion, eds. P. Marler and J.G. Vandenbergh, vol. 3, pp. 351-
     394. New York: Plenum Press.

(51) Waldman, B., and Adler, K. 1979. Toad tadpoles associate
     preferentially with siblings. Nature 282: 611-613.

(52) Wrangham, R.W. 1977. Feeding behaviour of chimpanzees in
     Gombe National Park, Tanzania. In Primate Ecology: Studies
     of Feeding and Ranging Behaviour in Lemurs, Monkeys and Apes,
     ed. T.H. Clutton-Brock, pp. 503-538. London: Academic Press.

Group on <u>Measuring Fitness in Social Systems</u> - Seated, left to right: Jerram Brown, Mildred Dickemann, Donald Sade, John Bonner. Standing: Frank McKinney, Bob Metcalf, Ulli Reyer, Eric Charnov, John Krebs, Tom Olivier.

Evolution of Social Behavior: Hypotheses and Empirical Tests, ed. H. Markl,
pp. 205-218. Dahlem Konferenzen 1980. Weinheim: Verlag Chemie GmbH.

Measuring Fitness in Social Systems
Group Report

J. R. Krebs, Rapporteur
J. T. Bonner, J. L. Brown, E. L. Charnov,
M. Dickemann, F. McKinney, R. A. Metcalf,
T. J. Olivier, H. U. Reyer, D. S. Sade

INTRODUCTION

The aim of this report is to discuss a number of problems which
relate to field tests of ideas about the evolution of social
behavior. After a very brief introductory discussion of the
notion of inclusive fitness, the report deals with the following
topics: studies of aid-giving in birds and social insects, some
alternative biological systems for studying the evolution of cooperation and conflict, the comparative method for studying
adaptation, and some problems which arise in trying to use the
idea of evolutionarily stable strategies in field studies.

SOME COMMENTS ON INCLUSIVE FITNESS

Direct and Indirect Fitness

Many field studies of sociobiological ideas involve making some
kind of estimate of fitness. The idea that individuals can
propagate their genes via relatives other than direct descendants (embodied in Hamilton's concept of inclusive fitness) is
central to studies of the evolution of social behavior. It is
sometimes useful to think of inclusive fitness as being made up
of two major components, 'direct' (measured in terms of genes in
direct descendants) and 'indirect' (measured as genes propagated
through other relatives), and some field studies have attempted
to assess the relative importance of these two components.

The value of the distinction between direct and indirect fitness is still controversial. Some members of the group argued that it is valuable because it allows one to ask questions about the difference made by the indirect component in explaining observed behavior (Brown). Brown also argues that the term 'direct' is appropriate for the component of fitness dependent on production of offspring because the genetic path linking parent to offspring is shorter than that linking sibling to sibling, even though the end result in terms of relatedness is usually identical. In the case of a mother in a species with internal fertilization, the relationship with offspring is more certain than that with siblings, but this is not necessarily true for males, or females with external fertilization.

The distinction between direct and indirect fitness was criticized on two grounds (Krebs). First it is somewhat arbitrary from the genetical standpoint. Since full siblings are just as closely related to one another as are parents and offspring, there is no genetic reason for treating parents and offspring as a special case. It is true that parental care is much more common and in historical perspective better known, than sibling care. But the answer to the question of why parental care is much more common is more likely to be related to ecological constraints than to genetic mechanisms. Second, the terms direct and indirect are sometimes taken to imply that direct fitness is in some way a more straightforward mechanism of evolutionary change. People talk of "resorting to indirect fitness if classical (direct) explanations won't do." As explained above, the distinction is meant to refer to the number of steps in the pathways linking two individuals genetically and not to the effectiveness of the two routes in bringing about evolutionary change.

Relatedness
The extent to which an aid-giver gains a contribution to its indirect fitness depends partly on the coefficient of a relationship (r) between donor and recipient. Occasionally a confusion

has arisen about the use of r. It is sometimes said, for
example, that if all the members of a species share about 90%
of their genes, they should all be altruistic to one another.
The fallacy of this argument can be illustrated as follows. If
an aid-giver donates benefit at random to other members of the
population, there is on average an equal increment in fitness
to all genotypes, so that no evolutionary change occurs. Only
as a result of differential increments in fitness will gene frequencies change. Therefore, regardless of the overall degree of
genetic similarity between members of a population, an altruistic trait will spread only if altruism is dispensed preferentially to close relatives.

Measuring Fitness and Relatedness

Although theoretical discussions of fitness usually refer to
differential survival of genes or genotypes, most field workers
measure survival and reproduction of individuals. There are
many problems inherent in using approximate estimates of fitness
(8), one of which is that of how to combine different components
such as survival and reproductive success into an aggregate
measure of inclusive fitness. Usually the measure adopted in a
study is constrained more by practical problems than by theoretical considerations. This raises the general question of whether
sociobiologists should focus their attention exclusively on
systems which are tractable for measuring fitness.

Two main methods have been used in assessing coefficients of
relatedness: direct studies of family pedigrees and genetic
markers identified by electrophoresis. The latter method has the
advantage of being quicker, but its accuracy may be limited if
only a few polymorphisms can be identified. The pedigree method
may give misleading results if paternity is unknown (see Harvey
et al., this volume).

FIELD STUDIES OF COOPERATIVE BEHAVIOR IN BIRDS AND INSECTS

Among the classical case histories of sociobiological field
studies are numerous investigations of cooperative behavior in

Hymenoptera and birds. Some of the disagreements which have
arisen as a result of these studies have stemmed from a confusion between the different types of questions which have been
addressed. The aim of such studies is not to 'test the theory
of kin selection' or distinguish between the theories of 'kin
selection' and 'individual selection.' Individual selection is
the special case of kin selection in which the kin are offspring,
so the two hypotheses are not mutually exclusive alternatives.

So what are the aims of studies of cooperative behavior in birds
and insects? Four closely related but distinct aims are often
confused: (a) to determine the relative importance of direct and
indirect contributions to inclusive fitness, (b) to ask ecological questions about the selection pressures which have determined the importance of direct and indirect components of fitness, (c) to speculate about the evolutionary origin of cooperative sociality, and (d) to identify alternative strategies or
decisions open to an individual in a social group. While it is
clear that most published studies have at least touched on more
than one of these questions, for the purposes of discussion it
will be helpful to consider them separately.

Determining the Relative Importance of Direct and Indirect Components of Fitness

Consider a bird such as the Florida Scrub Jay, in which a male
may spend the first part of his life helping his parents to rear
young (i.e., rear his younger siblings) and later on acquire his
own territory and become a breeder (5).

One can ask how much genetic profit such a male gains as a
result of helping collateral relatives (usually siblings) and
as a result of rearing direct descendants. The question can be
posed as a 'decision' facing a young male at the beginning of a
breeding season, in which case it is necessary to estimate the
following quantities in order to calculate the solution. If the
individual decides to help, it expects to make an immediate
gain of indirect fitness (production of siblings) and a future

gain, of indirect fitness (e.g., increase in skill at helping
in the future). If the male chooses to breed, it expects to
make an immediate direct gain in terms of offspring and a future
direct gain which might, for example, reflect an increase in
future breeding success as a consequence of experience. Some
future direct gain might also accrue to a helper if, for example,
the probability of gaining a territory in the future is greater
when surrounded by more younger siblings, or if experience
gained by helping improves future skill as a parent. The aim
of many studies of helping in birds has been to ask whether
helpers gain more from future direct or immediate indirect fitness. The relative importance of these two components may
determine whether one characterizes the helping as 'altruistic'
(indirect gain is the major factor) or mutualistic/selfish
(future direct gain is the major factor) (Brown, this volume).
In some birds it may be possible to completely separate the two
components. For example, in the Pied Kingfisher (16) some helpers
are kin and others are unrelated to the breeding pair.

Metcalf's work on Polistes wasps (10,11) provides a good example
of how components of fitness have been measured in a social
insect. Polistes wasps may found nests as solitary individuals
or as pairs of sisters. In a pair, one individual (the α or
dominant) does all, or virtually all, the reproduction, but the
second or β female contributes to nest building and maintenance.
Metcalf estimated fitness by measuring the relative success in
passing on genes of β, α, and solitary foundresses. His
results showed that an α foundress has a significantly higher
expected success than a β female, but that the β and solitary
females do about equally well. The measure of fitness involved
estimates of the coefficients of relatedness (using isozyme techniques) between members of a foundress pair and the number of
offspring produced by pair and solitary foundresses. Pairs of
females sharing the same nest are related on the average by 0.63,
and the calculations show that a β female's gene contribution
to the next generation is about 90% as a result of helping her
sister and 10% the result of direct production of offspring.
The study allows us to draw two conclusions. For β females

indirect fitness is a major component of inclusive fitness, and
β females would do no better by founding nests as solitary individuals, given that they are condemned to be βs.

The study of Metcalf was done in Illinois, and a parallel study
in Kansas revealed slight differences. In Illinois, pair nests
produced about twice as many offspring as solitary nests and had
a higher survival rate up to the time of reproduction. In
Kansas, however, group nests produced no more offspring than
those of solitary females, but the young emerging from group
nests matured earlier. It is not yet possible to say whether
the general conclusions from Metcalf's study also apply to the
Kansas population (Michener, personal communication).

Ecological Questions about Helping

One of the conclusions drawn from studies of helpers in territorial birds has been that helping tends to occur in saturated
habitats where young males have little chance to establish a
territory. This is an answer to a question about ecological
pressures which might lead to the evolution of helping and is
to some extent distinct from the type of question discussed in
the previous section.   The distinction can perhaps be illustrated by referring back to Metcalf's study of Polistes wasps.
While Metcalf addressed the question of how different kinds of
foundresses pass on their genes to the next generation, he did
not consider the question of why some females are solitary and
others are pair foundresses. One answer might be in terms of
habitat quality. If all suitable nest sites are occupied by
females, a newly arriving queen may have no choice but to join
another. This hypothesis, which might for example be tested by
removal of nests from occupied sites, refers to the ecological
conditions which favor joining as opposed to solitary nesting.
Ecological questions about helping have been more often posed
in bird studies than in studies of social insects.

The Evolutionary Origins of Cooperation

By its very nature this is a rather intractable question. There
has been more discussion of this problem in relation to the

eusocial Hymenoptera than for birds. One argument sometimes
used to favor the idea that eusociality in insects arose as a
result of parental manipulation is that many of the proximate
mechanisms of social communication in hymenopteran colonies are
such that the queen appears to be in control. For example,
worker reproduction can be suppressed by chemical cues from the
queen. Another line of argument is that the queen in primitively social bees and wasps is clearly more different from a typical solitary hymenopteran than are the workers. The queen has
relatively larger ovaries, has specialized behavior and lives
longer than solitary female hymenopterans, perhaps suggesting
that she has evolved specifically in the direction of parental
manipulation.

A more fundamental approach to the problem is to make a genetic
model of the evolution of parent-offspring conflict and ask
whether there are any particular reasons for supposing that
either parents or offspring will 'win' in an evolutionary race.

The answer seems to be that there is usually no particular genetic asymmetry which would favor the evolution of either parental
or offspring dominance. Genetic models suggest that the evolutionarily stable state will usually be a compromise (14,16).
Such models also underline the fact that 'parental manipulation'
and 'kin selection' should not be considered as alternative
hypotheses. As mentioned earlier, kin selection is a general
statement about routes of gene propagation, and parental manipulation is a special case within this framework. However practical considerations might often play an overriding role in
determining the outcome of parent-offspring conflict. Sexual
incompatibility mechanisms in plants (9) can be viewed as examples of parental manipulation; parent plants prevent pollen
grains from fertilizing their sisters. Presumably there is an
asymmetry in practical power which enables parental domination
in this case. As an example of offspring domination Williams
(18) cites the fact that parents appear to be unable to control
the sex ratio of their offspring in ways which would be adaptive
to the parent.

Charnov (3) has pointed out that there may be a special kind of
asymmetry in the evolutionary origin of sociality in wasps.
Imagine a hypothetical queen which manipulates her daughters to
stay at home and rear younger siblings. The daughters are
equally related to their own offspring and their full siblings
(assuming a 50:50 sex ratio) so that there is no penalty to the
daughters for looking after younger siblings. This holds as
long as the queen can provide each daughter with as many eggs
as she herself could produce, and the 'willingness' of daughters
to be manipulated may increase if good nest sites are in short
supply. The queen, however, gains a genetic advantage from per-
suading daughters to help, because she exchanges grandchildren
($r = 0.25$) for children ($r = 0.5$). Thus at the point of origin
of eusocial behavior there could be selection for parental
domination with no selection for offspring resistance to manipulation. This does not in any way contradict Trivers' and
Hare's (17) suggestion that after the establishment of eusociality workers might successfully retaliate and manipulate the
sex ratio in their favor.

Identifying Alternative Strategies

This question is discussed in more detail in the section on
ESSs. The point can be illustrated with reference to Metcalf's
wasps. In the earlier discussions it was assumed that the
alternative strategies open to an individual are solitary α and
β . It is possible, however, that the alternatives are 'found
a nest' and 'take over a nest.' Individuals adopting the second
strategy might sometimes end up as β females and sometimes as
solitary females. Although it seems very unlikely that this
interpretation is correct for Polistes, a similar argument has
been used to account for shared nesting in the great golden
digger wasp (Sphex ichneumoneus) (2). The general point is that
any study of the costs and benefits of cooperative behavior has
to make assumptions about the strategies available to an individual.

ALTERNATIVE SYSTEMS FOR STUDYING THE EVOLUTION OF COOPERATION
AND CONFLICT

The principles of Hamilton's kin selection theory can be applied
outside the conventional contexts of helping and cooperation in
animals.   Two possible systems which might be rewarding to study
from this perspective are the endosperm and embryo sac of higher
plants and the slime molds.

Embryo Sacs

The triploid endosperm of higher plants is usually formed by the
fusion of two meiotic products of the female and a sperm.   The
zygote is as usual formed by the fusion of one female meiotic
product (the egg) and a sperm.   The egg and the female contribution to the endosperm are often genetically identical because
all three cells arise by mitosis from one cell formed through
meiosis.   The male's contribution to the endosperm is genetically identical to the sperm which fertilizes the egg.   The role
of the endosperm is to 'feed' the developing zygote.   While it
has the potential to develop into a whole plant itself, the
endosperm so to speak altruistically sacrifices itself for the
zygote, to which it is very closely related.   However, sometimes
the female gene contribution to the endosperm is not identical
to that of the ovum, and it might be interesting to compare
plants with different degrees of relatedness between endosperm
and zygote.   The phenomenon could also perhaps be viewed as an
example of parent-offpring conflict.   Perhaps the parent plant
sets up an initial asymmetry such that the endosperm is condemned not to grow into an adult plant and can only increase
its inclusive fitness by feeding the zygote.   These are outrage-
ous speculations, but the point is that questions about conflict
and cooperation between close relatives might profitably be
studied in the system (4).

Slime Molds

Slime molds show apparent sacrifice when a group of cells aggre-
gates to form a fruiting body.   Some individuals (about 25% of
cells) form the stalk of a fruiting body and die, while others

form the spores and perpetuate their genes. Each cell has the
potential to become a stalk or a spore up to the moment of
fruiting body formation. Little is known about the genetic
relatedness of slime mold aggregations in the field, but in the
laboratory, they may be members of the same clone or genetically
mixed. In one study (1,6), a mutant which tended to get itself
in a position to form spores was identified. The mutant did
not, surprisingly, increase in frequency in the population,
presumably because it did less well at another stage in its life
cycle. Slime molds may provide in many respects an ideal model
system for studying aid-giving and indirect fitness (13).

COMPARISON BETWEEN SPECIES
Comparative studies of closely related species provided the
first clear indication of how social groups might be influenced
by ecological pressures. Among the advantages of comparative
studies are the following. They may help to identify possible
strategies. If species B, a close relative of A, has a particular trait (e.g., living in groups), it might be reasonable to
propose that the trait is an evolutionary option that has been
open to A. A second contribution of comparative studies has
been to generate hypotheses and identify questions. Much of the
experimental work attempting to relate group living to dispersion of food and the influence of predators uses ideas generated
by comparative studies. Questions such as why apes have abnor-
mally large home ranges for their body size, or why terrestrial
monkeys have exceptionally small home ranges in relation to
their daily matabolic needs would not have been recognized without comparative surveys of home range size, body size, and meta-
bolic requirements of primates. Among the limitations of comparative studies are the problems of disentangling cause and
effect, the choice of taxonomic units for comparison, and the
fact that most of the interpretations and hypotheses tested are
qualitative rather than quantitative.

EVOLUTIONARILY STABLE STRATEGIES (ESS) IN THE FIELD
One of the most important theoretical developments in sociobiology during the last few years has been the realization that the

costs and benefits of alternative behavior patterns may be frequency dependent. When two or more ways of achieving the same
end are observed, we have to consider the possibility that the
two strategies coexist in stable equilibrium because of frequency
dependent benefits. For example, if males of particular species
could obtain matings either by defence of a mating territory or
by sneaking, it is possible that the payoffs for the two strategies are equal at an equilibrium mixture (too many sneakers
favors defense, with too many defenders, sneaking is favored).
Without going into the intricacies of the theory it is worth
making three points about the attempts to test ESS ideas in the
field. The first is that such exercises should not be viewed
as attempts to test ESS theory. The theory is used as a tool to
generate ideas about the frequency dependent costs and benefits
associated with alternative strategies. The second point is a
methodological one. If the prediction of an ESS model is that
the net payoff for two or more alternative strategies is equal,
the investigator is faced with the difficult task of trying to
demonstrate that there is no difference between a number of sets
of measurements (e.g., the number of matings achieved by sneakers
and guarders). Since the null hypothesis is usually that there
is no difference between the groups of measurements, it may be
difficult to convince a skeptic that one has actually demonstrated equal payoffs. An alternative, and more powerful test of an
ESS hypothesis might be to perturb the frequencies of the alternative strategies away from the hypothesized equilibrium and
predict that the payoffs should be frequency dependent. In this
connection it is perhaps worth emphasizing the distinction
between cases in which the two strategies coexist in equilibrium
(mixed ESS) and the case where one strategy has a higher payoff,
and the other can be viewed as making the best of a bad job.
Thus sneakers could in some species be young males with no
chance of setting up their own territories but an occasional
chance of stealing a copulation. One of the tasks facing field
workers is to distinguish between this case and that of a mixed
ESS.

The third problem is one of correctly identifying the strategies.
This point can be illustrated by referring to the bluegill sunfish (Gross, in preparation). There are three kinds of breeding
male sunfish within a population, small (sneakers), medium
(satellites), and large (territorial) males. However, an analysis of the life history reveals that the three behavior types
result from two strategies. One strategy is to postpone breeding until the age of about seven years and then become a large
breeder. The alternative is to start breeding at the age of two
and pass through the small and middle sizes before dying at the
age of about five years. The decision point is at the age of
two, and the strategies are to postpone reproduction and grow,
or to reproduce early and grow less. Calculations suggest that
the two strategies coexist as an ESS.

Conclusions

This report has described some of the problems which have arisen
in trying to carry out field tests of sociobiological hypotheses.
There are a number of further points which are important but
have not been discussed, for example the question of whether
technical limitations in the ability of field workers to measure
fitness will set limits on testing hypotheses. The discussion
has not referred to trait group selection as a mechanism for the
evolution of aid-giving behavior (19). In one case, trait group
selection might have been important in the evolution of sex
ratios (8) and recent studies of migration between rhesus monkey
groups suggest that genetic isolation of groups may be greater
than previously thought (12).

Finally, a comment about applying sociobiological arguments to
human populations. At the moment most tests of sociobiological
theories with animals have been qualitative, and the same applies
with even greater force to human studies. However, there is
often a superficial concordance between qualitative predictions
of sociobiological theories and observations of human behavior.
This might suggest a hint of cautious optimism for the future
studies of human behavior using the neo-Darwinian framework.

REFERENCES

(1)   Bonner, J.T.   1959.   Differentiation in social amoebae.
      Sci. Am. 201 (No. 6): 152-162.

(2)   Brockmann, H.J.; Grafen, A.; and Dawkins, R.   1979.   Evolu-
      tionarily stable nesting strategy in a digger wasp.   J.
      theor. Biol. 77: 473-496.

(3)   Charnov, E.L.   1978.   Evolution of eusocial behaviour:
      offspring choice or parental parasitism.   J. theor. Biol.
      75: 457-465.

(4)   Charnov, E.L.   1979.   Simultaneous hermaphroditism and
      sexual selection.   Proc. Natl. Acad. Sci. USA 76: 2480-
      2484.

(5)   Emlen, S.T.   1978.   The evolution of cooperative breeding
      in birds.   In Behavioural Ecology, An Evolutionary Approach,
      eds. J.R. Krebs and N.B. Davies, pp. 245-281.   Oxford:
      Blackwells.

(6)   Filosa, M.F.   1962.   Heterocytosis in cellular slime molds.
      Am. Nat. 96: 79-92.

(7)   Hamilton, W.D.   1979.   Wingless and fighting males in fig
      wasps and other insects.   In Sexual Selection and Reproduc-
      tive Competition in Insects, eds. M.S. and N.A. Blum, pp.
      167-220.   New York: Academic Press.

(8)   Howard, R.D.   1979.   Estimating reproductive success in
      natural populations.   Am. Nat. 114: 221-231.

(9)   Lewis, D.   1979.   Sexual incompatibility in plants.   London:
      Arnold.

(10) Metcalf, R.A., and Whitt, G.S.   1977a.   Intra-nest related-
      ness in a social wasp Polistes metricus.   A genetic analysis.
      Behav. Ecol. Sociobiol. 2: 339-351.

(11) Metcalf, R.A., and Whitt, G.S.   1977b.   Relative inclusive
      fitness in the social wasp Polistes metricus.   Behav. Ecol.
      Sociobiol. 2: 353-360.

(12) Ober, C.; Olivier, T.J.; and Buettner-Janusch, J.   1980.
      Genetic aspects of migration in a rhesus monkey population.
      J. Human Evol. 9: in press.

(13) Olive, L.S.   1975.   The Mycetozoans.   New York: Academic
      Press.

(14) Parker, G.A., and McNair, M.R.   1979.   Models of parent-
      offspring conflict IV Suppression: evolutionary retaliation
      by the parent. Anim. Behav. 27: 1210-1235.

(15) Reyer, H.U. 1980. Flexible helper structure as an
      ecological adaptation in the Pied Kingfisher (Ceryle
      rudis rudis L.). Behav. Ecol. Sociobiol. 6: 219-228.

(16) Stamps, J.A.; Metcalf, R.A.; and Krishnan, V. 1978. A
      genetic analysis of parent-offspring conflict. Behav.
      Ecol. Sociobiol. 3: 369-392.

(17) Trivers, R.L., and Hare, H. 1976. Haplodiploidy and
      the evolution of the social insects. Science 191:
      249-263.

(18) Williams, G.C. 1979. The question of adaptive sex ratio
      in outcrossed vertebrates. Proc. R. Soc. Lond. B 205:
      567-580.

(19) Wilson, D.S. 1980. The natural selection of populations
      and communities. Menlo Park: Benjamin/Cummings Inc.

Group on <u>Genetics and Social Behavior</u> - Seated, left to right:
Christian Vogel, Ross Crozier, George Williams, Dorothea Brückner.
Standing: Francisco Ayala, Bengt Bengtsson, Marc Feldman,
Dick Wrangham.

Evolution of Social Behavior: Hypotheses and Empirical Tests, ed. H. Markl,
pp. 221-232. Dahlem Konferenzen 1980. Weinheim: Verlag Chemie GmbH.

Genetics and Social Behavior
Group Report

M. W. Feldman, Rapporteur
F. J. Ayala, B. Bengtsson, D. Brückner,
R. H. Crozier, C. Vogel, G. C. Williams,
R. W. Wrangham

INTRODUCTION

This group had the difficult task of attempting to determine
the extent and nature of the genetic contribution to the
variation in social behavior and its relevance to the evolutionary theory of such behavior.

The first question raised in this regard is whether comparisons
between species or other taxa in behavioral or morphological
factors might be informative. The answer is "No." It is
impossible, for example, to demonstrate that the difference
between two-leggedness and four-leggedness is genetic because
it is impossible to demonstrate experimentally genetic influences
on phenotypic differences between groups when crosses between
them cannot be made. The problem is analogous to that mentioned
by Metcalf (this volume), namely, that it is impossible to
compare fitnesses accruing to strategies some of which are not
observed. In fact, it is part of our cultural background to
assume that genetics is the underlying reason for specific
phenotypic differences between species despite the general
impossibility of proof.

The comparison of different populations of the same species
raises issues which are extremely difficult to resolve even with
optimal experimental materials. For example, in primates the
role of tradition differences between groups (transmitted cul-
turally) may be important. In general, attempts to exclude
learning as a source of behavior differences are difficult to
interpret for a number of reasons. Among them are that (a) the
distinction between environmental factors that instruct and
those required for normal development is somewhat arbitrary;
(b) the processing of its own odor or performance by the animal
of a particular action may provide the animal with relevant
information; and (c) rules of equivalence, not conceived of by
the investigator, may be used by the animal so that the investigator may not be able to insulate it from important stimuli.

Another approach to between-population differences is to correlate some easily measured genetic parameter such as heterozygosity at some enzyme loci with some behavior such as aggression. Such correlational analysis tells us nothing about cau-
sation.

The final level of variation is within populations. Here is the
true bone of contention which has bothered population geneticists for some 60 years: what is the relationship between normal phenotypic variation and genetic variation? There are some
behavioral traits which appear to vary discontinuously, but most
of the behaviors of interest to this meeting must be regarded as
varying continuously. These require the tools of quantitative
inheritance. With many discrete valued behaviors the possibility of gene-phenotype association is a priori greater than for
continuous traits. For the latter the analysis and results will
be statistical, and, unless extremely carefully planned, the
experiments cannot separate cultural from biological transmission.
Even if such a separation is statistically feasible, these tools
will not identify specific genes. This remark may be most relevant for the behavior of higher animals, but even in social
bees, as discussed by Hölldobler and Michener (this volume), the
process by which nestmates are recognized is one of imprinting

and as such would presumably involve an intricate confounding between learned and innate factors. However, if there is variation for the behavior, then, in principle, artificial selection experiments can be set up and heritability estimates made. Such statistics give no indication of mode or complexity of gene action, nor do they tell how susceptible the behavior is to environmental manipulation. For the higher animals, cross-fostering studies between different social settings under ideal conditions (e.g., using monozygous twins) may in the future contribute to our knowledge (2). In humans, such adoption studies are the only way nature-nurture differences are resolvable, but random adoption is unethical; in some primate species it might be possible and would be profitable.

A few examples exist where variation in social behavioral patterns in natural populations have a demonstrated genetic contribution, but the number is very small. In the fish Xiphophorus maculatus, Kallman and Schreibman (9) showed that a single sex-linked gene controls the approximate age of maturity. Sohn (15) demonstrated that inhibition of maturity occurs when an individual is not dominant near its genetically determined age of maturation, if a dominant individual is also present. There is an interaction between the maturity gene and the social behavior. In the crickets Teleogryllus commodus and T. oceanicus, females identify conspecific males by their song. Hoy and Paul (8) showed that F_1 hybrid females prefer the song of the hybrid male over either parental song. This implies some level of genetic influence over song recognition and transmission. In honey bees, some races clean their hives of dead nestmates while others do not. Rothenbuhler (13) showed some segregation of this behavior in crossing experiments but the evidence for his two-locus hypothesis is not conclusive.

There exist studies on inbred lines of mice which exhibit different aggression patterns and Craig et al. (4) have selected for social dominance in chickens. However, the interpretation of these data in terms of social behavior in nature is difficult to make. In a few insect species there is the possibility of

using parthenogenetic strains to generate lines completely identical by descent. Between-line studies here might even address
the neurological antecedents of behavior. The interpretation
of these experiments and extrapolation to other organisms
must be done with utmost care.

GENETIC STRUCTURE OF POPULATIONS AND VARIOUS MODES OF SELECTION
What can we learn from studying genetic structure of populations
about the action, present or past, of kin selection or other
modes of selection?

Genetic structure of populations can mean many things in population genetics: (a) pattern of heterozygosity or (b) pattern of
the number of alleles. (These two are correlated and it must
be remembered that current theory for the evolution of social
behavior applies only to the two-allele single-population situation.) (c) Actual (observable) subdivision of a population
into hives, groups of hives, etc. The effect of this, even in
the absence of true inbreeding, is to simulate a loss of overall
heterozygosity. (This is called Wahlund's effect.) It takes
very little gene flow between subpopulations to produce an
equilibrium situation which appears to be panmictic. (d) Models of gene flow generally take the migration rate to be constant
in time and ignore changes in population size. Genetic differences in the rate of dispersal are rarely treated. Any of these
factors, or even the possibility of a non-equilibrium situation
with constant migration, could produce the interesting effect
discovered by Olivier (personal communication), namely, significant gene frequency differences among neighboring groups at
the Cayo Santiago rhesus colony, and by Schwartz and Armitage
(14) in the marmot. (e) By careful experimentation, dispersal can be measured even in insects. In primates dispersal can be extremely frequent and very careful observation is
required before an apparently partitioned population can be
accepted as a set of genetic isolates. (f) Observable inbreeding: This can be measured using known pedigrees if these are
available, which is not often. Both Metcalf and Crozier (this
volume) point out that measured inbreeding is low in those eusocial Hymenoptera for which electrophoretic data are available.

In all cases the result of population structure is uneven gene
frequency distribution, but the population must be very highly
structured for this to be noticeable or important for evolution.
On the other hand, gradients over space or time in selection
pressures can be very important in determining patterns of gene
frequency. However, selection at the genetic level is very
difficult to measure.

The result of this difficulty in population genetics has led
to correlational treatments, i.e., correlations between gene
frequency variation and variation in environmental parameters
are computed. Of course, the same could be done for kinship
levels, but to allow the inference from this kind of analysis
that kin selection is operating, selective differentials must
be enormous (see Lewontin (10)). Standard errors of estimated
fitnesses are generally very high (see Metcalf, this volume).
In populations genetics, selection coefficients are measured in
terms of mating propensities, fecundities, viabilities, gametic
fitnesses, etc., by a sequence of experiments called "selection
components analysis" in a framework of high replication to reduce standard errors (see e.g., Christiansen and Frydenberg (3)).
This same level of rigor is required before the existence of
kin selection on a specific phenotype can be inferred, and even
then concomitant selection at the genetic level would be very
difficult to show.

Group selection, i.e., the extinction and recolonization of demes
promises to be even more difficult to demonstrate because in
those animals where it might be invoked, the level of migration
is very high so that extinction is unlikely. In those cases
where it has been invoked in genetics (usually cases of meiotic
drive), deeper experimentation has shown that individual selection can suffice as an explanation (e.g., Curtsinger and Feldman (7)).

Sexual selection presents some fascinating problems and may be
the most fruitful avenue for the demographic assessment of its

evolutionary importance. Observations are possible although
tedious, and since the agent of the selection often appears to
be morphological (color, size, etc.), there is some optimism
that scales of mating success can be developed and demography
carried out.

GENETIC RELATEDNESS

Even at the theoretical level, there are apparent difficulties
concerning the quantification of relatedness between individuals.
These theoretical difficulties concern the definitions of coefficients as used in modeling and speculation.

One recent definition of relatedness is that of Crozier and
Pamilo (6) (see also Crozier (5)). The relatedness of B (say,
a potential beneficiary) to A (say, a potential altruist) was
defined as

$$G_{B(A)} = \frac{\text{mean identity by descent of A's genes with the genes in B's gametes}}{\text{mean identity by descent of A's genes with the genes in A's gametes}} \cdot$$

This formula indicates the "worth" of B to A. For haploid-
diploid interactions, however, as in Hymenoptera, a further weight-
ing of $\nu = 1$ for males and $\nu = 2$ for females is required:

$$G'_{B(A)} = G_{B(A)} \cdot \frac{\nu_B}{\nu_A}.$$

How can we estimate relatedness between individuals in natural
populations? One way is to determine the pedigrees involved
and from the G (or other coefficient) values derive the average
relatedness between individuals for the categories involved.
But this way is not open if we cannot obtain this pedigree information, such as when we deal with larger multi-lineage
groups (including many mammal and some social insect species).
If we obtain genotypic data on individuals in these groups, we
can follow up a suggestion of Orlove (11) and estimate the regression coefficient of relatedness by using either the genetic
similarity between the individuals of interest or, as Pamilo

and Crozier have done (manuscript in preparation), between
each individual and the rest of its group.

The regression used here depends on there being two alleles
per locus and Hardy-Weinberg equilibrium. Further statistical
analysis concerning departures from these limitations would
be most desirable. The pedigree and regression methods each
have characteristic strengths and weaknesses besides those
just mentioned:

Pedigree:
   (a)   An estimate is possible even if only one group is
         available.
   (b)   If the pedigree information does not go back far
         enough, relatedness may be severely underestimated.
         How far back one should go is very difficult to pre-
         dict in the absence of precise knowledge about the
         degree of inbreeding in progenitors, which might it-
         self change over time.
   (c)   As the number of lineages per colony increases, the
         data become harder to obtain and the analysis increas-
         ingly more difficult and, ultimately, impossible.

Regression:
   (a)   One group alone is useless; a number (say, at least 20)
         is needed for analysis.
   (b)   While the pedigree method potentially gives an exact
         result, the regression method always yields an estimate
         with confidence intervals.
   (c)   Low levels of genic polymorphism in many vertebrates
         and Hymenoptera may reduce the applicability of this
         method; use of several loci is advisable.
   (d)   If several loci are used, tests for homogeneity of the
         estimates can be applied. Heterogeneity may imply
         selection but could conceivably result from linkage.

The spatial distribution of related groups may be important.
Pamilo and Varvio-Aho (12) found adjacent Formica sanguinea

nests to be highly related. Such findings imply that competition effects cannot readily be directed at non-relatives, unless
special behavioral mechanisms occur to guarantee this.

GENETIC CONSEQUENCES OF SOCIAL STRUCTURE

Selection and drift (gene flow) are the main evolutionary mechanisms which result from the mating structure of a population.
The effect of these mechanisms depends on the effective size,
the spatial dimensions of the population, and the mating pattern within the population. These parameters, particularly the
social pattern of the population, affect the gene frequency
distribution during consecutive generations and hence evolutionary process by causing departures from random mating. It may
be useful to look at these phenomena differentiating between
intergroup mechanisms and intragroup mechanisms. Of course,
social barriers may not always result in genetic isolation.
Intercaste concubinage and interdeme wife capture are examples
of behaviors which mediate genetic mixing despite the social
disguise.

Intergroup Mechanisms

Size and spacing of social groups in terms of reproductive units
are important factors influencing the genetic structure. Territoriality or home range distribution of social subunits of a
population are especially important cases of spatial heterogeneity. As Baker and Marler (this volume) point out, defensibility of food resources and/or mates appears to be important
in determining such mating patterns. The relative isolation of
resulting subunits of a population may cause diversification.
There are several social mechanisms (e.g., communication systems)
which can produce and maintain the subdivision of populations.
These are opposed by migration between reproductive subunits.
The pattern as well as the intensity of these variables is
severely influenced by ecological conditions and, what concerns
us here, by the pattern and mechanisms of the social structure
of the reproductive units or subunits.

Intragroup Mechanisms

The social pattern of reproductive units has an essential impact on the degree of relatedness within these groups as well as on the distribution of kin throughout the population. The degree of relatedness is a consequence of the structure of the social unit. The main types of mating systems have been described in typological terms such as monogamy, polygamy, polyandry, and promiscuity (most commonly among mammals and birds in the form of so-called "patterned promiscuity").

These systems may or may not be species-specific and may or may not be special adaptations for ecological conditions. For example, special types of social structure might lead to competition for mates which in turn could lead to selection on the components of this competition. Thus to estimate the degree of selective forces, monitored by social structure, it would be necessary at least to know the proportion of each sex-class which is really reproducing.

If there are stable rank hierarchies of one or both sexes and if the reproductive success of a given individual is correlated with its position within this rank order, the gene frequency distribution within the consecutive generations will probably shift to somewhat higher frequencies of genes directly or indirectly (even by chance!) associated with higher rank.

The distribution of kin (e.g., siblings) is monitored by social structure. Dispersal is often sex-biased: for instance, in primates migrants are mostly males, in birds females (see Baker and Marler, this volume). In primates immigrant males seem to be favored as mates over home-born males, thus decreasing inbreeding. There are many special mechanisms of (direct) incest-avoidance. For example, in primates: (a) in monogamous forms the offspring has to leave the native family before becoming sexually mature (gibbons), or it remains infertile as an adult (marmosets), thus giving them the opportunity to become something like "helpers at the nest"; (b) in polygynous systems,

tenureship of the only reproductive male on the order of magnitude short enough to prevent father-daughter incest (Presbytis
entellus) is limited, juvenile females are "stolen" by outgroup
males (hamadryas) or juvenile males have to leave their native
troop, thus avoiding son-mother as well as intersibling incest.
Such social factors must be important contributors to the rate
and direction of evolutionary change.

It should be remembered that some social structures such as those
which promote inbreeding or reduced population size will have
different effects from others such as stable rank hierarchies
which, at the level of the whole population, may have only slight
influences on gene frequencies.

In humans, social systems are presumably of importance in producing and maintaining genetic differences between populations.
Castes, religions, races, or socioeconomic factors can contribute to the maintenance of partitions in such a way that gene
frequencies for blood groups, proteins, and diseases can differ
widely. The adoption of Western eating habits has (presumably)
contributed to a higher rate of hypercholesterolemia in Japan.
Any heritable component of this disease must therefore be subject to this dietary influence, and the same can be said for
coeliac disease and lactose intolerance. Marriage between relatives, perhaps inspired by economic considerations (as appears
to occur in some Middle Eastern societies), results in an increase
of genetic diseases. Different linguistic groups of the Yanamamö
or Bougainville Islanders have different gene frequencies. A
similar situation has been described by Baker (1) for song dialect
and genes in California populations of the white-crowned song
sparrow. In humans, at least, it is highly unlikely that the
genes studied influence language.

OPTIMIZATION THEORY AND POPULATION GENETICS
In the analysis of genetic systems themselves, i.e., the properties of meiosis, of mutation, of sex-ratio, the past ten years
of genetic theory suggest that simple rules of optimization will

produce at best approximations to the exact evolution. How
close the approximations are likely to be is open to question,
but in certain circles the argument is made that the poor field
biologist does not understand the theory anyway so give him
the quick and dirty way. In some situations, e.g., foraging
strategies, which are intrinsically economic in nature, there
may be agreement as to what should be optimized (e.g., reproduction per unit investment). Unlike the situation of genetic
perturbation to the genetic system itself, such as might occur
with genetic control of recombination, modes of gene action on
such traits as foraging strategies are pure speculation, and in
such cases, as much information might be obtained from the
econometric approach as from the exact genetic modeling. In
between the genetic system problem and the foraging strategy
problem lie such questions as inclusive fitness. Here there
may not be gross quantitative differences between the approaches,
but in using the exact models the theoretical structure of the
assumptions in the model are revealed as well as the limits to
application.

REFERENCES

(1) Baker, M.C. 1975. Song dialects and genetic differences
     in white-crowned sparrows. (Zonotrichia leucophrys).
     Evolution. 29: 226.

(2) Cavalli-Sforza, L.L., and Feldman, M.W. 1973. Cultural
     versus biological inheritance: Phenotypic transmission
     from parents to children (a theory of the effect of paren-
     tal phenotypes on children's phenotypes). Am. J. Hum.
     Genet. 25: 618-637.

(3) Christiansen, F.B., and Frydenberg, O. 1973. Selection
     component analysis of natural polymorphisms using popula-
     tion samples including mother-offspring combinations.
     Theor. Pop. Biol. 4: 425-445.

(4)   Craig, J.V.; Ortman, L.L.; and Guhl, A.M.   1965.   Genetic
      selection for social dominance ability in chickens.   Anim.
      Behav.   13: 114-131.

(5)   Crozier, R.H.   1970.   Coefficients of relationship and the
      identity of genes by descent in the Hymenoptera.   Am. Natur.
      104: 216-217.

(6)   Crozier, R.H., and Pamila, P.   1980.   Asymmetry in related-
      ness: who is related to whom?   Nature.   283: 604.

(7)   Curtsinger, J., and Feldman, M.W.   1980.   Experimental and
      theoretical analysis of the sex-ratio polymorphism in Droso-
      philia pseudo-obscura.   Genetics, in press.

(8)   Hoy, R.R., and Paul, R.C.   1973.   Genetic control of song
      specificity in crickets.   Science.   180: 82-83.

(9)   Kallman, K.D., and Schreibman, M.P.   1973.   A sex-linked
      gene controlling gonadotrop differentiation and its sig-
      nificance in determining the age of sexual maturation and
      size of the platyfish, Xiphophorous maculatus.   Gen. Comp.
      Endocrinol.   21: 287-304.

(10) Lewontin, R.C.   1974.   The Genetic Basis of Evolutionary
      Change.   New York: Columbia University Press.

(11) Orlove, M.J.   1975.   A model of kin selection not invoking
      coefficients of relationship.   J. Theor. Biol.   49: 289-310.

(12) Pamilo, P., and Varvio-Aho, S.L.   1979.   Genetic structure
      of the nests in the ant Formica sanguinea.   Behav. Ecol.
      Sociobiol.   6: 91-98.

(13) Rothenbuhler, W.C.   1964.   Behavior genetics of nest clean-
      ing in honey bees IV.   Response of Fl and back cross genera-
      tions to disease killed brood.   Am. Zool.   4: 111-123.

(14) Schwartz, O.A., and Armitage, K.B.   1980.   Genetic variation
      in social mammals: The marmot model.   Science.   207: 665-667.

(15) Sohn, J.J.   1977.   Socially induced inhibition of genetically
      determined maturation in the platyfish, Xiphophorus maculatus.
      Science.   195: 199-201.

Evolution of Social Behavior: Hypotheses and Empirical Tests, ed. H. Markl,
pp. 233-242. Dahlem Konferenzen 1980. Weinheim: Verlag Chemie GmbH.

Conclusion

G. C. Williams
Department of Ecology and Evolution, State University of New York
Stony Brook, NY 11794, USA

It is unlikely that any participant in this conference would
expect me or anyone else to achieve any sort of success, in a
few pages, at stating conclusions for a week of intense discussion by fifty scientists. Such a task is especially difficult for a field like sociobiology, which engenders a great
diversity of views and convictions. All that I will try to
do here is to state some of my own conclusions from discussions I have heard at this conference.

Studies of animal social behavior have proliferated rapidly
for the last few decades and have grown ever more explicitly
Darwinian. Any child could tell us that the study of animal
behavior is fascinating, and the intuitive appeal of the
phenomena may partly explain why so many biologists want to
study them. There may now be an additional motivation in the
intellectual rewards that can be reaped in a Darwinian
approach to animal behavior. This approach is especially rewarding in studies of complex social interactions among members of a single population, because modern biologists can
make some critical uses of theory in attempts to explain
these phenomena.

Before discussing such current rewards and future promises,
I would like to observe that earlier generations of field and
museum zoologists seldom made critical demands of the theory
of natural selection. Studies of such topics as the fossil
record, ecotypic differentiation, and comparative physiology
merely demanded that evolutionary theory imply phylogenies
with certain properties. Organisms must always (a) evolve
gradually, on a time scale that would satisfy adherents of
punctuated equilibria and related earlier views, (b) evolve
new organs only by modifying old ones, (c) remain closely
adapted to some way of life in some environment. This sort
of a purely descriptive theory of evolution suffices for most
of the data of natural history. So does the Darwinian theory,
but so also would a modified Lamarckism.

Darwinism triumphed, not by being better supported by comparative evidence, but by faring better in direct tests of its
premises. These general axioms, stated by Lewontin and restated here by Feldman et al. (this volume), are all empirical
generalizations. That like begets like is a matter of direct
experience. The physical scientist's major theories are of a
different kind. They are all constructions based on untestable
postulates (for instance, on the combining properties of the
oxygen atom). They are testable only indirectly by deduction
of consequences from the whole theoretical package (e.g., for
macroscopic combining weights). Evolutionary scientists enjoy
the luxury of being able to investigate their most general
premises directly.

The failure of natural history (more currently the comparative evidence) to support traditional Darwinism decisively
over rival theories results from a flaw in the original theory,
not any deficiency in the evidence. The summary phrase "survival
of the fittest" makes grammatical sense from the trick of using
an adjective as a noun. Conceptually the idea is incomplete
until someone specifies the fittest what, as Dawkins (2) has
pointed out. He and I and many other biologists would maintain
that natural selection is the survival of the fittest genes,

if not as our unshakable conclusion, at least as a routine
working hypothesis. If selection of the fittest genes takes
place through independent effects on phenotypes, we can immediately conclude that selection maximizes a certain phenotypic
property called mean inclusive fitness.

Of course we know that matters are not that simple. Genes
can be selected on the basis of segregation ratios, mutation-
rate influences at other loci, hitch-hiking opportunities,
and other properties that influence the number and kinds of
phenotypes in which they may be found, but are independent
of the genes' effects on these phenotypes. More serious is
the fact that epistatic interactions and linkage can cause
deviations from optimality and phenotypes that are less than
maximally fit. I assume that these problems are mostly minor
and cause inaccuracies that are small compared to measurement
error. The maximization of inclusive fitness may follow from
premises that are inaccurate, but so do the gas laws, which
remain useful nonetheless. My reasons for optimism on the
validity of the inclusive fitness concept are essentially those
stated here by Oster et al. (this volume). It seems to be generally true that, whatever variability is needed for response to
a certain kind of selection, it will be available. It will be
available even if demands are extremely stringent, like the
requirement that the requisite genetic variation be found in
the minute proportion of the genome that is closely linked to
some specified locus. Turner (7) maintains that this genetic capability is required for the evolution of certain kinds
of mimicry, and he calls it genomic largesse.

To maximize the remote theoretical property of inclusive fitness requires that certain measurable properties of organisms
be optimized. It is entirely appropriate that we inquire into the limitations and misleading aspects of the optimality
concept, especially in relation to social behavior, as was
recommended by several workers at this conference. It is not
at all appropriate to question optimality as a general feature

of the design of organisms. The idea is at least as old as
Aristotle's "History of Animals" (1), although I do not find
his examples convincing. Paley (4) in his "Natural Theology"
was much more successful, and his 1836 work may still be
read with profit by modern biologists. Paley's nineteenth
century understanding of mechanics, optics, and chemistry,
and his detailed knowledge of anatomy, enabled him to develop
his God-as-Engineer concept with a great profusion of examples
of functional optimization found in the bodies of living organisms.

I regard optimization, not as any sort of modern abstraction
of limited credentials, but as the most obvious set of phenomena to be explained. The important recent advance is the
proposal that all the goals for which Paley recognized optimization, such as vision or locomotion or food processing,
are tributary to the most general goal of inclusive fitness.
This explicit focusing of the optimality concept enables us
to specify and predict optimization in aspects of biology far
beyond Paley's grasp. Only for these recent extensions via
game theory into social relationships would I agree with the
Oster's et al. report (this volume) that "Optimization is a
subjective tool for rating the relative merits of a set of
strategies..."

The inclusive fitness concept provides powerful intellectual
appeal and a conceptual unification for studies of behavior.
It gives us a clear statement of the essence of behavioral
adaptations that is especially useful for understanding interactions among members of the same population. I cannot imagine
that anyone using Lamarck's premises, or any other theory that
fails to give adaptation a single explicit meaning, would
be able to expain why there is more cooperation in hymenopteran
societies between sisters than between brothers or between
brother and sister, or why it is mostly mature female and
immature male ground squirrels that try to murder their neighbors' infants, or why adult male langurs try to murder their

mates' infants, or why postzygotic parental investment is under-
taken mostly by female mammals, by male fishes, and by both
sexes in birds. Only with an exact idea of the nature of adaptation, as Hamilton achieved in 1964 with the concept of inclusive fitness, could we dream of predicting the relative weights
of male and female reproductives emerging from an ant nest, or
the relationship between reproductive effort and age in various
iteroparous populations.

That we have a new Rosetta stone for interpreting the beguil-
ing phenomena of social behavior must account for a large
part of the recent profusion of sociobiological studies. The
reproductive behavior of the sunfish discussed here by Krebs et
al. (this volume) was a matter of high interest even when it was
merely a group of items in a catalog of zoological wonders.
How much more exciting it is to be able to treat the individuals
at a breeding aggregation as participants in a complex game
and to have explicit criteria for measuring their success. How
much more satisfying it is to understand the strategy being
employed by each contestant, and its reasons for using that
strategy rather than some other.

Sociobiological theories were devised in an attempt to understand animal behavior, but it may be that their main value
will relate to somewhat different sorts of phenomena. Two of
these were discussed by Krebs et al. (this volume). One was
the effect of genetic heterogeneity on slime-mold morphogenesis,
which assigns some cells an altruistic somatic function that
aids the reproduction of possibly unrelated cells. The other
is the presence of genetic heterogeneity and conflicting interest in the embryo sac of a higher plant, especially the possible conflict between diploid embryo and triploid endosperm.

Relatives must often deal with each other cytologically or
physiologically rather than behaviorally. Examples can be
found in relationships between mother and young in utero or
among litter mates in any viviparous animal. Seeds in a pod

on a parent plant are an obvious analogy. For such individuals
any deception, threat, or transmission of useful information
must depend on chemical messages, but each individual is expected to react to any detected stimulus in a way that would
favor its own inclusive fitness. Genetic heterogeneity makes it
likely that the ideal allocation of resources for one party in
such a system will be less than ideal for another. Such conflict
may sometimes be resolved by compromise, achieved perhaps after
some wasteful wrangling, or there may be total victory for one
party and adoption of an optimal loser strategy by the other.
Victory for a parent may imply equitable compromise for sibling
rivalry.

Resolution by compromise can probably be illustrated by weaning
conflict as a behavioral example, although I would expect some
bias in favor of the mother. Any good example of distributive
justice in biology, whether produced by behavior or some other
process, must result from compromise. An example would be
meiotic division of a protozoan or algal zygote with each gene
in each tetrad assured of representation in one daughter cell,
and each cell given almost exactly the same resources. Whenever
one sex is entirely responsible for parental investment, the
other may be considered to have won a contest. Males are generally the winners among mammals. In fishes, females are commonly the winners with respect to postzygotic behavioral invest-
ments (e.g., defense against predators), but only rarely
(Syngnathidae) even partly victorious with respect to nutritive
investment. Parent-offspring contests are often unfair in that
the parent has greater resources for waging a contest, and is
therefore more likely to win. For example, chicks hatching
from large grackle eggs have an advantage over those hatching
from average eggs (3). Average egg size is less than optimal
for the offspring. This is expected if egg size is optimized
by the hen to maximize her rate of return on investment, as
envisioned by Smith and Fretwell (5). She wins this contest
easily by completing yolk provisioning before there is any

genetically different individual to dispute the issue. Parental
victory here implies equitable compromise as the outcome of
sibling rivalry.

One contestant's superiority of resources may be less decisive
for conflict over microscopic events. Suppose that fitness
for some female mammal would be maximized by her producing a
litter of two, one son and one daughter. She achieves this
by ovulating enough eggs to assure getting both sexes, has
them fertilized, implants the first applicant of whatever sex,
then one more of the opposite sex, and then rejects all
others. If this were the normal sequence of events, it would
select powerfully for any device a rejected embryo might use
to overcome the mechanism of rejection. This would substi-
tute life for death for the embryo, but would only cause a
finite reduction in fitness for the mother. I recently used
such reasoning to explain why parents seem to exercise so
little control on the sex ratios of their litters or clutches (8).

The special promise of fertilization processes, gametogenesis,
the early events of pregnancy and seed set, and similar phenomena in a wide range of animals and plants lies in their
amenability to precise observation and experimental control.
It is easier to provide for normal placental growth in the
laboratory than for a normal dominance hierarchy. It should
be easier to characterize and quantify the hormonal changes
responsible for parturition than the stimuli necessary to
make a male bird switch from parental behavior to cuckold
behavior. I do not plan to undertake any study of these phenomena on my own, but I will remain alert to the possibility
of non-behavioral uses of sociobiological theory, and to the
availability of collaborators in relevant fields. If surprises
turn up, so much the better. They may be just what we need for
important refinements in our theories, which could then be re-
applied in a more enlightened way to animal behavior.

I wonder also if there is not some possibility for human
sociobiology to be especially enlightening. The biological

study of human behavior is made immensely difficult by the
overwhelming importance of culture, as any number of people
have emphasized. It is nevertheless true that some important kinds of data are much more readily derived from human
subjects than from animal. I refer to cognitive information,
on the desires, hopes, fears, attitudes, and motivations that
underlie social behavior. Symons (6) has recently tried this
approach for an understanding of male-female contrasts in
sexual behavior. He succeeds well enough to suggest to me
the possibility that human sociobiology may become not merely
a controversial extension of general sociobiology, but a
special source of refinement for the general field.

REFERENCES

(1) Cresswell, R. (Translator). 1902. Aristotle's History
     of Animals. London: George Bell & Sons.

(2) Dawkins, R. 1978. Replicator selections and the extended
     phenotype. Zeitschr. Tierpsychol. $\underline{47}$: 61-76.

(3) Howe, H.F. 1976. Egg size, hatching asynchrony, sex, and
     brood reduction in the common grackle. Ecology $\underline{57}$: 1195-
     1207.

(4) Paley, W. 1836. Natural Theology, vol. 1. London: Charles
     Knight.

(5) Smith, C.C., and Fretwell, S.D. 1974. The optimum balance
     between size and number of offspring. Am. Nat. $\underline{108}$: 499-
     506.

(6) Symons, D. 1979. The Evolution of Human Sexuality. New
     York, Oxford: Oxford University Press.

(7) Turner, J.R.G. 1977. Butterfly mimicry: The genetical
     evolution of an adaptation. Evol. Biol. $\underline{10}$: 163-206.

(8) Williams, G.C. 1979. The question of adaptive sex ratio
     in out-crossed vertebrates. Proc. Roy. Soc. London B $\underline{205}$:
     567-580.

Afterthoughts

INTRODUCTION
During the five days of hard work, the various participants
composed the following limericks and presented them at the
end of the meeting.

Homage to William D. Hamilton

There once was a chap who for fitness
Helped his brother do more what he did less
And explained: thus I am able
To keep gene frequencies stable
But I would still rather perform than just witness.

Jim Markl

To the Master of the Sussex School

Remarked John the famed theoretician
Of evolution I have just a faint vision
And I am glad if I'm able
To make it evolutionarily stable
Whether it's true is beyond my ambition.

Jim Markl

For Jerry Brown

Remarked an altruistic girl with respect
Indirect fitness I would not neglect
So I enjoy helping mother
To produce sister and brother
But I prefer much the direct effect!

Jim Markl

There once was a poor field worker called Joe
Who worked very hard watching a Doe
He measured her fitness
But lacking a witness
People believed not him but his foe.

Ross Crozier et al.

There was a young man from Bodensee
Who knew much of Sociobiologie
Without any witness
His inclusive fitness
Deserves to spread throughout West Germany.

Mike Baker

There once was a man named Corrother
Who aspired to have sex with his grandmother
He said: "T'would be fun
To brag to someone
My son is my own father's brother."

           George Oster and Brian Charlesworth

A Worker's Prayer

"Sister tell me where are the genes
That determine who cooks and who cleans"?
"They're all in your head,
Now Quiet," she said,
"And get on with helping the queens."

           Marc Feldman

Population genetics analysis
Has warts and carbuncles and calluses
Maths isn't for me:
I like logic, you see,
And Dawkins has twelve lovely fallacies!

           Jeremy Cherfas and Dick Wrangham

Said Darwin, "It's all too absurd,
The distinctions are getting quite blurred.
They've abandoned, R.S.;
To I.F. they say 'yes';
O! When will the selfish be heard?"

           Jeremy Cherfas and Dick Wrangham

To Be Read By A Man

The latest genetic machine
Fuses alleles to make up <u>one</u> gene.
Now, if one's from a bee
And the other's from me,
It leads to this beautiful scene.

The allele for keeping bees clean
At first thinks her partner obscene
But she loves to entwine
With his helical line
When he tells her "me Tarzan, Hi Gene!"

           Jeremy Cherfas and Dick Wrangham

List of Participants

AYALA, F.J.
Department of Genetics
University of California
Davis, CA 95616, USA

*Field of research: Evolutionary
biology, philosophy of science*

BAKER, M.C.
Department of Zoology and
Entomology, Colorado State University
Fort Collins, CO 80523, USA

*Field of research: 1) Avian vocal
dialects: behavioral mechanisms and
genetic population structure; 2)
Social hierarchies and optimal
foraging*

BATESON, P.
Sub-Department of Animal Behaviour
University of Cambridge
Cambridge CB3 8AA, England

*Field of research: Development of
social behavior*

BENGTSSON, B.
Institute of Genetics
223 62 Lund, Sweden

*Field of research: Genetics of
evolution*

BISCHOF, N.
Psychologisches Institut
Biologisch-Mathematische Abteilung
8044 Zürich, Switzerland

*Field of research: Human social moti-
vation (proximate and ultimate causal
analysis)*

BONNER, J.T.
Department of Biology
Princeton University
Princeton, NJ 08544, USA

*Field of research: Developmental
biology, especially of social amoebae;
evolution of social systems*

BRADBURY, J.W.
Department of Biology
University of California
La Jolla, CA 92093, USA

*Field of research: Social evolution in
bats*

BROWN, J.L.
Department of Biological Science
State University of New York
Albany, NY 12222, USA

*Field of research: Sociobiology: field
studies of helping behavior in birds
aimed at estimating fitness parameters
of social behavior*

BRÜCKNER, D.
Zoologisches Institut der
Universität München
8000 Munich 2, F.R. Germany

*Field of research: Ecology and evolution
of social insects*

CHAMPE, P.C.
Department of Biochemistry
CMDNJ-Rutgers Medical School
Piscataway, NJ 08854, USA

Field of research: Medical education

CHARLESWORTH, B.
School of Biological Sciences
University of Sussex
Falmer, Brighton BN1 9QG, England

Field of research: Population genetics

CHARNOV, E.L.
Department of Biology, University of Utah
Salt Lake City, UT 84112, USA

*Field of research: Evolution of patterns
of sexual reproduction in plants and
animals*

CROZIER, R.H.
School of Zoology
University of New South Wales
Kensington, N.S.W. 2033, Australia

*Field of research: Evolutionary
genetics, especially of ants*

CURIO, E.
Ruhr-Universität Bochum
Abteilung für Biologie
Arbeitsgruppe f. Verhaltensforschung
4630 Bochum 1, F.R. Germany

*Field of research: Behavioral ecol-
ogy with emphasis on predator-prey
interactions*

DICKEMANN, M.
Department of Anthropology
Sonoma State University
Rohnert Park, CA 94928, USA

*Field of research: Human social
biology; mating strategies in
stratified societies; unpredict-
able environments; the evolution
of female infanticide, celibacy
and claustration*

EMLEN, S.T.
Section of Neurobiology and Behavior
Langmuir Laboratory
Cornell University
Ithaca, NY 14850, USA

*Field of research: Social behavior
and adaptive strategies in birds*

FELDMAN, M.W.
Department of Biological Sciences
Stanford University
Stanford, CA 94305, USA

*Field of research: Population ge-
netics, cultural evolution and
human genetics*

HAMMERSTEIN, P.
Universität Bielefeld
Fakultät für Biologie
4800 Bielefeld 1, F.R. Germany

*Field of research: Game theoretical
models in sociobiology*

HARVEY, P.H.
Department of Biology
University of Sussex
Falmer, Brighton BN1 9QG, England

*Field of research: Behavioral ecology
of birds and mammals*

HAUSFATER, G.
Langmuir Laboratory, Cornell University
Ithaca, NY 14850, USA

*Field of research: Primate sociobiology,
computer models of social and mating
systems*

HELLER, R.
Ruhr-Universität Bochum
Abteilung für Biologie
Arbeitsgruppe f. Verhaltensforschung
4630 Bochum 1, F.R. Germany

*Field of research: Behavioral ecology
with emphasis on optimal foraging*

HÖLLDOBLER, B.
MCZ-Laboratories, Department of Biology
Harvard University
Cambridge, MA 02138, USA

*Field of research: Behavioral ecology
and sociobiology of invertebrates*

KRAMER, B.
Fachbereich Biologie
Universität Regensburg
8400 Regensburg, F.R. Germany

*Field of research: Species specificity
of electric signaling and communication
in weakly electric fish*

KREBS, J.R.
Edward Grey Institute of Field
Ornithology
Oxford OX1 3PS, England

*Field of research: Optimal foraging,
bird song evolutionary ecology*

LINSENMAIR, K.E.
Zoologisches Institut III
Universität Würzburg
8700 Würzburg, F.R. Germany

*Field of research: Behavioral and
physiological ecology, especially
of desert invertebrates; sociobiology; orientation physiology*

LUMSDEN, C.J.
Museum of Comparative Zoology
Harvard University
Cambridge, MA 02138, USA

*Field of research: Theory and
modeling of insect societies,
mathematical biology*

McKINNEY, F.
Bell Museum of Natural History
University of Minnesota
Minneapolis, MN 55455, USA

*Field of research: Evolution of
social systems and communication
methods in dabbling ducks*

MARKL, H.
Fachbereich Biologie
Universität Konstanz
7750 Konstanz, F.R. Germany

Field of research: Animal behavior

MARLER, P.
The Rockefeller University
New York, NY 10021, USA

*Field of research: Animal communi-
cation and behavioral development*

MAY, R.A.
Biology Department
Princeton University
Princeton, NJ 08544, USA

*Field of research: Population biology
and community ecology*

MAYNARD SMITH, J.
School of Biological Sciences
University of Sussex
Falmer, Brighton BN1 9QG, England

*Field of research: Evolutionary
biology*

MENZEL, Jr., E.W.
Department of Psychology
State University of New York
Stony Brook, NY 11794, USA

Field of research: Primate psychology

METCALF, R.A.
Department of Zoology
University of California
Davis, CA 95616, USA

*Field of research: Evolution, genetics,
and behavior of social insects*

MICHENER, C.D.
Department of Entomology
University of Kansas
Lawrence, KS 66045, USA

*Field of research: Biology of primi-
tively social bees and especially
recognition of degree of relationship among such bees*

MILINSKI, M.
Ruhr-Universität Bochum
Abteilung für Biologie
Arbeitsgruppe f. Verhaltensforschung
4630 Bochum 1, F.R. Germany

*Field of research: Feeding strategies
in social context*

OLIVIER, T.J.
Anthropology Department
Northwestern University
Evanston, IL 60201, USA

*Field of research: Population
genetics, especially micro-
evolution in cercopithecoid
monkey species*

OSTER, G.F.
Department of Entomology and
Parasitology, University of California
Berkeley, CA 94720, USA

*Field of research: Sociobiology,
developmental biology*

REYER, H.U.
MPI f. Verhaltensphysiologie
8131 Seewiesen über Starnberg,
F.R. Germany

*Field of research: Social struc-
ture and breeding success of
African kingfishers in relation
to ecological conditions*

SADE, D.S.
Department of Anthropology
Northwestern University
Evanston, IL 60201, USA

*Field of research: Population
biology of primates*

SHERMAN, P.W.
Department of Psychology
University of California
Berkeley, CA 94720, USA

*Field of research: Evolution of
social behavior, behavioral
ecology*

TRILLMICH, F.
MPI f. Verhaltensphysiologie
8131 Seewiesen über Starnberg,
F.R. Germany

*Field of research: Social structure
and breeding success of Galápagos
pinnipeds and European starlings*

VOGEL, C.
Lehrstuhl für Anthropologie
der Georg-August-Universität
3400 Göttingen, F.R. Germany

*Field of research: Sociobiology and
ontogeny of social behavior in non-
human primates, especially Presbytis
entellus*

WICKLER, W.
MPI f. Verhaltensphysiologie
8131 Seewiesen über Starnberg,
F.R. Germany

*Field of research: Evolution of social
behavior in animals, selective consequences of traditions (especially
in birds)*

WILLIAMS, G.C.
Department of Ecology and Evolution
State University of New York
Stony Brook, NY 11794, USA

*Field of research: Evolutionary
theory and marine ecology*

WRANGHAM, R.W.
King's College
Cambridge CB2 1ST, England

*Field of research: Primate social
evolution*

Subject Index

Author Index

Dahlem Workshop Reports

Life Sciences Research Report 9

verlag chemie

Morality as a Biological Phenomenon

Dahlem Workshop Report on
"Morality as a Biological Phenomenon"
held in Berlin between 28 November and 2 December, 1977.

Editor: Gunther S. Stent, University of California, Berkeley.

Contents
Introduction: The Limits of the Naturalistic Approach to Morality:
G. S. Stent. – The Concepts of Sociobiology: *J. Maynard Smith.* –
Analogs of Morality Among Nonhuman Primates: *H. Kummer.* –
On the Phylogeny of Human Morality: *N. Bischof.* – Social Morality
Norms as Evidence of Conflict Between Biological Human Nature
and Social System Requirements: *D. T. Campbell.* – The Biology
of Morals from a Psychological Perspective: *P. H. Wolff.* – Prosocial
Behavior of the Very Young: *H. L. Rheingold and D. F. Hay.* – The
Development of Moral Concepts: *E. Turiel.* – Psychiatry, Biology
and Morals: *F. A. Jenner.* – Literacy and Moral Rationality:
J. Goody. – The "Moral Universal" from the Perspectives of East
Asian Thought: *W. Tu.* – Biology and Ethics: Normative Impli-
cations: *C. Fried.* – Ethics as an Autonomous Theoretical Subject:
T. Nagel. – Evolution of Morals? Morals of Evolution? (Group
Report): *H. S. Markl, Rapporteur; E. Butenandt, D. T. Campbell,
F. J. G. Ebling, L. H. Eckensberger, C. Fried, H. Kummer.* –
Psychology (Group Report): *G. W. Kowalski, Rapporteur; N.
Bischof, J. R. Searle, J. Maynard Smith, H. L. Rheingold, E. Turiel,
B. Williams, P. H. Wolff.* – Sociobiology, Morality, and Culture
(Group Report): *R. C. Solomon, Rapporteur; C. Geertz, E. A.
Gellner, J. Goody, F. A. Jenner, T. Nagel, G. S. Stent, W. Tu, G. W.
Wolters.* – Conclusion: *B. A. O. Williams.* – List of Participants –
Author Index.

1978. 323 pages, with 4 figures.
Softcover. ISBN 3-527-12013-1

Fields of interest: Anthropology, Behavioral Science, Biology,
Philosophy, Psychiatry, Sociology, Theology.

...kshop Reports

...ical Sciences Research Report

...eawater
                                        ISBN 3-527-12003-3